D1074079

The Mainland *Haole*

Afternoon tea in a Honolulu garden, 1908. Mrs. Edmund Johnson serves tea in the garden of the renowned photographer Ray Jerome Baker. This comfortable, genteel group symbolizes a paradise gained. The mythic landscape is domesticated with all the familiar traditions of home. Bishop Museum.

The Mainland *HAOLE*

The White Experience in Hawaii

Elvi Whittaker

New York   **Columbia University Press**   1986

Columbia University Press
New York   Guildford, Surrey
Copyright © 1986 Columbia University Press
Printed in the United States of America

Library of Congress Cataloging in Publication Data

Whittaker, Elvi W.
    The mainland *haole*.

    Bibliography: p.
    Includes index.
    1. Whites—Hawaii—History.   2. Whites—Hawaii—
Social conditions.   3. Whites—Hawaii—Cultural assimila-
tion.   4. Whites—Hawaii—Ethnic identity.   I. Title.
DU624.7.W45W48 1985   996.9′004034   85–454
ISBN 0-231-05316-9
ISBN 0-231-05317-7 (pbk.)

This book is Smyth-sewn and printed on permanent and durable
acid-free paper.

For my parents,
Marta and Aksel Roman Waik

Contents

Preface

Writers invariably use a preface to reveal their aspirations and to apologize for their pretensions. They also attempt to guide the reader in how the work is to be interpreted, and what place the ideas are to assume in some intellectual landscape. This extraordinary privilege accorded to people who write permits us to give our efforts an unabashedly personal cast. This is doubly true for me. Not only have I had the opportunity to choose to study the people I did and not only did I put my own idiosyncratic methodological and theoretical stamp on the work, but I was myself one of these people. Thus what I write is a subjective document paralleling my own experiences.

In a substantive sense the monograph has a dual goal. First, it sketches an impressionistic portrait of the two actors who assume a major role in this piece. Most directly center stage in the work are a group of people called the *mainland haole*, who live in the Hawaiian Islands and who have come there of their own volition seeking a better life. In adopting the style I did, in writing as I did, it was my intention to honor their experience ethnographically as they discover what it is to know a place in its existential possibilities. I have tried to be faithful to their experiences as they related them to me.

The other leading actor on the stage is a set of ideas called the Western consciousness. This invisible actor, residing in the persons who live and articulate the ideas, is as central to the encounter as the flesh and blood persons themselves. The book is a biography of these ideas, how they influence me in analyzing and writing, and how they confront the challenges of a growing malaise, a waning cultural hegemony, and a demanding new context.

The second goal is made of the stuff of my pretensions and my long term commitments to various positions I hold on the business of producing knowledge. In this sense the book is really not about Hawaii, nor even about the *mainland haole*, nor about the imperatives that make them think and act as they do. Rather it is a book about method. By this I do not mean methods in the traditional sense employed in the social sciences, but the melding of ideas, theoretical positions, and intellectual preferences which lead us to choose particular instruments of methodology and analysis and wield them as we do. I have claimed for myself the luxury of trying out arguments that have long intrigued me, and of seeing how they resonate with data.

I have exercised three converging commitments. My first indulgence has been to try to write ethnography reflected through my favorite paradigm, the sociology of knowledge. This has allowed me some insights into the rich possibilities of ethnography and has produced the inevitable temptations, put aside to be satisfied on some future work. My second commitment was to view anthropology not only as the discipline within which I write, not only as a depiction of the subject studied but as a powerful form of criticism, a special, privileged moral critique of the human condition and the human endeavor. And finally, I have cast covetous eyes at anthropological epistemology, felt committed to understanding it better as it now prevails, and perhaps contributing at some fictitious future time to its possible moral and aesthetic alternatives.

Perhaps these awarenesses have been visible only to me. So much the better. I have tried to give the book a structure with a conventional logic. The prologue permits me to air my analytic possibilities as a kind of backdrop, to leave with the reader the notion that neither data nor analyses are preordained. After this, however, I have conformed, more or less, to the dictates of what we have come to recognize as the order that anthropologists place on their work, and expect to see in the work of others. Hence there is a history chapter which posits not only the history of white people in Hawaii, but also a short introduction to the history of the ideas that govern them. Next there is a chapter recognizing method, which shows how I did the work, that it was done in 1971 through 1973 and again in three separate summers after that, most recently in the summer of 1982. The next chapters deal with selected experiences of the *haole* as they adapt to the physical and moral order. There is no conclusion, for that particular assertion belongs to a language I do not claim to speak, and which I quite happily disavow. Conclusions belong to a paradigm which espouses hypotheses and findings. Mine lie in my preface and prologue, and in any implications this work might have.

Implications in themselves are interesting. The people I talked with, the *haoles* I interviewed, expressed a variety of attitudes about what I was doing and what consequences it would have. Some were diffident ("why would anyone be interested in me?" or "why would anyone want to know about white people?"). Others were grateful ("at last someone is going to tell our story"). A few were suspicious ("this might make our situation worse"). Some forecast the book's reception ("you may not be safe in this town again"). Others analyzed its political import ("it'll be seen as reactionary" or "it'll be the most radical book around"). My own hopes are much more modest than these predictions. I see the truth of C. Wright Mills' claim that political implications, if any, are directed by the fact that any writer offers a certain reality. Any influence, therefore, would lie in how this reality is accommodated.

The preface has one further use. It affords the opportunity to thank those to whom I owe so much. As such recognition always comes to be written at the end of a work, it becomes suffused with the relief that finishing brings, and thus one is in danger of choking with effusive gratitude and sentiment. As sentiment is definitely unfashionable and moreover tends to be embarrassing, I shall attempt to be direct and simple. Most importantly I want to acknowledge all those whose experiences have become part of this book. Some of them have become friends to be visited on each successive trip, and I recall hours of interesting conversation. Others are unnamed strangers whose inadvertent comments and actions have added to the fabric of my data. Especially to be thanked are those who, over the years, have conducted a personalized clipping and information service and have made it their business that I knew how the political and social winds were blowing. They sent me copies of letters to the editors of the newspapers, information on changes in ecological and economic policy, on the latest activities of the *yakuza*, and other matters which they knew would be of interest to me.

The influential ideas of those who have worked in the areas I touch, or related areas, are acknowledged in the usual manner in the text and references—old intellectual heroes like Kenneth Burke and George Herbert Mead, and appealing new discoveries like Edward Said and the existential geographers. There are yet others still more influential, whose presence is pervasive and on whose thinking I rely quite shamelessly. They seldom appear by name, but the reader will immediately recognize my debt to the phenomenological philosophers, the sociologists of knowledge from Marx to the sociolinguists, many of the radical social scientists and the anthropological and sociological ethnographers. I wish my own productions more clearly honored the stunning insights of the former thinkers and incomparable eloquence and polish of some of the latter. Other debts are of a more personal kind, pervasive in ways which the reader cannot immediately discern. I have learned much from both Gerald Berreman and Virginia Olesen, both intellectually and in seeing where the powers of the social sciences lie. Both read and commented upon early drafts of this manuscript. John Brown donated ideas from his own imaginative repertoire, challenged my assumptions and helped with the editing. Michael Ames, Ken Burridge, May Diaz, Carole Farber, and Roy Turner were kind enough to read various portions and versions of the work, offered suggestions, and were encouraging. When my own writing most repelled me Beverley Lee, Joanne Richardson, and Erik Whittaker read, edited, and saved me the embarrassment of going public with too much clumsiness.

On the Hawaiian scene I thank the following for their time and the specialized knowledge they shared with me: Agnes Conrad of the State Archives of Hawaii, Ernest J. Donehower of the Hawaiian Visitor's Bureau, and Ah Quan McElrath of ILWU. The generosity of friends made each field trip a pleasure, especially to be remembered are Fred Bail, Lida Chase, Jim Charlton, Pete Dunn-Rankin, Pat Leong, and Momi Naughton. Generosity is too banal a word to recognize such diverse gifts as: places to live, loans of cars, hours of time photocopying materials I needed, outings to theaters and to picnics, patient chauffering on rush errands on days of departure, good-natured responses to disparate requests made by long-distance telephone, dinners bought for me at restaurants and cooked for me at homes, leis at the airport, and, above all, continued good companionship.

I have yet further debts to acknowledge. Over the years David Whittaker has given scholarly and professional advice and material help of many kinds. My friends Else von Rosen and Martha and Bert von Rosen-Olds gave me the extraordinary luxury of a quiet, scenic place to write. The Canada Council is to be acknowledged for the financial freedom it permitted me. Yvana Christie and Ria Rowe uncomplainingly confronted my messy scratches and with speed and smoothness turned them into a manuscript. I especially want to mention the ongoing impetus given by my youngest son who continually asked, "Isn't it finished *yet?*"

Creating Anthropological Knowledge

Anthropologists are often asked an innocent question: "Why did you do the kind of work you did?" It arises out of polite curiosity and asks why anthropologists elect to go to the places they do and study those whom they come to study. Moreover, it reveals interest in how anthropologists analyze their data. On the surface this query is simple enough. Yet it is deceptively so, for it challenges the anthropologist's theoretical commitment, and ultimately conscience itself. By virtue of the anthropology I write I must deal with it. Only by doing so can I begin to honor the most fundamental issue in anthropology, the creation of anthropological knowledge itself. This creation deserves careful scrutiny, as do the ideological tenets behind it, and the presuppositions that make these possible.

The question carries a strong moral tone. It seems to ask for justification, as if the work had important relevance for human understanding and well-being. Eventually I came to see it as a question put to the very existential core of anthropology. Behind its seeming innocence lies a cosmic demand, and it is no wonder that answers I have heard given have been evasive. They tend to be carelessly amusing, cynically self-effacing, or merely cryptic. They acknowledge the importance of the question, but imply a reluctance to address the hidden challenges. Anthropologists seem unwilling to become involved in potentially the most troublesome intellectual and ethical debates of our time.

The question recognizes the truth that any writing is, at least behind the scenes, poignantly self-conscious. Prevailing conventions, however, ignore this self-consciousness and present the written product, like Venus in her shell, purified and liberated from the toils of birth. Such evasion creates a dangerous illusion, for it implies that knowledge is gained ready-made, unsoiled by biases and engineering on the part of the researcher. One glaring omission in this assumption is the presence of the anthropologist, and the work done by that person in the name of research. This is the way that science is always presented, and in most cases, it is also how the results of anthropological fieldwork are portrayed. It is deeply antithetical to the whole endeavor.

No knowledge arises in a vacuum. In anthropology it requires, in the first instance, "seeing" and "hearing," which in themselves are no simple matters. They are possible through decisions and strategies, which in their turn demand a highly developed sense of what are data and what are irrelevancies. While the latter can be allowed to remain in oblivion, data themselves are not possible without underlying theories which shape strategy.

The invisibility usually accorded such matters is not a conscious attempt to conceal, but follows naturally from two beliefs. The first is that the facts are there, absolute, awaiting discovery. This, of course, is basic to science. The second belief is that the methods of getting there are so widely known and accepted that an exploration of them is superfluous and can safely be ignored. There is a scientific cast to this belief as well, in that most scientific routines are already so familiar that they require only the briefest of acknowledgments.

Yet knowledge and fact do not stand pristine. They reflect their producers and the methods of their production. In addition they must be put into a particular order and processed for our understanding. Anthropology is one of the ways of ordering knowledge. It has routines for doing this which, not surprisingly, inspire the label of "discipline." Disciplines, after all, are merely specific systems for perceiving and transforming observations into adequate knowledge.

Innocent questions from the merely curious, therefore, address the kinds of issues that anthropologists do not write about, although they occasionally discuss them with fellow anthropologists. Anthropological fact and anthropological analyses come from field-work experiences and decisions made there. They cannot be pre-planned; they occur situationally. In addition, steps are taken for which there are no immediate visible rationales. The anthropologist essentially treats the experiences, the decisions, and hidden ration-ales as non-data. These matters are seldom recorded, reflected upon, or remembered as relevant or as data. The folklore of an-thropology, however, retains some facets of these silent methods. It is possible to see that these choices and experiences have humble origins. Some future investigation of the epistemology of anthro-pology will define these very matters as primary data. It can then be shown, ethnographically, how ethnography is actually done. We may all be a little surprised, if not even awed, with the cognitive and intellectual complexities of the actual process that stands for fieldwork.

The informal talk of anthropologists, however, shows that ethnography often begins with naked romanticism, with moral or political fervor, or with a personalized odyssey. Yearnings to visit an esoteric location, determination to show the plights of poverty or oppression, and even the austere expediency of available grants have provided acceptable rationales for undertaking specific kinds of fieldwork. It is always more satisfying, or perhaps more credible, to claim that decisions in ethnography are prompted by anthro-pological problematics, such as specific issues in kinship or in ac-culturation. While these abstract and essentially emotionless inter-ests contradict the humanism and romanticism deeply engrained in the anthropological ethos, they are considered quite legitimate.

After initial decisions are made, something akin to a tourist's fantasy takes over. In pleasurable and safe imagination an-thropologists see themselves in the setting. These ruminations permit a rehearsal of some of the personal issues involved in any piece of fieldwork. Undoubtedly much of the time spent in planning, and some of the time actually spent in the field have all the trappings and experiences common to the tourist. It could also be argued that the moral fervor and the commitment resemble the missionary more than the tourist. While "getting to know the people" is a purpose common to all three, the sharpest distinctions among anthropologist, tourist, and missionary become obvious upon return home. The average tourist seems keen to retain facets of the experience as a life accomplishment to be displayed at will as claims to sophistication. The average missionary gains increased knowledge of the human condition and his own personal ongoing moral growth in the commitment to his chosen calling.

The ethnographer, in contrast, is seldom permitted these particular informalities. A peculiar transformation, unknown to tourist and missionary alike, takes place. A massive symbolic attack and intellectual purging occurs. Commonsensical views are obviously inappropriate, and early fantasies must be distilled into anthropological proprieties. The transformation presumes a world of respectable anthropology, to be gained through various ritual exercises, by translating observation and ordinary living into anthropological idiom.

There is a preliminary stage prior to going to the field, which should be mentioned. A "proposal," a document of studied frugality and skeletal-like impersonality is pared out of the initial daydreams. The product is destined to meet the critical scrutiny of granting bodies or dissertation committees. This step lifts the project out of the imaginative milieu in which it was created, and introduces an epistemological break. This kind of break is a necessity in science and is practiced assiduously in anthropology. By eliminating the presumably polluting romanticizing and the everyday planning it is believed that objectivity can be introduced.

The canons of conventional ethnography further prescribe that previously established knowledge pertinent to the area be accumulated and incorporated. In this recognition of accumulated knowledge, anthropology again follows the lead of science. One must become familiar with knowledge "in the area" and display this in the document produced. The failure to show such precedence becomes immediately suspect, while, on the other hand, displaying it shows membership with anthropologists. The conventions thus monitor the ordering appropriate to the discipline and ensure that the project addresses the issues the discipline considers properly its own. For example, a commitment to a geographical location and to an identifiable people is considered necessary. Anthropology is always performed in some "place" and with some "people." Further, it has a deep sense of history, not only in using the contemporary event of fieldwork to reconstruct the past, but in using historical resources as well. The assumption appears to be that meanings cannot be established without a history, that the present is only possible because of the past. Initially the history is always a positivistic, Westernized history. In doing the actual work, however, such histories may be compared to those held by the people studied, although just as often the latter become labeled as "oral tradition" or even "mythology." It is further assumed that understanding is impoverished if attention is not given to ecological adaptation, subsistence patterns, food production, language spoken, and the like. These matters are familiar to all anthropologists and emphasize the scientizing, formalizing, and officially condoned ways of providing meaning. I raise them only to draw attention to the disjunctures between sentient traveler and anthropological fieldworker.

The revered ambience of science is thus adopted for ethnography. What it seems to do, however, is to separate what is known from the knower, the fieldworker from the product. In the scientific enterprise this might be well and good. Yet in the endeavor called anthropology the procedure suggests a questionable posturing. Ignoring the anthropologist's experience is a little meaningless, and even ludicrous, when the main epistemic underpinning of fieldwork is to use this very experience, sensemaking ability, and creative perception as the basis of the knowledge created. Thus, essentially everyday encounters become transformed, shaped, and modified by the rigors peculiar to the discipline. The anthropologist's day-by-day involvement with people, the way he or she comes to understand these people, is forced into becoming a body of recognizable objective and formally accredited knowledge. The ethnographer is forced to engage with existing paradigms.

Yet any conceptual or theoretical knowledge entertained before entry into the field must be suspended in order to operate there. In the field the demands are specific and personal. The fieldworker is thrust into common-place dialogue with the very people to be known and understood. This requires some renuncia-

tion, in an immediate sense, of most anthropological positions previously taken, for they represent a culture curiously foreign to the
ongoing interaction. People do not interact in the models of developed paradigms, preordained concepts, and formalized categories. Another epistemological disjuncture occurs.

A scientific gloss is sometimes passed over the fieldwork
process by according it the status of "method." Yet its practices
are far removed from the kinds of rationalities preferred by science,
the method without peer. Fieldwork rests its ultimate sanctity and
validity on the elusive, and at the same time invaluable entity, human
experience. This highly complex instrument, shaped by a lifetime
of cultural involvement and a more limited period of anthropological
training, becomes the means of creating knowledge. Yet it remains
in itself almost completely unexplored and little understood as an
instrument.

The final transformation comes when the knowledge
shaped by the fieldworker's experience is molded into the studied
proclamations of ethnography. This experience is made intelligible
by casting it into legitimated paradigms. It is as if "the way the
world is experienced" is to be changed into "the way the world
is." The dialectic now shifts to the reader to whom the experience
must make anthropological sense.

The doing of ethnography then involves a series of epistemological shifts. Anyone who has done fieldwork has intimate
knowledge of them. Yet despite their obvious importance they have
been relegated to the annals of undisclosed autobiography. What
seems important to do, therefore, is to examine such matters and
to describe how they relate to the knowledge finally presented.

Having set the frame of necessary transformations, I can
now return to the original question. Anthropologists seem of two
minds with regard to explicating decisions and field experiences.
One set considers it *de rigueur* as a part of method and claims that
ethnographies without it are meaningless. Another set views it as
"confessionals," tainted either by surreptitious attempts to write
autobiographies or by publicizing unnecessary closet guilt. I belong
to the former and thus for some time I have listened to and collected
the accounts of other anthropologists. They seem to have much in
common in that they are rather consistently organized as parables.

The earliest involvements I had with the Islands were as a cross-Pacific traveler, and as a convention goer. In the practiced clichés of a mainland imagination the experience was familiar. These clichés alternated between the depiction of a South Seas' paradise of racial harmony and the pejorative intellectual version of exploitative tourism and bottled experience. I had fallen for the inevitable warmth and palms, yet also encapsulated in my mind were images of a crude commercial Hawaii banalized with plastic pleasure. I was liberated from these tiresome superficial metaphors by the parable I am about to relate.

My particular story takes place outside the Pioneer Hotel at Lahaina, on the island of Maui. I have related it so often that it has assumed apocryphal status. It is no longer clear to me which parts would be considered local folklore, which parts would be considered brute fact, and which parts have simply been created and recreated in many tellings. Perhaps most revealingly none of this matters any longer. The experience captures for me an appropriate intellectual genesis.

Beneath a rather nondescript tree in front of the hotel lives a man, more legendary than real. He sleeps in a blanket-roll which, for safe-keeping and convenience, is stored behind the hotel bar during the day. The man, supposedly the gentlemanly product of an Ivy League education, is said to share his tree with a dog of untidy appearance and uncertain pedigree. Evidence of his permanent commitment to this particular unpretentious abode is provided by a mailbox where he presumably takes delivery of ghostly copies of the *New York Times*, if only to remind himself of the lifestyle and consciousness he has renounced. I do not clearly remember seeing either the blanket-roll, the mailbox, or indeed the man himself. But from my memory and the story I have constructed around the raw possibilities has emerged a bearded unprepossessing character, someone reputed to have relinquished a comfortable position in life for this simple existence, a Hawaiian compromise between a tropical Thoreau and an American Gauguin. Rationality suggests that this person may have the face of the original narrator, or another seemingly fitting visage onto whom I mapped the story at the time. The tale had an undeniable familiarity and provided a contrast to much of what I had learned to take for granted. Whether it was actuality sluiced with lore, or appealing metaphor, is largely irrelevant. The parable serves in some way as a symbolic synopsis of the anthropology to come.

From these beginnings I progressed through the stages known to all who do academic anthropology, and found myself in the field for the first time in 1971. This monograph should reveal some of the transformations from original fantasy to recognizable ethnography. It relates my experiences and those of the people who, in terms of the anthropological idiom, were to become "my people."

Once in the field I entered an apparent crosscurrent of disparity. The tidy and unproblematic world of early metaphor and solitary imagination was challenged. Previous certainties became uncertainties with everyday demands. Conceptualizing about what I was learning became, not more and more obvious as I had expected, but increasingly complex and elusive. I was studying strangers in a new land. At the same time I was a stranger myself attempting to begin a life in this new land. Finally, I was also an anthropologist, thus self-consciously a stranger, a stranger by methodological requirements. Were there then three or more existences of which I had to be aware and of which I had to make sense? Realities of all kinds were continually presented to me by the people I was studying. There were also the many realities of my own life for which I supplied conventional meanings. Finally, there were the conventions of what anthropologists are supposed to think and do.

How were each of these conventions to be honored? How much disparity should the anthropologist permit between what she knows and what the informants know? Between what is experienced as person and as anthropologist? Should the nature of these disjunctures be revealed? Are the conventions for living and creating these realities the same as those for talking about them? Is one of the aims of good anthropology to make these realities somehow coincide? Was this to be a study about dialectics, for surely that is inherent in all knowledge? Was it then to be a study of how epistomology, in the name of anthropology, emerges? Was it to be a study of moral choices? I must admit to willingly compounding these problems by making them a part of the analysis and the subject of critical reflection.

As a newcomer to Hawaiian soil I was in the continual position of having to reexamine what I thought I knew. Despite my professed eagerness to learn and to relearn, there was an almost unconscious move to protect what I knew. This reluctance to give up a past of certainty is surely true of all strangers undergoing acculturation. At the same time the demands of anthropology are to suspend belief in past beliefs and foster the new, the culture to be known. There must be ways in which this dualism is conventionally accommodated. It is seldom, however, made a topic for reflection.

When I first went to the field in 1971 I had long ago given up dependence on the value-freeness of social science or, indeed, of science itself. Reliance on that established security no longer provided satisfaction. I could not roll value-freeness out like a well-oiled machine, with assurance, nor believe that it would stand unquestioned as producing knowledge without bias. Knowledge without bias is merely the ideal of a culture of rational formality.

The final recognition of value-freeness as a never-to-be-reached haven, however, had confusing implications. There was now a smorgasbord of possible choices for what is usually called "method and analysis" and no clear directions on how to make them. The choices seemed to me to be moral and aesthetic ones. This subsumes, of course, what others might consider political or cultural. Obviously the choices must not be solipsistic, but must presume on being legitimated by some convention. While at one time I had thought movement away from positivism might be possible, it now seemed that if indeed this could be achieved, it would be a relatively hollow victory. Positivism is, after all, part of the language we all speak, both commonsensically and anthropologically. Further, the recognition of some convention, whatever its nature, must suggest established, recognized, and agreed-upon fundamentals. Surely this is a case of some kind of positivistic knowledge. It seems to be a barren exercise to evoke the familiar dichotomy between positivism and nonpositivism, where each stands at the furthest ends of a polarity. Surely it does a kind of disservice to understanding the very nature of knowledge? Surely all knowledge can be viewed as starting phenomenologically and passing through definable gradations of positivistic purification? The state of purification considered acceptable is undoubtedly a cultural or a moral decision. No doubt one becomes morally fervent about one's choice of position on the polarity. Anthropology in particular occupies various complicated positions comparatively close to phenome- nonological origins. The paths of positivism, on the other hand, are those of conventional wisdom, condoned and tried. They evoke ready consensus. One is faced, however, with the notion that these methods do not present the "true facts of the matter," but are the accumulated and officially respectable interpretations taking their authority from centuries of epistemological approval.

The choice of nonpositivistic methods is then a pointed one, and somehow begs justification. For me the choice was made without hesitation. Phenomenonological awareness was morally pleasing as a protest against invisibility and depersonalization, those formalities of positivism. Meaning, culture, and consciousness, the themes I wanted to understand and to address, had lent themselves but meagerly to positivistic investigation. Phenomenology was heav- ily woven into the intellectual idiom of the time at which I began this work. It refreshed that old axiom that persons be treated as persons, that a respect for paramount reality be elevated to claim its due attention and that the world be depicted as it was experi- enced. The "as it was experienced" was to be understood as "ex- actly as it was experienced." This meant unadulterated by erstwhile interpretations. What could be more accurate, therefore, than the language and depiction of those doing the experiencing? Moreover it was the time when the prevailing morality was that research in itself was exploitative. The only really "moral" research was to study one's own kind. Furthermore, intellectual ideologies tended to de- pict positivism as the epistemology of the establishment and, as befitted the times, the establishment was seen to have had a clumsy hand in producing some of the greatest troubles of the age. I even- tually came to think of phenomenologically inspired knowledge as meeting some of the standards of objectivity, and as both a morally and aesthetically pleasing version of the truth.

Having decided upon this theoretical perspective and having let go of the notion of finding out "the ultimate and real facts" about the matter, a different kind of puzzle emerged. I had hoped that the choice of the method would recommend some worthwhile way of putting order into the material. It did not seem to do so. So I had a choice about analysis and presentation to consider. While there were in the literature ongoing discussions about the epistemic core of anthropology pointing to parts-wholes and similarities-differences as fundamental issues, they suggested no order that appealed to me. Picking on a "part" of some known whole, or striking as "similarity" or "difference" to what is already known would certainly be acceptable anthropologically. Such solutions were probably rote and unavoidable. Yet, what material to present, and how to order and present this material, continued as nagging and intriguing problems.

At an early stage I had assumed that tape-recorded conversations with "informants" would solve some of the problems of rigor and purity. On occasions these had a "pregnant moment" sanctity which consoled me, if nothing else. Ordinary ethnography seemed so laden with unreflexive description, obscure premises, and indigestible tacitness. Yet, unavoidably, it was immediately obvious that my own experiences structured the interviews, which could then, after all, be viewed only in the cultural context in which they happened. The dialectic between myself and the setting was undeniably accountable.

Some argue that the very ordering of data somehow pollutes their sanctity. If so, then the very existence of something we can call "data," and the use of fieldworkers' experience and orientations would do the same. These are the things, however, that suffuse the material with meaning. The pointedly cultural organization of knowledge makes possible the existence of anthropology, or "data," and of the sense which is to be given to it. This is what positivism means. It is true some have produced successful documents essentially unadulterated at first glance by orders and rationalities, by categories and selectivity. Studs Terkel is one. Elliott Leyton's work on dying miners and Manuel Gamio's autobiographical collection on the Mexican immigrant are others. These do not have, however, a vested interest in, nor do they make overt claims to be, works of academic anthropology. Rather they are works of strong moral fiber, the full impact of which is possible by the authors opting out of the positivistic neutering that social scientific analysis renders.

My problem was that I *did* wish to write anthropology and indeed had contracted to write anthropology. Given this, then, what kind of ordering of the knowledge would I take? What kinds of responsibilities for order would I adopt as my own, and thereby advocate to the reader? Should I advocate the life situation of the people studied and document their discomforts and pains? Should I permit these very data to speak further to some more overriding moral or political ethos about the Hawaiian Islands? Should I project some familiar problematics about the human condition, or about a universal human consciousness? There were precedents for all of these things "in the literature." Obviously these precedents had also prepared reading audiences. As ways of doing anthropology they had become formalized, their ways of making sense and being understood had already been prepared and significant deviations would, no doubt, appear ludicrous. Such precedents and conventions were overriding enough to become a necessary prerequisite to successful work.

This question of what themes or what data to write about led me to become engaged with an enduring and familiar puzzle. It is sometimes referred to by those who write social science, and not without considerable amusement, as the "many books problem." It refers to the awareness by most researchers that many books could come out of the same piece of fieldwork, and even out of the same specific pieces of data. I began to be aware of it in the days when the work was a mere fantasy, when I wondered what kinds of conversations or interviews I might initiate with my informants. It continued through two years of initial fieldwork and subsequent field trips when it assumed an immediacy and intensity obvious in every daily encounter. It intrigues me now even in the writing. At the moment all I can produce from this experience is the well-worn conventional wisdom that knowledge is culturally, ideologically and temporally organized. Knowledge, its order and implications reflect the writer and her experiences if not entirely, at least as much as they do the situation presumably under study. It will take more than the knowledge of the Lewis-Redfield debate, or the Mead–Freeman dispute about adolescence in Samoa, to show how differences in writers' perspectives affect anthropological epistemology. Yet the only possibility seemed to be to permit the intellectual and ideological times to guide me in these choices. Thus it would be of some interest to me to reflect upon my final choices and to consider how it might have been done a few decades ago, or, alternatively, a few decades hence.

To make these problems and analytical queries visible seemed an imperative prelude to the work. It would permit the reader to make a considered evaluation of the kind of knowledge I finally decided to produce. This purposeful visibility suggests several attributes of knowledge. First, it shows that knowledge is constructed, and it is constructed ideologically from previous materials. Second, it seems important to attempt a reconstruction of the early choices and decisions in attempts to understand the ultimate rendering. We may have been liberated from reliance on value-free-ness, yet the choices now posited for us are, after all, a burdensome freedom. In view of this I want to present a few of the choices that were open to me.

No doubt some would argue that the use of a known frame is merely a form of elitist conservatism, and the previously honored and condoned analytics are simply strengthened by additions of newly-found "evidence." Others would argue that *any* frame or analytic mode, merely by producing discourse and discovery, eventually acquires recognition. Recognition undoubtedly has power, and can lead to advocacy positions in analysis, thereby eventual conservatism is inevitable.

Turning to the substance of the analytic frames, I should report that an early influence for me, and one which continually reappeared, was given enthusiasm and verve by an almost forgotten schoolgirl fascination with Milton and the Bible. The celestial dramatics and the awesome mysteries of Heaven, Earth, and Satan seemed to be revisited in the experience of the newcomer from the mainland. Paradise gained and paradise lost were epitomized in the enlightenment and the pain. All of the mythic features of seeking the promised land, of committing the forbidden act, and of being expelled seemed to be there. The quest was there, and the fall from grace. This frame also permitted me some of the indulgences I had previously been denied. I could humor my inclinations toward the imagery and promise of the South Seas myth, to the evolving cultures of Utopia, and to the richness of European liter-

ature celebrating the geographic imagination. I could make an anthropological topic out of that impenetrable domain of artists and
poets, the Western consciousness. These possibilities were heavy
with the kind of excitement that Lovejoy must have experienced
when he documented his various excursions into the history of ideas.
It was a theme that I knew I shared with many a writer on the
subject of Hawaii, as I shall point out later. The romanticism, the
primitivism, the millenarianism were all there. This seemed a fitting
stage onto which I could bring the seeker after the Golden Age and
his own fortunes, the person called the *haole*.

     Interlocked with this was another frame which satisfied
my anthropological conscience as well as that of the liberated North
American of the mid-twentieth century. This conscience, like some
of the others I discuss, was fanned by the ideological winds that
blew across Berkeley in the sixties and which I willingly claimed.
In my mind it acquired a rather sardonic title—How the West Made
Hawaii Possible. It did not suggest an occurrence to celebrate, but
rather something which, with equal vividness, could be depicted
as the rape of Polynesian culture. The ideological engagement of
contemporary anthropology with the topic of colonialism and its
ravages made this an inviting theme. I could clearly engage my
anthropological and personal sympathies with the Hawaiian people
against a steady stream of *haoles,* venturing to the Pacific world in
the aftermath of James Cook. More importantly, however, I viewed
Hawaii, the place we know, as being created by the Western world.
At this time I had not yet encountered Edward Said's incomparable
Orientalism, with its proposition that the Orient is a discourse produced ideologically, imaginatively, politically, and in other ways by
European culture. Nor had I yet come upon Billington's scholarly
account of the American frontier as depicted through European eyes,
Land of Savagery, Land of Promise. Their work would have sharp-
ened my views and enriched them considerably had I discovered
it before the first draft of this manuscript was completed.

     Part of the sensitivities of this time at Berkeley was the
notion of "anthropological imperialism" made into a classic state-
ment by Kathleen Gough. Thus I was also engaged by reflections
upon the unwitting aggressions of my own kind, whether they were
the omnipresent Occident or the omnipresent anthropologist. There

was a strong motivation to analyze my data in terms of a white hegemony. The multiple problems narrated to me by *haoles* residing in Hawaii could become evidence for an account of a waning hegemony. Certainly for an ever-persevering Protestant, the attractions of such self-condemnations seemed satisfying enough and particularly poignant as they were shared by so many of my informants. Moreover, they were ideologically sound from the anthropological viewpoint.

The continuing convention of defining the contemporary age as one of unprecedented agitation suggested yet another frame. It was, and still is, pressingly of the times to review old commitments and to find them wanting. One such taken-for-granted commitment was causing controversy and even anarchy in the written word and on the streets. Progress, and our commitment to it, was up for reexamination. Though given sanctity in biblical lore, it seemed to be having a less than holy effect on the human world. Oppression and colonialism, the military-industrial complex, and the untrammeled exploitation of nature and innocence were, in this paradigm, all laid at the door of progress. The mainland migrant to the Pacific seemed an embodiment of the protest against the inevitabilities of the future. The romantic quest was for a more primitive existence with its reasonable absence of uncertainty, where all the puzzles were solved. Yet the migrant seemed to find there, and indeed to carry there himself, even more progress.

Parallel to this frame is another which could evoke an appropriate anthropological discourse, namely that of cultural ecology. In this paradigm the notion of progress becomes translated into the relationship of humans to the environment. It was apparent to me that the study of the mainland *haole* could be told in terms of the politics of space, the existential satisfactions of what it means to be in a place. This again borrows from the image of paradise where islands in the South Seas are imbued with the myth and lore of centuries. They promise freedom from those conditions which are culturally decried as antithetical to human well-being. The evils of society from which relief is to be sought are recognizable enough—industrial carnage, encroachment on time and space, violation of culturally mediated notions of beauty, excessive inhibitions, and so on. The enticement of an easily gained Utopia with its promise of relegating these abnegating conditions to another world could be mapped onto Hawaii.

This frame readily transposes into one that I developed and found satisfying, namely that of expatriate pilgrimages. This notion amply fulfilled a familiar romantic fantasy. It has given us pioneers, Russian émigrés, self-imposed political exiles, transplanted scientists, and an array of Shelleys, James Baldwins, and Gertrude Steins. In more modest anthropological versions, migration might be the appropriate focus. Conventional notions of "push" and "pull" could be infused with perhaps fresher themes of a good life and ideological commitment.

A volume about acculturation was an obvious choice. I constantly found myself embroiled in issues which could be labeled as problems in existential becoming. The suggestion of strangers in a strange land had enough appeal for imagination, enough fictive and biblical lore to tease every ounce of possible romance from the experience. While the hardships and exigencies of the everyday were certainly there, I could not help but be engaged by the transformations imposed on the journeying selves who came to Hawaiian shores. A fairly "ordinary, average mainland person" becomes, by virtue of a reasonably commonplace decision to migrate, that alienating entity called the mainland *haole.* Not only was the person now a *haole,* but also a colonial, and the heir to a string of surprising descriptions—privileged, arrogant, stupid, lazy, rich, and exploitative. How does an ordinary North American learn to live with this?

In periodic incurable involvements with the notion of pure form, I fantasized about producing a manuscript about method. It would be unadulterated by any obligation to discuss the people studied except peripherally as illustrations. In the world of imagination this satisfied some private fantasies about being the Walter Mitty of anthropology, pointing to radical revelations which forge new directions in the discipline. With Walter Mitty and Horatio Alger aside, there were clear attractions in doing a preliminary ethnography of the ethnographic process. Anthropologists like Gerald Berreman have been calling for this for some time. I could talk about the epistemology of encountering and knowing, surely the process through which knowledge becomes established in fieldwork. I could write of the many dialectics introduced in the process, such as the dialectics between my own autobiography and those of the people whom the study purports to discuss. I could reflect upon the nature of the phenomenological endeavor and its transformations, upon ethnography and the nature of description, and upon the many disjunctures that arise. I could look upon the fieldwork encounter as a process requiring certain performances and itself creating a definitive culture. I could categorize the coherent and tacit repertory of beliefs which make fieldwork a possibility. What needs to be negotiated in doing it and what does this portend? It would not be a book about Hawaii at all, but rather a book about method and meta-method, about the cultural organization of knowledge, about social epistemology. Perhaps I could even evoke the claim to *Wissens-anthropologie*? This particular scenario of possibilities was exciting enough to have many private rehearsals, and to be played at frequent intervals like any perennial favorite. Obviously, many parts of it could be salvaged and legitimately produced, even *pro forma*, as part of any conventional ethnography. Method, after all, is considered an appropriate and desirable topic for anything produced, even remotely, in the name of science. All ethnographies have to recognize it.

The imagined scenario also ran through other choices of aesthetic, moral, or political import. What if I wrote it as a treatise on ethnic relations? This had many disciplinary forerunners and had a body of ready-made knowledge where it would fit. If I expanded my scope in subsequent fieldwork endeavors I could write about the Americanization of a cultural plurality, or perhaps the ebb of the Anglo-American hegemony and the possible rise of the Japanese one. Or, in recognition of the contributions of folklore, the whole work could be synchronized in terms of folk beliefs, folk theories, and folk explanations. It could be written on folk beliefs about ethnic and racial equality, about the dominion of the good life and how these become implemented, practiced, and rationalized in a multi-ethnic society. Perhaps I could produce it as a history of the white person in the Pacific with the mainland *haole* I came to know constituting the contemporary actors in the historic process. In short my choices were legion. They forced upon me decisions which were necessarily positivistic, demanding of me an authoritative stand. Yet the nagging problem of making considered epistemological decisions continued to concern me.

In some academic and social scientific circles positivism has come to be a cause for denigration. It has become associated with unsavory qualities such as authoritarianism, oppression, and impoverished single-mindedness. As nonpositivism is probably not a possibility in some pure form, a recognition of some of the kind of work it could do is subsumed currently under the label of "interpretive" anthropology. This permits interpretations with all their varieties, vagaries, and seemingly endless numbers of possibilities. Yet there is much about the very presentation of each interpretative endeavor that is surely positivistic. There is a curious disparity here. Does the condoning of interpretive work then really suggest the break with positivism? Does the *very accepting and condoning* of interpretations (however many of these there are) as appropriate forms of the truth, then become nonpositivism? At the same time is the substantive content of each and every interpretation, the inescapable matter of "the knowledge itself," really always positivistic? Perhaps nonpositivism should not be merely interpreted as "truer" knowledge or "actual" knowledge? Perhaps instead it should be seen primarily as an ethical position, a methodological or theoretical stance that countenances all kinds of conventional wisdoms, or new insights, however contradictory, with the awe and respect previously accorded "truths"? Is it a new kind of liberalized conscience? Certainly Anthony Giddens captures this notion very aptly by calling it post-positivism. Can it be that the two positions are a new version of the old dialectic between form and content? For me nonpositivism captures a new morality for the social sciences. It allows me, under the guise of the theoretical-methodological position this creates, to view anthropology, not as the vehicle for the discovery of truth, but rather as a form of criticism.

Perhaps it is not necessary to evoke the imagery of literary criticism, political criticism, journalistic criticism or other kinds of purposeful organizing of knowledge to a specific end. It is most importantly for me a social and cultural criticism and recognizes what has always been *tacitly* present in anthropology and indeed in all kinds of knowledge—a moral position. For me, however, it is always a disciplinary criticism in that it recognizes a body of existing knowledge, in this case of course, anthropological knowledge, and attempts to work within these bounds. In this perspective positivism and phenomenology are inextricably intertwined as cultural necessities in the organization of a knowledge that makes sense to us. Yet it gives the writing of academic anthropology, despite all of its inevitably positivistic overtones, new moral and aesthetic possibilities. It permits me to organize themes both in terms of how they arise in the consciousness of my informants and how they could be ordered in recognizable anthropology. It permits me to render appropriate connections to the growing historical body of ideas subsumed by the discipline and give full account to the choices and thoughts of the people being depicted. It allows me to use, with a clear conscience, already documented, authorized, and otherwise prepared-for-consumption knowledge. It also condones that I too, as the anthropologist, prefer analyses, make choices, and intrude my personal views and life into the document I present. Most importantly, this intrusion does not become a canker or abomination to be eliminated and condemned, but rather part of the natural order of producing anthropology.

It is not necessary to agonize about the truth-value of it, but rather to see it as the kind of knowledge arising out of a common foundation, with a shared language. Rigors from the past and positivistic knowledge are combined with phenomenology. The latter gives full legitimate credit to interpretations and the elusive nuances which might otherwise disappear in the elimination and reordering fervors of positivism. It does this whether these interpretations arise with the people studied or with their scribe.

Understandings such as these, but more importantly, the acceptance and legitimation of such understandings within a consciously reasoned frame, surely makes the writing of an ethnography tailored to my own choice academically appropriate. It surely permits me to choose frames with discretion, to mingle them as I wish, and to declare facts in a manner chosen by me. It also suggests the presence of an anthropological audience who would accept these postures.

Having proposed the foregoing, I can now do what inclination has prompted me to do. I can address the *haole* from the perspective of a critical consciousness. I can attempt an anthropology of the *haole* as well as deal reflexively with my own endeavors at ethnography. I can write an ethnography with reflexive asides and weave my ideas around sets of notions like "Western consciousness," "the *haole*," "the place called Hawaii," and around the experiences of my informants. Most pertinently, I can make epistemological and anthropological choices and not be beholden to the impossible and improbable need to "discover the ultimate truth."

The Mainland *Haole*

Dialectics of Enterprise, Hope and History

. . . that far-off home of profound repose, and soft indolence, and dreamy solitude, where life is one long slumberous Sabbath, the climate one long delicious summer day, and the good that die experience no change, for they fall asleep in one heaven and wake up in another . . . but no other land could so longingly and so beseechingly haunt me, sleeping and waking, through half a lifetime . . .

Mark Twain (1889:145)

ka palekani wahi
heaven on earth

When the sun rose to affirm Sunday, January 18, 1778, as yet another golden Pacific day, it witnessed a momentous event. The entry that documents the occasion, however, was terse and undramatic. It carried no hint of its profound significance, or of the excitement and promise that day was to suggest.

we however saw [no land] till day break in the Morning of the 18th when an island was descovered bearing NEBE and soon after we saw more land bearing North and intirely ditatched from the first;

both had the appearance of being high land. At Noon the first bore NEBE½E by estimation [left blank] leagues distant and an elevated hill near the east end of the other bore N½W; our Latitude at this time was 21°12′30″N, Longitude 200°41′E. We had now light airs and calms by turns so that at sun set we were not less than 9 or 10 leagues from the nearest land.

Monday 19th. On the 19th at Sun rise the island first seen bore East [left blank] leagues distant at least; this being directly to windward there was no geting nearer it so that I stood for the other, and not long after discovered a third island in the direction of WNW and as far distant as an island could be seen . . .

Thus wrote Captain James Cook in his log of the events of two January days in 1778 (p. 263) and by doing so he set down the first encounter of the Western world with the Hawaiian Islands. His Britannic Majesty's survey sloops *Resolution* and *Discovery* dropped anchor off Kauai near the village of Waimea. Cook believed that he had discovered merely another of the many inhabited or uninhabited islands he had come upon in his voyages. Barely a fortnight ago he had left Christmas Island. Also he had recorded in his log the discovery of the Cook Archipelago, New Caledonia, Norfolk Island, the Isles of Pines, and the rather awesome encounter with Australia. What he had now come upon, as he was able to intuit from the reticence and wonder expressed by the natives who came aboard, was an island which encountered Europeans for the first time. He bestowed upon the group the name Sandwich Islands in recognition of the First Lord of the British Admiralty.[1] The first *haole* had arrived.

The notion of discovery, of the resulting wonder, is a familiar Westernized way to begin an account of the Hawaiian Islands. It seems to provide an adequate overture not only to histories, but often to travel books, sociological treatises, works of political economy, and fiction as well. Yet, though in many quarters Cook is still accorded the distinction of being the "discoverer" of the archipelago, this is a construction of European ethnocentrism and Westernized history. If discovery or precedence is at issue, this perspective is neither anthropologically accurate nor ideologically appropriate. Rather it is merely a reflection of the cultural transformation by which all cultures make sense of matters outside their usual interpretive domains. Obviously, if dates of arrival are to determine discovery, the rights to this event belong to ancient Polynesian mariners of inordinate skill, who are believed to have cast off from the shores of the Marquesas and the Society Islands. Archaeological dating of their first settlement has been put forth tentatively as A.D. 124 (Ferdon 1968:100), while sites on Oahu have a possible date of A.D. 375 (Kirch 1974; Tuggle 1979:189). There seems to be general agreement that Polynesian settlers were there in the early years of the Christian era, and new knowledge is being continually established with the promise that a more comprehensive prehistoric settlement pattern will eventually emerge. It is often pointed out, in addition, that Polynesian discoveries, migration, and later two-way voyaging occurred at a time when Europeans were still timidly splashing around in the Mediterranean. Such comparisons are part of the romantic vision which can be expected of a culture with a well-developed technology. To such a culture feats achieved with "inferior" technological skill are the objects of wonder and awe. The Western world, and anthropology as part of it, is often in the position of wondering about such human ingenuity and how it could be possible without adequate technological support. Such supposed paradoxes make it inevitable that there would be much speculation as to whether the Polynesians came to Hawaii in a deliberate search for land or were carried there inadvertently by gale and current. Not surprisingly no serious weight is given to native versions of origin and settlement. The emergence of the various islands due to the coupling of the gods Papa and Wakea are accounts relegated to the scholarly concerns of the collectors of mythology. Chants and traditions of voyages from the mythic homeland Kahiki become mere esoteric asides to the facts assembled by Western histories.

Even in a discussion of how the white world came to Hawaii, it is a matter of speculation as to whether the precedence actually belongs to Cook and his men. If the sheer weight of documentation over the last two centuries alone were to determine the decision, undoubtedly discovery should be placed with him. One of the more intriguing mysteries of Pacific navigation, however, places doubt on this decision. For example, Cook records that the Hawaiians had iron artifacts in their possession: "a piece of iron hoop, about three inches long, fited into a wooden handle in the same manner as their stone adzes and a nother edge tool which was supposed to have be[en] made of the point of a broad sword. . . . How they came by them I cannot account for" (1967:285). Admittedly these could have been traded with other island groups. It does not seem possible that they were washed ashore. More believably they indicate the presence of other Europeans at an earlier time.

There is evidence that the Spanish could lay claim to the title of discovery. That they have not been able to do so in significant ways is possibly the result of the flimsy status of navigational recordings made before the use of the chronometer. Any assertions by the Spanish also face the sheer weight of British claims. It comes as no surprise that the majority of work dealing with early and contemporary Hawaii is in English, and the history promoted as authoritative has been filtered through that language. Yet Balboa had stood in the waves of the Pacific Ocean and claimed those waters for Spain in 1513, and seven years later Magellan pierced its vast mysteries. In 1493, Pope Alexander VI had given Spain the authority to claim dominion over discovered and undiscovered lands west of a meridian a hundred leagues from the Azores. Therefore, before Drake brought the British flag there, the Pacific was known as the Spanish lake.

Spain had established trade routes from Acapulco to Manila with at least one vessel a year making the voyage. The Solomons, New Hebrides, and eastern Polynesia were visited by the Spanish captains Mendaña, Quirós, and Torres between 1565 and 1606 (Schurz 1939; Beaglehole 1966). Whether the Spanish reached the Hawaiian Islands or not has been a matter of ongoing debate. Despite some vigorous dissent (Dahlgren 1917; Stokes 1939), the evidence proposed seems solidly constructed. The whole debate is a problem in the negotiation of historical fact and like the notion of first discovery itself, a product of European culture.

Several pieces of evidence to support the Spanish presence are usually put forward. A native tradition of white men landing at Kealakekua Bay on Hawaii was apparently in good currency in the early years after Cook and well into the middle of the nineteenth century. It has been independently recorded by the missionary Ellis (1831:438), the Russian explorer von Kotzebue (1830:166), the American seaman Townsend (1888:17) and the Hawaiian historian Malo (1838:106). It was supposed to have occurred during the reign of the high chief Keliiokaloa. By setting a specific time for the duration of a generation, and knowing the genealogy of the chief, some have estimated that the event might have occurred sometime after A.D. 1500. This suggests that the castaways were from the lost ships of the Saavedra expedition to the Moluccas from Mexico in 1527 (Alexander 1892). Other tales of castaways appear in early works, and mention is made of an ancient anchor. Some have proposed that even the feathered cloaks and helmets so idiosyncratic to the Hawaiian chain were an adaptation of those worn by the Spanish (Langdon 1975:273).

The evidence of two ancient manuscript charts is sometimes put forth. In 1865 a letter from the Hydrographical Department in Madrid was published in the Hawaiian newspaper *The Friend*. It stated that the Madrid archives possessed a map with a group of islands named Islas de Mesa on the same latitude but some 17° to the east of the Hawaiian Islands. The Spanish claimed that Juan Gaetano had discovered them in 1555. Further supportive evidence for this event is said to have occurred in 1743 when the British man-of-war *Centurion* captured a Spanish galleon carrying a chart of Pacific discoveries. The same set of islands were depicted, the largest was named La Mesa, probably Hawaii, north of this La Desgraciada (the unfortunate), possibly Maui, then three called Los Monjes (the monks), which could have been Kahoolawe, Lanai, and Molokai (Alexander 1892:4; Peirce 1880). Both Captains Vancouver and La Perouse, however, failed in their efforts to locate these legendary islands, and their existence is relegated to historical tracts, where the question of their status is raised from time to time.

In providing these accounts of discovery as a beginning to a discussion of Europeans in the Islands I have followed a well-established tradition. It becomes apparent in comparing various volumes about the Hawaiian and Pacific islands that, although there are several variations on the theme of discovery, some widely held symbolic conventions are being tapped. That dozens of authors choose this method of opening, in contrast to those who write about

Africa or South America, signifies some recognizable cultural assumptions, a commitment to activating tacit understandings in the reader.

A few of the beginnings evoked are cosmic and biblical in their awesome breadth. They report how some twenty-five million years ago, give or take a millennium, a cone thrust itself above the water line. Curiously, such beginnings seem almost irrelevant to the subject matter to be discussed. A work of demography, liberally illustrated with tables, opens this way (Nordyke 1977:3), as does Michener's epic novel:

> Millions upon millions of years ago, when the continents were already formed and the principal features of the earth had been decided, there existed, then as now, one aspect of the world that dwarfed all others. It was a mighty ocean, resting uneasily . . . (1959:1).

These ethereal forces of creation are evoked also as a familiar metaphor, which serves to herald the particular calling of the writer, as in the following case:

> Darkness covered the earth and gross darkness the people. This, for ages, was emphatically applicable to the isles of the great Pacific Ocean. But the voice divine said, "Let there be light."

The writer was the renowned Hiram Bingham, of the first company of missionaries to reach the Sandwich Islands in 1820 (1849:2).

Some historical reporting finds the beginnings with Cook (Day 1960:3; Daws 1968:1). Others begin with the arrival of the Polynesians, creating in that very arrival the wonder we have come to expect. The feats of these ancient people become contrasted most favorably to the achievements of other early cultures. One anthropological treatise notes that the accomplishments of the classical world on the waters of the Mediterranean and the seafaring courage of northern Europe's proud Vikings are dimmed in comparison to the brilliance and skill of Polynesian navigation (Buck 1959:3). A historical account of the distribution of power in the Pacific opens its pages with the greatness of the Polynesian discovery reflected against the civilizations of China, Japan, Mexico, and Peru, which are seen as unable to match that particular achievement (Morrell 1963:3). One work chronicling the economic and ecological exploitation of the Pacific considers the only appropriate comparison to be the cases of Egypt and China (Wenkam 1974:3). Such beginnings reflect the romantic interpretations so characteristic of our times where the achievements of the "primitive" are treated with respectful awe.

Another traditional beginning takes advantage of the reader's experiences with arrivals, anticipations, and discoveries, a state of pleasurable anxiety common to all. It asks the reader to become transplanted into the role of sojourner or stranger approaching the Hawaiian islands. A book, destined to inform the casual visitor of the history, society, and approved touristic images of the Islands, includes a chapter entitled "Origins." In it the authors issue this invitation: "It all begins with journeying. The visitor flies in search of the sun across the time zones, and his first discovery is that his biological clock has gone wrong" (Goodman et al. 1971:9).

Two frequently cited histories adopt this beginning. Judd opens with an arrival by air:

> Hawaii has a history . . . Going to Hawaii for the first time is a memorable experience . . . Glimpses of land flash by, soft green and brown, edged by a white and blue ribbon of beach and sea . . . (1961:13)

Similarly, Loomis' history of the arrival of the missionaries in 1820 creates a fictional picture of the event:

> Elisha heard the thud of running feet on the deck and a shrill Hawaiian voice crying, "Land ho!" . . . High over the island of Hawaii a snow-crowned peak gleamed wan and rosy above the clouds, like a sign set in the heavens. (1966:9)

In fact the arrival by sailing ship is common enough to be used by Jack London, Mark Twain, Robert Louis Stevenson, and Gauguin, as well as by sundry travelers such as the French diplomat Barrot (1839), and by contemporary anthropologists on their way to the field (Suggs 1966; Marshall 1961).

> I saw that island first when it was neither night nor morning. The moon was to the west, setting, but still broad and bright . . . (Stevenson 1892:3)

The dark jagged outlines of the Marquesas Islands inspire a certain feeling of awe in a visitor making his first landfall. (Suggs 1966:3)

One of the great classics of anthropological reporting begins in this very familiar manner. In the opening lines of *We, The Tikopia,* Raymond Firth writes

In the cool of the early morning, just before sunrise, the bow of the Southern Cross headed towards the eastern horizon, on which a tiny dark blue outline was faintly visible. Slowly it grew into a rugged mountain mass, standing up sheer from the ocean. (1936:1)

Surely the preponderance of such beginnings requires some interpretation? Surely such knowledge is constructed to some end? There must be some covert hypothesis which either heralds the writing of history or makes a fitting introduction to the South Seas. Not surprisingly these openings tell us more about ourselves than they do about the world of the Polynesians. They serve as appropriate seminal metaphors for our interpretation of the world, or more particularly, specific parts of it.

What the writers of these beginnings do not point out is that they are producing and reproducing cognitive predispositions by which the world is infused with meaning for Occidental cultures. They are displaying Western consciousness. Thus when Captain Cook steps ashore, in actuality or in print, the very act of doing so has become possible only because of a world view which has "making discoveries" as a way of making sense of the world. Is it part of a cultural predisposition—this coming upon, unearthing, and making into certainties what is mythic and elusive, tacit and hazily comprehended? As an orientation to the world it is well worth considering as central to the structure of the knowledge we have produced.

This is a rather elaborate way of making a point about discovery, about coming upon something for the first time. It is noteworthy that so many writers attempt to create this experience for the reader. They seem to be doing something else as well. It seems important, for example, to remind the reader that even though the work may be about demographic patterns it is importantly situated in a place. The implication is that the material to be discussed cannot be understood without this reference to place, nor can it be apprehended without adequate notions about its beginnings. The message suggests that all knowledge is, on the one hand, dependent upon its past and on the other can only be understood within the context introduced for it. This introduced context is both blandly forthright, as in the example above, and by implication subtly evocative.

The story of Hawaii, any story of Hawaii, can have a perfect, a "natural" beginning. To a culture obsessed with origins, such openings are rich with satisfaction in providing the kind of undisputed "facts" that only the authority of vulcanologists and geologists can produce. To a people who believe themselves fashioned by celestial power, their habitat created for them in the same manner, the rising of islands out of the sea in the dim stretches of the past manages to recreate Genesis in oceanic form.

Genesis and beginnings imply a duality of views which serve to orient one to the cognitive ecology of Occidental cultures. They point to a descending and an ascending view of human evolution. One point of origin arises from the creative acts of God, from whose enviable position of grace humans have continued to descend, taking one giant step toward their inevitable decline, the expulsion from paradise. Most significantly the expulsion is into an unremitting wilderness. At the same time Western culture has produced an opposing view. Humans are depicted ascending from an initial wilderness to an even better future, from the untamed animal world of their origin to civilization, or a promised land. At first glance these cosmic paradoxes appear irrelevant to a story about whites in Hawaii. Nevertheless they produce the dialectic that creates a cognitive tension in these people. This duality becomes importantly manifested in the shaping of contemporary Hawaii. It is woven into what I propose is an ecological imperialism or an ecological hegemony, and the inherent paradoxes poignantly present in these states.

Some relevance is served by posing an untrammeled creation, perhaps an Eden, against the particular reality I plan to create in the ensuing work. The pristine and Elysian beginning contrasts with present woes. Former bliss and present turmoil, such juxtaposing is a common device in Western discourse. By posing the opposite, the condition under discussion is presumably suffused with new clarity. Original purity contrasts with later fall from grace.

These openings then suggest pervasive tautologies (Burke 1966:55). Two unmistakable ones are present in the works on Hawaii revealing themselves as untapped presuppositions. As discrete, generative, dominating ideas they appear and reappear as epistemological tenets. Both lie tacit in the openings I have discussed, prevail implicitly in the story of the mainland *haole*, and serve to make some initial sense of the white presence in the Islands. They both concern Nature. One is the peculiarly Western notion of the relationship between humans and their natural environment. It is a complex relationship perhaps best revealed in Christian belief and lore. It lends itself to ready analysis through the doctrines of conflict theories. The common cliche "man against nature" probably encapsulates it most efficiently. The other is Nature as nostalgia. Again, biblical writings and their fervent message about a future utopia probably reflect the nostalgic view most succinctly. A pleasurable, remembered past defines a future in its image. The present, almost by definition, cannot encompass complete happiness. Happiness is an experience of the past and a promise of a future in which perfection is to be regained. The cliché here is probably "the promised land." These two themes are the dialectic which governs the Western presence in Hawaii, and, in some sense made Hawaii what it is. The imagery evoked by the depiction of creation, or of discovery, essentially taps this ecology, massively persuasive, yet effectively hidden, in the Occidental world view. It is an unwritten script, an obscure treatise on geographical or ecological knowledge, and yet it could be said to have transformed the world. The postulates are consensual, unquestionable, and as morally dictatorial as any of the Ten Commandments. The resulting truths are self-evident.

The Ecology of Enterprise:
Wilderness and Progress

The whole of nature, as Emerson once noted, is a metaphor of the human mind. It is this metaphor, the vision within, that sees equivalents in the environment around and, by doing so, creates and actualizes the metaphor. It permits a place to become exotic and foreign, or alternately to be familiar and known. A necessary continuity with views of the world held previously is thereby made possible. "Every image and idea about the world is compounded, then, of personal experience, learning, imagination, and memory" (Lowenthal 1961:260).

The notion of "discovery" is a part of this environmental cognition which resonates through Western perceptions of nature. As vision and knowledge are discontinuous, some geographical objects acquire a mysterious salience, others do not. We see islands and oceans, but, unlike Polynesians, have no developed and differentiated sense of waves. We are obsessed with a primacy of land which we acknowledge by sight and touch, but have no sense of specific points on the ocean. We glorify the unusual and the pristine and permit the usual to remain unseen and fade into insignificance. Being the "first to see" is an experience which carries some rights to ownership. "Seeing is believing" as Dundes (1972) maintains, and with the added act of touching, usually by foot, it becomes property. Discovery does, however, also require legitimation. It is as though the failure of the Polynesians to document their find, and the failure of the Spaniards to do it publicly and convincingly enough, has been held against them. Their claims are relegated to the dusty tracts of archives and histories and, in the case of the Polynesians, to the romantic accounts of anthropologists. They are marginal to officially condoned and politically sanctioned validations. Some of the troubles in Hawaii stem from the fact that Polynesians are still reporting, many centuries after the fact, their rights to discovery and ownership. The ultimate success of these claims is left up to public consciousness in the now familiar form of "aboriginal land claims."

The notion of ownership and control, of finding, and perhaps subduing, is revealed in the concept of discovery. To "discover" requires a particular view of humans in relation to nature. It is a state of eternal tension with natural forces, where the opponents hold positions of separateness, in a struggle for dominance. Each has a will and a discrete body of truths in this paradigm. The inherent conflict is not something that can be ultimately eradicated, but is a necessary and ongoing component of the relationship. A sense of moral appropriateness pervades it. After all, following the creation of the natural world, God fashioned man in His own image, central to the universe, and in no way a part of the world shaped before his arrival. Man was His greatest creation and he was given full dominion over the natural order. There was to be a "relationship" not a symbiosis, congruence, or common core (Rust 1953; Glacken 1967). The initial Eden seemed nontroublesome enough, yet, as is more evident, it had its hidden menace. Nature has continued to be capricious and to conceal its threats. The fall from grace merely exacerbated and made visible these threats. It is not surprising, therefore, that seventeenth-century philosophers saw the fall as the origin of disorder in the natural world. The notion of a chaotic and untrustworthy wilderness had become apparent.

This separateness of humans from the encroaching threat of the natural world makes other notions possible. Nature becomes an adversary, powerful and mysterious. It is infused with strangeness, remoteness, and can command shock, wonder, and awe. We live in perpetual anxiety in relation to it, and spend considerable energy in seeking new and more foolproof ways of harnessing it. The idioms developed to deal with the relationship reveal the human toils necessary: "conquest of nature," "man against the elements," "tame the wilderness," and "the jungle reclaims its own." Seas are angry, clouds threaten, mountains loom, rains blind, winds howl, volcanoes erupt, cliffs menace, and waves break and dash. The threatening and fearful world of nature is even attributed to South Sea islands which are usually given, in most imagery, an idyllic calm. Volcanoes and tsunami are the classic aggressors. In the imagination of mainland North Americans, however, at least those who produce movies, the dangers are legion. An analysis of 125 feature-length films made about the Pacific Islands during the years 1913–1943, shows that geography constituted a constant hazard to human life. Volcanic eruptions, earthquakes, hurricanes, typhoons, crocodiles, sharks, and octopi appeared as perennial favorites (Schmitt 1968a). As many as twelve films depicted volcanic eruptions, some erasing complete islands.

The relationship depicted above, alienated and aggressive, with its ongoing efforts to force nature into subservience, can be further illuminated by comparing it to Chinese attitudes to the natural world (Tuan 1968). Formal European gardens can be compared to Chinese naturalistic ones. Western gardens provide a stage for humans, while the Chinese lay aside such pretensions in order to be one with a benign nature. The oneness with the natural order, so apparent in the Chinese world view, is presumably something that we from the Occident can only occasionally experience. To be able to "commune with nature" seems to require the lyrical subtleties of the poet, the innocent and untutored imagination of childhood (Cobb 1977), or some rare ecstatic experience of mystic origins.

Nature-as-foreign extends, in the Western view, to include those of human form but of strange ways and unfamiliar habitat. The "primitives" or "savages" of most parts of the non-European world occupied in the past a status in the natural order rather like natural curiosities of the plant or animal kingdom, worthy of the attention of gentlemen scholars. In particular, the peoples of the Pacific came within the purview of the West during the eighteenth century, the era when a romantic ethos imbued Nature with a new kind of exoticism (Schenk 1966). Despite its capriciousness, a deep affinity was felt for the natural world. This included a new appreciation for humans of lowly status at home, despite their unsavory ways, and for the savage beyond the horizon, despite his perversity.

The savage, in particular, seemed to encapsulate a nostalgia for greater happiness and to suggest an ideal perhaps beyond the grasp of European civilization (Baudet 1965; Fairchild 1955; Sinclair 1977; Street 1975). So the ascending and descending views of human civilization, ascending to better things from a primitive past and descending to lower and lower degradation after the fall, were both encompassed in the discovery of the South Sea islanders. This is exemplified in the attitude of Sir Joseph Banks, gentleman, scholar, and scientist, during his voyage with Captain Cook in 1768–71. He clearly pronounced the nobility of the savages of Otaheite by giving them the names of classical Greek heroes. Yet, at the same time he subjugated them to the status of scientific specimens by wondering why he could not take one of them home as "a curiosity, as well as some of my neighbours do lions and tygers at a larger expence" (p. 313). Remnants of these views persist today in Western attitudes toward Hawaiian culture, mixing a respect for an existence at once nobler than its own, and at the same time, in need of elevation by the techniques of "advanced" cultures.

Despite the human characteristics of vengeance and ire sometimes attributed to the natural, it is often imbued with a peculiar static quality. It is seen as coming to life, being meaningful and changing only after the relationship with humankind is established. The Pacific was "opened to the world" after the coming of white men, and untouched island communities presumably were "revealed." This untouched and untampered quality has particular appeal to the romantic and had much to do with the waves of Europeans who came to Pacific shores after Cook and the early explorers. Nor is this sense of isolation and stillness missing from the endeavors of anthropology. Indeed Oceania, and New Guinea in particular, must be among the most anthropologized places on earth. Even anthropologists, faithful as we are to notions of social change, have unwavering preconceptions about Oceania (Clark and Terrell 1978:296). Most important for the present argument is that apparently anthropologists depict the cultural traditions of the Pacific as changing very little before European contact. Thus, anthropology, the recalcitrant stepchild of the West that it is commonly seen as being, merely duplicates wider cultural assumptions.

There is a distinctly entrepreneurial view of the environment in the Western mind. Wilderness and savagery in biblical, talmudic, and classical sources is repulsive and its challenge to the puritanical mind is obvious. Unfettered nature, whether animate or inanimate, sets up a symbolic resonance in the world view of the West and signals a call to action. Wilderness needs development and inevitably needs to be exploited (Nash 1967). It is uncivilized and must be appropriately tutored. It is unruly in growth and must be tamed or ordered. It is pristine and uninhabited and thus suggests a frontier and the inevitable pioneers (Turner 1893). It is raw material and thus implies opportunity. The "natural" is distasteful and calls for improvement. Nature, a powerful adversary, and wilderness, a threatening presence, deserve to be addressed with all the powers and benefits of technology. North America is the archetype of what can occur when antagonism is felt for the environment and this antagonism is combined with technology, democracy, and capitalized zeal (Moncrief 1970).

The Western world view on nature was manifested early after European contact. Ellis notes in his *Journal* that large tracts of land "lie waste" (1827:18). The notion of "waste lands" is a concept out of the European agricultural tradition depicting the morality for ordering and using nature. Land in a state of nature is wasteful. Ellis also looked forward to the day when the natives would reach the desired, and undoubtedly the inevitable, stage of being more industrious and more civilized. Similarly, an American, William Ladd, one of the three co-founders of the first sugar plantation, noted in a speech to the Sandwich Islands Institute, that the chiefs were ignorant of the "value of their natural resources" (1838:68). They had, consequently, he argued, "neglected the soil." Befitting the mercantile consciousness of the nineteenth century, Ladd evokes the paradigm that typifies the relationship to nature, by issuing a puritanical call for industriousness and the fullest utilization of natural resources. Consonant with his world view, he suggests that the accomplishment of this would be expedited by the methods of Western scientific and economic knowledge. He calls for correct information on matters such as "composition and properties of the soil," "the humidity of the atmosphere," "the requisite elevation of the land," "the cost of labor," as well as other matters such as transportation to market, influence of mountains and trade winds, and the effects of sea vapor (1838:74).

Suffused with apparent goodwill and morality, such views nevertheless project the familiar commitment to progress. They depend on the notion that happiness and advance are inextricably entwined and that some form of paradise can be gained only by moving ahead. It is synonymous with reaching for the promised land, with social and cultural evolution, and with an ascending image of human history. Our orientation to the future resonates with these assumptions, as do our notions that life in the present century is eminently superior and preferable to that of previous centuries which, depending on their distance from us in time, approach some dark age of human understandings and welfare. All of these past ages become rehearsals for the present and the future. This particular world view is patently similar to that held by seekers after paradise and the coming of the Golden Age. Yet in essence paradise is not necessarily in accord with progress. Progress, with its built-in technical optimism, finds its greatest hope in the development and promise called science, while paradise usually finds its fulfillment in a denial of science.

While the paradigm of progress seems beyond immediate reproach, it has in recent decades come up for a reevaluation. Its previously undoubted association with betterment and well-being has been questioned. In fact, one of the major themes of an ongoing debate in contemporary Hawaii involves the notion of progress and all its concomitant possibilities. Such recent books as Creighton's *The Lands of Hawaii: Their Use and Misuse* (1978) raise the very question of unexamined presuppositions and unreflective commitments.

The Ecology of Hope:
Nostalgia, Paradise and the Promised Isles

The celestial paradises of our myths are responsible for an earthly search to satisfy uncompromising yearnings for a better life. The search may lead to millennial movements or utopian plans, but quite often it seems to be arrested at some "place" liberally endowed by nature. To those with enterprise and progress on their minds, liberally endowed nature merely seems to suggest that all that is required is a reordering, a new and better order. In contrast, for others paradise stands beckoning in imagination, already perfected and untampered by thought or deed. Human intervention would be, of course, superfluous. Paradise must carry with it the implicit trust that its perfections have been molded by divine wisdom. It is paradise precisely because it meets, or more appropriately, suggests, all the tangible and intangible horizons of psychic optimism. It is paradise only because it is complete *in situ*. It requires, by definition, neither planning nor labor, human intervention nor technological development. An ultimate paternalism is assumed to be operating, for it forsees, predicts, and makes into visible form what is yet largely unformulated. Unerringly it puts shape to what is tacit, formless, and inconceivable. "The image of Paradise taken by itself, would seem to be at once an image of desire and an image

for the release of desire, an image for the realization and fullfilment
of self and an image for the surrender of self" (Sanford 1961:265).
The idea of paradise is a method by which out of amorphous and
untextured inclinations, possibilities are implied. Once possibilities
are implied, probabilities become expected.

How is it that Hawaii has become synonymous with
paradise in the consciousness of most Occidentals? Probably only
because paradise is an unknown terrain. Certainly there is ample
knowledge about the lushness and plenty of Elysian fields, and
biblical tracts constantly remind us of the bounties and pleasures
associated with Eden. Of course, such paradises are appropriately
only for the deserving. We also know that for Aristotle paradise is
an island world; Hesiod and Pindar claim that it lies in the Western
Ocean; and Lucian records it as being "bathed in atmospheric perfume of many flowers, with calm harbors and calm rivers, and soft
breezes" (Lovejoy and Boas 1935:299). Certainly academic knowledge about paradises, utopias, and millennial dreams is legion. Yet,
despite the analyses generated, no adequate cultural ecology of
paradise exists. Using the words of Clifford Geertz, paradise has no
"thick description" (1973:3). Therein, of course, lies its allure, its
pervasiveness and its long history in human consciousness. All people have a paradise. Its face is determined, as one might indeed
expect, by culture, history, and the winds of prevailing ideologies.
By analyzing the visions of paradise one learns more about the
culture, and the despair of the people who uphold them. Paradise
is an ecology of hope.

Images of possible utopias come within reach when
appropriate markers are tapped. The tourist industry, intent on main-
taining and spreading the notion of Hawaiian paradise, relies on
such markers. A single hibiscus, a single undulating palm, or an aptly
chosen brown limb seem to be enough to foster the desired imagry.
The ability to recognize, or exploit, hidden paradises depends simply
on their very existential poverty. The significance lies not so much
in what features the Islands do or do not offer, as much as the fact
that Western imagination is stubbornly fixated on creating and knowing a paradise. Even the most rudimentary of cues brings the whole
gestalt into view. An existential and commercial facilitation process
sees that this imagery is mapped onto Hawaii.

Thus paradise involves a dialogue with the past, about

the problems of reshaping a less than perfect present toward a future detached from either. This is a kind of prophecy, and prophecy suggests a promised reality. Visionary landscapes become possible only if there is a belief in their existence. Paradises require an ability to bring parts of an obscure possibility to a particular "place" and annotate the features of this place with meaning.

Freud has it that civilization is at the root of much human despair, and thus, paradoxically, civilization can be seen as shaping paradise. Are Western paradises then a return to a past, a more primitive, a more natural state? If science and technology are leading proponents of contemporary civilization, are they then somehow instrumental in shaping visionary utopias? Undoubtedly such thoughts are produced by a romantic consciousness and interpretation of the world. They are based on the notion that utopias and paradises have their genesis in relative deprivation (Aberle 1970), stress (Ames 1957), or disaster (Barkun 1974).[2] They can result in millennial visions, in revitalization or messianic movements, or in migration as in the case of the *haole*. The stresses that lead to them are culturally and ideologically conceived, and historically bound. Thus the paradises that emerge can differ markedly depending on the contexts that produced them. Mumford's survey of utopias makes clear their essentially ideological character (1922); and Manuel's classification of paradises according to the tenor of the eighteenth, nineteenth, and twentieth centuries shows the changing ethos of those times (1965). Paradises are psychic ceremonies to deal with prevailing discontent. "We 'choose' our past and our future from the bondage of present experience thereby to transform it" (Harper 1966).

If paradise is an envisioned possibility born out of discontent, then Hawaii is the product of puritanism, guilt, constrained sexuality, unrewarding labor, malignant surroundings, and racial threats. The assumption is that those seeking the Pacific paradise are escapees from these forces. The logic lies in the commonly held images attributed to the Islands: bounty, leisure, and guiltless indulgence. In the most recently produced visions Hawaii is also a melting pot, a cultural crossroads, and a racial paradise (Hammons 1976; Ige 1968). It would be difficult to explore the two centuries of white presence without considering these particular facets of ecological consciousness.

There is a triad of indulgences promised as alternatives to the combined restrictions of Christianity and industrialization. Sensuality, indolence, and aesthetics entwine in a view of nature antithetical to enterprise and exploitation. This laissez-faire paradise suggests a bounty of things natural and beautiful, and somehow in accord with what is viewed as basic human nature. Mark Twain captures this promise in the opening paragraphs of an unfinished novel about Hawaii:

> The date is 1840. Scene the true Isles of the Blest; that is to say, the Sandwich Islands—to this day the peacefullest, restfullest, sunniest, balmiest, dreamiest haven of refuge for a worn and weary spirit . . . Away out there in the mid-solitudes of the vast Pacific, and far down to the edge of the tropics, they lie asleep on the waves, perpetually green and beautiful, remote from the work-day world and its frets and worries, a bloomy, fragrant paradise, where the troubled may go and find peace, and the sick and tired find strength and rest. (1967:xiv)

Nurturing and succoring, nature is abundant and requires no maintenance. It renders the artifacts of technology superfluous. The inspiration for many a commitment to indolence must have been born out of such obvious promise (Hall 1931).

Other promises endow Hawaii with a guiltless sexuality. The women who swam out, unwittingly enough, to the ships to meet explorers and traders for, what appeared to the nautical imagination, no other reason than to offer their persons, established a male paradise. Cook noted, with his usual understatement, that it was impossible to keep the women from the ships. They were typically to be found in the first company of natives who came aboard with items for trade. All of his best efforts to keep the sailors and Polynesian women apart seemed of little avail as Thomas Edgar, master of the *Discovery* reported—for, either the sailors dressed them as men in order to smuggle them on board, or, if the sailors were permitted ashore, the women "used all their arts to entice them into their houses and even went so far as to endeavor to draw them in by force" (Daws 1968:6). Not surprisingly, the first Hawaiians to travel to North America were two young women from Niihau who stowed away, or were kidnapped, on the *Jenny* and had to be returned from Nootka Sound by Captain Vancouver (Anderson 1960:114). The symbolic promise was of an unconditional surrender to sensuality without the presence of the gatekeepers of sexual propriety.

Much is made of this particular promise of paradise. Bevies of enticing females of elusive ethnic origins constitute an adequate travel poster, augmented perhaps with the suggestion of the hula, synonymous in Western consciousness with sexual invitation. Indeed Schmitt found interethnic sexual relationships the most popular theme of all in the movies of the first half of the century (1968a:436). There seems to have been more than mere convention in the names given island groups by early explorers— the Friendly Islands, the Society Islands.[3] The promised pleasures depend on a combination of factors. The very isolation of island worlds offer concealment from the guardians of morality and the work ethic. Paradoxically, however, an important component is the half-conscious recognition that full and absolute freedom would rob the apparent licence of much of its pleasures.

The metaphors that connect nature with hope are necessary fictions. Like much of fiction, if they are recounted often enough they become crystallized as truths, where they tend to become so soaked with rationality that their original contexts disappear. They become self-evident, unquestionable, and in some senses tiresome from overuse. This is true of the metaphors of nature commonly associated with Hawaii. The earlier contexts which gave them birth have long receded and they live on in sparse outline to entice future generations of whites and anthropologists. These earlier contexts, however, make the present more meaningful. Alternately they themselves derive their sense from present perspectives and ideologies. The mainland white about whom this volume is written does not stand alone, but rather has some centuries of ancestors who have shared their consciousness and have attempted to realize the possibilities. Ever since Cook claimed the Sandwich Islands, whites have come to them in ever increasing numbers, and continue to do so. This volume isolates a small group of them from this steady stream of human movement and pauses to examine their experiences and expectations, their hopes and discontents. It asks what can be learned from the meanings they give to their experience and the interpretations they provide for their world. How do knowledge and place merge?

Terrae Incognitae
and the Culture of Possibility

Hawaiian history, in the formal, documented, and Western sense, dates from an entry in the *London Gazette* on January 11, 1780, announcing the death of Cook: "At the Island of O'-why'ee, One of a group of new discovered Islands . . . in an affray with a numerous and tumultous Body of the Natives" (Kittelson 1971:195). Yet this was not so much a beginning as another addition to an ongoing excitement in European culture. Wavering between legend and fiction, between wild probabilities and limited certainties, there lay in Western consciousness the kind of knowledge that continued to tantalize generations. This tenuous domain, a *terrae incognitae*, was called the South Seas. The knowledge of such a possibility, the mystique of its dimensions, and its attraction for interpretations of all kinds burst upon the "known world" in the early years of the sixteenth century. Remnants of the heady mythology remain, firm enough, to inform even present generations.

All the imagery about the relationship between nature and humans was tapped and the South Seas were to be reworked in terms of established realities. It became important to know the size of the islands, the precedence of national claims, the possibilities for commerce and enterprise, the invitation to scientific enquiry, and perhaps whether they offered something in the way of utopias.

The most revealing way the knowledge became shaped, in Britain in particular, was reflected in the formation of the South Seas Company, incorporated in 1711. Supported by the attractions of untapped natural resources and burgeoning trade, the company became highly successful. It was able to gain several advantages from the British government such as the monopoly on trade with South America and the Pacific islands. In 1719, by offering to take over all of the national debt, a staggering sum of £ 51,300,000, it won even further concessions. By this strategy the annuity holders could be persuaded to exchange their annuities for stock in the company, which was to be sold at a high premium. Success was almost immediate as the stock rose about 700 percent, and five million shares were sold. Imitations, hoaxes, and uncontrolled speculation led to a fall in stock, and further to the revelation of embezzlement and of the bribery of government officials. Thousands were ruined, many fled into obscurity, and history christened the event "The South Sea Bubble." Despite this adverse past, however, the South Sea Company continued into the nineteenth century.

The South Seas were still largely a geographical concept, a possible trading area, and a place where an ordinary man could perhaps make his fortune. But to the culture of imagination its boundaries were vague only to be demarcated, its inhabitants illusory only to be painted in detail. Pierre d'Ailly's *Imago Mundi* had placed a possible paradise in Ethiopia, but the inferences drawn from St. Brendan's adventure and Columbus' positive assertions that paradise lay south of the equator on a mountain top shifted the locale to the South Seas. But it was a land no farther west than Brazil that inspired the society depicted in Francis Godwin's science fiction of 1599, *The Man in the Moon or a Discourse of a Voyage Thither by Domingo Gonzales*, and Cyrano de Bergerac's book of 1656, *Voyage dans la lune*. Then a series of writings, together with the published reports of some explorers, focused attention on the South Pacific and on island paradises.

There was a confluence of European sentiments shaped in a fundamental way by the magic that islands seem to exude for Western culture (Manley and Manley 1970). In 1709 Woodes Rogers and William Dampier rescued from Juan Fernandez Island a Scotsman, Alexander Selkirk. Selkirk had disputed with his captain some years before and had asked to be put ashore. There he remained for four years, epitomizing human intuition and fortitude against the elements. Much was made of his story when he returned to England. There is sufficient evidence, however, that he himself was far from enthusiastic about his self-imposed solitude. His views, however, have been largely ignored by the legend, as it diffused its way through Western culture, and by history as it recorded his story. This is frequently the fate of real and legendary figures when interpretations are produced to fit ongoing value systems (Whittaker and Olesen 1964).

Daniel Defoe met Selkirk at Bristol and was inspired to write one of the great classics of a man against nature, *The Life and Surprizing Adventures of Robinson Crusoe*. The book appeared in 1719 to great acclaim. Even in the days of a more restricted reading audience it went through an edition a month. So unprecedented was this success, so appealing was it to the imagination, that it spawned dozens of imitations and gave birth to European Crusoe cults. Defoe again gauged the tenor of the times with great sensitivity and set his considerable imagination to work on an unadulterated fabrication, inspired somewhat by the published adventures of Dampier and Anson in the South Seas. The result, *A New Voyage Around the World by a Course Never Sailed Before*, appeared in 1725. Such was the high level of expectancy vested in discoveries, so apparently wide the geographic possibilities, and so eager the public to map their fantasies appropriately, the hoax remained uncovered for many decades.

Meanwhile, Jonathan Swift had created his own science fiction. He published it privately in 1720 to avoid bringing to public attention a keen satire directed at the foibles and malevolences of the social circles with which he was acquainted. The authorship was attributed to one Lemuel Gulliver, surgeon and captain, and the book bore the title *Travels into Several Remote Nations of the World*. The kingdoms of Lilliput, Brobdingnag, and Houyhnhnms were all placed within recognizable new lands of the Pacific. The climate of opinion at the time was such that the adventures of Gulliver brought to a head entrepreneurial inclinations and scientific curiosity and directed much of it to the Pacific (Rogers 1975).

It was the voyages of accepted reality, however, that seemed to put the final touch to the South Seas excitement. Baudet maintains that it was Bougainville's *Voyage autour du monde* (1771), and his sojourn in Tahiti in particular, that was most influential (1965:29). Whether this work deserves such a status is debatable. Literature on voyaging, however, was emerging in many places and in many languages and was well placed in the romantic ambience of the time. The published discoveries and adventures of Quimper, Dampier, von Kotzebue, Arago, Belcher, Bennett, Archibald Campbell, Choris, Freycinet, Meares, and others illuminated the South Seas and fanned the fascination at home. Some of the publications dealt specifically with the Sandwich Islands and did much to provide some texture for what a prospective visitor, settler, or trader could expect. An account of Peter Corney's trading voyage appeared in the *London Literary Gazette* in 1821; and Charles

Stewart, an evangelist from Boston, had his *Private Journal of a Voyage to the Pacific Ocean and Residence at the Sandwich Islands in the years 1822, 1823, 1824, 1825* published in 1828.

The works of the missionaries Ellis and Cheever appeared in 1831 and 1851 respectively. In 1843 Munroe of Boston published a volume about the Sandwich Islands, *Scenes and Scenery . . .* penned by James Jackson Jarves, the first editor of the Hawaiian newspaper *The Polynesian.* Jarves was a not overly successful businessman who had turned his hand and mind to writing. This is by no means a full account of the various early writing on the Sandwich Islands. Bernice Judd's rather thorough bibliographic survey of the years before 1960 lists 193 items (1974).

The Judd collection contains those voyages or sojourns either solely devoted to the Sandwich Islands, or those which mentioned a period spent there en route elsewhere. On these lengthier voyages, the Islands were written about in a variety of European languages, some of them translated into yet another. French works appeared between the years 1798, when La Perouse penned his experiences, and 1866. They included the writings of Peron, Arago, Thiercolin, Laplace, La Salle, Lafond, and Freycinet, the latter famous for having brought the artist Choris to the Islands. Choris made some of the earliest pictorial records of native Hawaiian life. Skogman and Egerstrom wrote in Swedish in 1856 and 1859; Golovin and Dobel in Russian in 1822 and 1842; von Kotzebue, Meyen, and von Rosen in German; Boelen and Andersson in Dutch; and Arago in both Italian and French. There is listed, in addition, a rather intriguing volume by a French-speaking missionary, J-B.Z. Bolduc from Quebec.

Not surprisingly, therefore, most of the works are in English and have been written by English and American explorers, travelers, traders, and missionaries. Perhaps this is to be expected as the books listed in the collection are those from the Hawaiian Historical Society and Hawaiian Mission Children's Society. Collections such as these, given over to developing documentation and a historial image of the Hawaiian Islands possess only a couple of non-English language works devoted solely to the Islands. They are among the very few which permit the Islands to be transformed into anything but products of Anglo-American culture and interpretation. Quimper's Spanish work in 1822 is one exception and John Guy Varigny's *Quatorze ans aux Ils Sandwich*, published in Paris in 1874, is the other.

Documents and literary tracts constitute artifacts, one form of the material culture of literate civilizations. They have a magical authority, a supernatural power to order the world and to decree the kind of knowledge that makes up a large part of such cultures. One can view with some amazement the powers vested in written artifacts and their ability to formalize meaning and to bring about beliefs. Anthropological inferences aside, however, what these writings on the Sandwich Islands imply so forcefully is not only the existence of the white hegemony, but of the Anglo-American hegemony. Hawaii as it is known was produced in terms of American and English cultural idioms, symbols, and universes of meaning.

The Expatriate Idiom:
Beachcombers, Derelicts, and Sailors

In 1790 there were about ten Caucasians in Hawaii. They belonged to a category of expatriate, isolated and socially itinerant, for whom a new name was coined in the culture of the Pacific—beachcombers. There is enough in their histories to suggest that most of them had some kind of deviant status. They were disputatious rejects from a ship's crew, or convicts from Botany Bay, or socially disaffected drifters seeking insulation from Western societies. What distinguished them from the traders, merchants, and missionaries who were to follow was their eagerness, not so much to set up an outpost of white culture in the Pacific, as to escape from it. They did so by joining native communities or living on the margins of them (Maude 1964). There were some legendary castaways, some even reputedly kidnapped by natives, but the majority were there of their own volition, bent upon carrying out their expatriate sentiments.

These expatriates, eager to avoid their own kind,

seemed to congregate around the high chief Kamehameha. Among them were John Mackey, an Irish surgeon on the *Imperial* who arrived in 1787, two younger men called Samuel Hitchcock and S. I. Thomas, a carpenter's mate Isaac Riddler, who deserted in 1789, Isaac Davis, the only survivor from those killed aboard the *Fair American*, and John Young, a boatswain retained by Kamehameha from the merchantman *Eleanora* (Cartwright 1916; Bradley 1942:33).

Both Davis and Young became favorites with Kamehameha, and after a few years they showed no inclination to depart. Davis acted as a co-regent to Kamehameha during the latter's absence in battling with the chiefs of Oahu and Maui. Young came to be a governor of both Hawaii and Oahu. Unlike some of their fellow beachcombers, who were described as "naked and wild among the natives, wretched and unprincipled vagabonds" (Ross 1849:46), Davis and Young were notably enterprising and essentially "made their fortunes" in good European tradition.

There was a major distinction between the communities of the beachcombers and those of the traders, whalers, and merchants who appeared next. It was as if entirely different dimensions of the ecological image were being activated. Undoubtedly this next wave of Caucasians to come had enterprising zeal on their minds and their pursuits distinguished them from their predecessors. The beachcomber community was part of the native community, however imperfectly. Regardless of whether they gained some of the symbols of worldly success, or remained drifters, deserters, and unprincipled degenerates, they were either supported by Hawaiians, integrated into their families, or seemed to be considered the responsibility of the king or the chiefs. Even this handful of men displayed the diversity of national backgrounds which was later to distinguish the Islands. Among them were English, American, Irish, Portuguese, and Genoese.

The numbers of beachcombers and, later, those who were part of what Ralston (1973, 1978) has called "the beach communities," encompassing both drifters and traders, were swelled by increasing waves of shipping which moved through Honolulu harbor. Forty years after Cook, in 1824, there were 103 vessels in and out of the harbor every year, and in 1852 there were 585.

Between these two dates, 5,016 vessels sailed into the harbor at Honolulu; of these, 2,886 were whalers, 1,992 were merchant ships, and 138 were ships of war (A *Haole* 1854:33). In the 1850s, for example, as many as sixty ships could be found in the harbor at any one time. A man of trade, Stephen Reynolds, whose journal colorfully depicts much of early European life in the islands, notes with amazement in an entry for May 16, 1836: "This is the first time for several years the Harbor has been left without a vessel" (Reynolds 1836).

From these ships ordinary seamen seemed to desert in large numbers, for they found themselves in the materialization of a sailor's paradise. In the middle years of the nineteenth century the deserters numbered anywhere between one hundred and two hundred or more each year. Captains took unforeseen precautions to control desertion, and managed to recover the majority, who were returned to their custody or to the confines of Oahu prison. Some were never recovered. Other seamen were legally discharged for being troublemakers or because more appealing replacements wished to sign on. In 1860, for example, 1,041 were discharged in Honolulu to idle in grog shops and brothels, to sign on to another crew at a later time, to set themselves up in their own shipboard occupations which were in great demand, or to establish a small business enterprise.[4]

As these unattached men, often destructive and of "low character," became the responsibility of the king and his constituted government, Kamehameha I very quickly found himself in the business of deciding upon desirable and undesirable residents and of acting on the matter. His action was often direct and, by white standards, harsh. One man who, for example, assaulted the seducer of his Hawaiian wife, was banished to Fanning Island (Reynolds 1825). Indeed Liholiho, who assumed the monarchy on the death of Kamehameha I, exiled many deserting sailors to Fanning Island, some 1,500 miles south, not a very promising place for settlement. However, most of these were permitted to return later.

Suspicious of most of the new foreigners, distrustful of their ambitions and influence, and cognizant of the plight of Hawaiian women, Kamehameha I began to take action in 1815. The women, in particular, concerned him. A generation of deserters, drifters, and adventurers had formed alliances with Hawaiians, "married" them in superficial acknowledgment of white practices and in placatory recognition of their own residual puritan consciences. By this, however, the women became disaffiliated from their own traditional kin. They were in most cases deserted within a few years. With no kin support and with several children, they became conspicuously derelict and constituted one of the many emerging social problems. Kamehameha conceptualized a form of citizenship where those not holding land were requested to depart. It seemed a simple enough scheme to give the privileges of native subjects to those whom he personally liked, and especially the six on whom he had already bestowed the privilege of land. It was an easy way to eliminate undesirables. The favored six included John Young and Isaac Davis, who had moved with him to the emerging town of Honolulu, and who performed many services for him, either as counselors or in the operation of his first American sailing vessel. Both men married into Hawaiian aristocracy, Young becoming the grandfather of Queen Emma. There were two other Englishmen— Alexander Adams and William Sumner. To Adams the king had given large tracts of land at Waikiki where Adams worked with diligence and an industry that was frequently remarked upon by the natives, presumably for its novelty as a practice among white men. He married and fathered an extensive part-Hawaiian lineage. Sumner, who had arrived in 1807, was also a holder of considerable lands. On occasion he continued to work as a sea captain. Another landholder was Don Francisco de Paula y Marin of Spain, the king's physician and confidant, as well as a botanist of some learning. The last of the six was Elliot de Castro of Portuguese extraction, also a physician to the king, but apparently an adventurer who finally found his unprincipled way to a San Francisco prison. This particular move by the king could be seen as the first act of naturalization. Landing seamen were placed under a bond of $60 for good behavior. Later, in 1838, oaths of allegiance to the king were required. Finally, marriage was permitted only upon formal naturalization or a residence of two years in the island, plus a substantial indemnity of $1,000.

The era of castaways and beachcombers, of sailors and drifters began to wane with more evidence of a community forming around commerce, trade, and, later, the mission. The idyllic paradise offered to these early seekers was slowly being eroded and changed for them into repressed similes for life at home. The community of which they were forced to be a part began to operate more and more according to the dictums of the familiar puritanical societies of North America. The licence and the promise had disappeared. While the merchants seemed to support the existing indolence by setting up grog shops and the like, they were essentially men of industrious bent, and cast disapproving eyes on the unsavory exploits of their fellow countrymen. With the missionaries, however, the doom of licence and promise was sealed and salvation was unbecomingly thrust in the faces of the beachcomber.

Seeking One's Fortune: Commerce and Trade

For many centuries the European world at home maintained the fiction that one could go to the "new world" to do that most desirable of things: make one's fortune. While the colonies of the New World were for a long time the locale for doing this, in their turn they developed their own version of a geography for promised riches. For them it was a continual "go west, young man." Many a young man, spurned and unsuccessful, set out to seek his fortunes on the frontiers of California or Hawaii. To these fledgling entrepreneurs the Islands suggested a sort of Lockean *tabula rasa*, a rebirth. It was a place to do something the European world had always cherished as a result of its fixation with Genesis and beginnings: to "begin again," or to "make one's stamp." One's own idiosyncracies and fantasies could be projected onto the existing social arrangements and a society created to one's own specifications. This, of course, presupposes a strong sense of cultural evolution where "less civilized" societies are delighted with the onset of young men, finding in them skill and wisdom where the society at home found none, and supplying for them accommodating, respectful assistance in the search for a fortune. It presupposes for natives, and for those already inhabiting the islands, a rather simple, unformed, or childlike mentality. This was, of course, a common vision in Europe and was amply documented.

The new world had the promise of a community of strangers in which the past could be eliminated and some idealized version of the self implemented. One could project upon the new setting all one's previously frustrated visions about the future. One could acquire by personal endeavor, by concerted effort and puritanical persistence, what one could acquire at home only by lineage. Abraham Fayerweather, an expatriate from New England, captures a version of it in a letter: "allow me to tell you that a man is looked at here for *what he is*; not *who* his *relations are* and people in Oahu are as ignorant of me and mine as when I first landed here" (May 8, 1833).[5]

In a less sympathetic version, an anonymous writer for the Hawaiian Club of Boston, provides a general satirical denigration of both Hawaiian culture in change and of white foreigners who have grasped what opportunities they could. New Englanders, he writes, affect life-styles similar to those of a higher social position, despite the fact that "they are not to the 'manner' born" ("Social Life" 1868:562). One soon learns, he claims, that many of these "distinguished foreigners" have histories which make "a residence away from their own country convenient, if not necessary." Offended by what he sees as the ludicrous presumptions of a white minister in Kamehameha V's retinue, he describes the man as one who has become

> . . . lost in the magnitude of the fact that he is an official; this is written upon his face in unmistakable characters. All traces of a more plebian life have been erased, when as barkeeper, footman, or peddler, he gained his bread in his native land. Instead you read: "Clear the way! I, the Minister of Foreign Affairs, Attorney General . . . I come! / help to steer this ship of State. (1868:563)

Honolulu rapidly became a headquarters for various traders—a stopping place and a wintering spot for the Northern Pacific whaling fleet. It was a brisk port in the sandalwood trade, the Islands themselves supplying a considerable quantity of the commodity, the returns from which went largely into the coffers of

Kamehameha I, his son Liholiho, and some of the chiefs. It also
occupied an important position in the fur trade until that began to
decline before the 1820s.

Retail trade was already well established by the time
the missionaries arrived, for Reynolds notes in his journal that some
of the missionary women were slightly disconcerted to find Hawaiians better clad than they were (May 21, 1828). There was
competition among large American retail trade stores which were
attempting to establish a secure foothold. In 1823 an ideal cargo
for Hawaiian retail outlets might consist of superfine cloth, calico,
ready-made clothing, shoes, hats, rum, wine, lumber, copper, paint,
rigging, tables, pumps, wheelbarrows, trunks, writing desks, hand-
carts, and carriages. The king was even reported to want a steamboat
and one chief wished for a billiard table (Bradley 1942:86).

One kind of retail establishment appeared in far greater
numbers than in European or American towns of similar size. This
was the grog shop. In 1822 there were as many as seventeen grog
shops in Honolulu, all operated by foreigners. Clearly, Honolulu
catered to a nautical culture. Liholiho himself was reputed to be so
enamoured of strong spirits that foreigners who kept diaries found
it simpler to note the days on which he was sober. Indeed, despite
the price of the imported liquor, life in many quarters seemed to
be one long bacchanal.

After the decline of the fur trade and the depletion of
sandalwood, the economic future of the Hawaiian Islands appears
to have become uncertain. Many companies ceased to be interested
and the Islands supported themselves by providing supplies to whalers and merchantmen and by making repairs to ships. While enterprising agriculturalists may have cast eyes on what the Hawaiian
soils could produce, the land system was rigidly set in old ways.
Ladd and Company had gained some concessions and set a pre-
cedent, but it was not until 1845 that significant change became
possible. In December of that year the Land Commission or the
Board of Commissioners to Quiet Land Titles was established "for
the investigation and final ascertainment or rejection of all claims
of private individuals, whether natives or foreigners, to any landed
property acquired anterior to the passage of this Act" (Chinen
1958:8). The Great *Mahele*, the division of land, heralded the end

of the feudal system in Hawaii and made the widespread acquisition of Hawaiian land by foreigners possible. The Hawaiian commoner was thus suddenly in the position to possess fee simple property. From this point, however, dispossession set in. Although Hawaiians now for the first time owned land, they had no understanding of what was implied by this imported foreign concept. Often they thought it more in their interests to sell the land rather than to keep it. The waning of the century thus saw huge tracts of land amassed by whites.

Before the Great *Mahele* foreigners had been able to lease land for only twenty-five years, now they could own it in perpetuity. It was this advantage that saw probably the greatest display of enterprise. Plantation cultures on the colonial model were born, and with them the possibility of the Islands as a plural society. At first, moderate success had come with the cultivation of coffee, rice, tobacco, and bananas. It was, however, when the indigenous sugar of the islands was turned to profit that the enormous Hawaiian plantation culture fully manifested itself. Further, John Parker from Massachusetts developed a huge cattle ranch on the island of Hawaii, and Dole, who controlled the pineapple industry, which was introduced later in the century, was able in 1922 to purchase the whole of the island of Lanai.

It was land and enterprise that finally made large fortunes. But it was the more modest striving of the Abraham Fayerweathers that typifies the *haole* of the nineteenth century and makes him an appropriate ancestor to those of the twentieth. Fayerweather's letters provide a chronicle of modest ambitions that provided for New Englanders the conviction that Hawaii could be a land of opportunity. He writes of his endeavors to earn enough as a clerk to wealthy Honolulu merchants in order to further his "own prospects" to set up a business. He writes of his despair over the theft of $75, and of his careful accounting of how he spent his wages. He admits to his reluctance and embarrassment about returning to New England without his fortune amassed, to be "made a butt of my misfortunes" by friends and neighbors. Despite homesickness and a desire to be reunited with his family, he writes:

> It is not the fine climate, the many attractions and beautiful scenery that still keeps me in this place. If that were all I would give them up now. But there are considerations in the way of business which

induce me to remain untill [*sic*] I have amassed something to put me upon a stand with some of the best and wealthiest of my Native Country—viz. a good independent property. (January 13, 1837)

Indeed, despite several reversals, his hopes appear to have been realized. Though he died at the early age of thirty-eight, without seeing his native land again, he became a man of property, owning, at one point, a plantation of his own. Many years after his death, his sisters learned that he had left the rather large estate, at least for the times, of $180,000.[6]

Dialectics of Sin:
Women and Missionaries

If the white male culture of the Sandwich Islands, profligate, inebriated, and troublesome, was not enough to concern the righteous, the condition of the Hawaiians themselves was generally deplored. Even Abraham Fayerweather noted with alarm on the occasion of the visit of two American women in 1832:

God forbid that any female relations of mine should ever visit this part of the world. Curious people however have an excellent opportunity to examine the shape of a *part* of the human race, in these Islands, for you may at all times see a naked man or woman . . . (April 13, 1832).

Ships' captains, while willing to transport males to the Sandwich Islands, thought the environment so depraved that under no conditions would they take women aboard.

In recognition of the freedom with which native women engaged in liaisons with sailors, and using contemporary fertility percentages it has been calculated that on the various Polynesian islands 7.5 percent of the women would conceive within the first week of a crew being ashore, 30 percent within the first month, 20 percent in the next month, and 15 percent in the third month (McArthur 1966). If the pure abstraction of a mathematical percentage can be taken to reflect actuality, there should be 150,000 surviving descendants of the original beachcombers in Polynesia.

In Hawaii in particular, the native historian Malo complained in 1838 that his Islands resembled a "giant brothel."

If some whites came to the Sandwich Islands in search of hope and paradise, and others came to tame, conquer, and exploit, what attracted the missionaries was sin: sin in its natural habitat. The sermon which marked the ordination of the Reverends Hiram Bingham and Asa Thurston as members of the first missionary group to the Sandwich Islands was delivered at Goshen, Connecticut, and was appropriately entitled "The Promised Land." All the notions of a sad and savage land in need of saving were behind their mission. The words of Bingham himself convey the full extent of the horror he faced. He could see there nothing but "unrighteousness, fornication, wickedness, murder, debate, deceit, malignity, whisperers, backbiters, haters of God, despiteful, proud, boasters, inventors of evil things, disobedient to parents, without natural affection, implacable, unmerciful" (Bingham 1849:23). There was sinning against all the known laws of God and righteous men. Casual nudity, thievery, to say nothing of public fornication, polygamy in both its forms, and even incest seemed to be endemic. It was no wonder that many in the group wept and feared that they might well die there. But, the Gospel had to triumph, and when the *Thaddeus* brought the band of missionaries to Honolulu in 1820 they set to work with determination and fortitude.

Their achievements were not small. They quickly acquainted themselves with the Hawaiian language and gave it a written form. The printing press they operated not only put the newly coded language into printed hymnals and biblical texts, it even provided a printing service for the government. The early missionaries may have been oddities, with their strange "long-necked women," but they represented a new and powerful addition to the white influence over the Hawaiian way of life. Andrew Peabody, in his review of *The Hawaiian Islands: Their Progress and Condition under Missionary Labors* written by the missionary Rufus Anderson, was moved to profound admiration and noted that Anderson's tour among the Hawaiian Islands "seems to us the most magnificent progress recorded in history . . . so entirely devoid of egotism and exaggeration" (1865:3).

By 1832 more than half of the adult population had

reading skills and many were able to write. The hula, that licentious dance, had been somewhat suppressed, as had nakedness. Liholiho, deciding to become a scholar of renown in his kingdom, sent two representatives to the mission school to accomplish this for him. Furthermore, Christianity had already been recognized by such powerful people as the female chief Kapiolani who successfully employed it to defy Pele, goddess of the volcano, at the crater of Kilauea. This act persuaded thousands of ordinary Hawaiians of the efficacy of the new religion.

More deeply ingrained values, so much a part of the world they took for granted that an attempt to change them would have been ludicrous, remained untapped. Royal incest and polygamy continued. The marriage service imposed on hundreds of commoners remained a rote and meaningless series of verbal maneuvers muttered in nautical responses of "aye, aye." Further, the attempt to define sexuality as taboo, as the harbinger of eternal hell, could not be made comprehensible to a people accustomed to construing it as enjoyable, natural, and incurious. Thus the British consul Charleton, with expected Victorian prudery, left a mission school in disgust because "he had, with his own eyes, seen four couples fornicating during prayers" (Smith 1956:62).

Other evidences of Puritan handiwork are still visible on all sides in contemporary Honolulu. Despite its industrialization and modernization, it still bears the unmistakable stamp of nineteenth-century New England folkways. White frame houses and small modest churches, predominantly Protestant, literally cover much of rural and suburban Oahu and the other islands. The changes seem to have been small since Nordhoff reported the same in 1874 (1874:22). The *muumuu* and the *holoku* (as Grundian answers to nakedness) and the famed Hawaiian bed quilt (as representative of feminine industry in the face of apparent native indolence) are not only seen in abundance, but have acquired the status of regional symbols. They have taken their place as such along with their "heathen" predecessors—the grass skirt, the flowered lei, and the hula. Perhaps, in view of their relatively early arrival in the Islands and the swiftness of their impact, the Puritan mission could be designated as a great facilitator for white hegemony, a powerful agent of change.

Division and Rank:
The Dialectics of Pluralism

Until the coming of the missionaries the white community was a male one, largely undifferentiated, of beachcombers, men of trade, and the transitory population from various ships in the harbor. To these were added the missionaries, their wives and children. With regard to this lack of variability, Mark Twain, in his inimitable fashion, noted in a letter to the *Sacramento Union* in April 1866 that, when confronting a stranger in Honolulu, one should

> strike out boldly and address him as "Captain." Watch him narrowly and if you see by his countenance that you are on the wrong tack, ask him where he preaches. It is a safe bet that he is either a missionary or a captain or a whaler. I am now personally acquainted with seventy-two captains and ninety-six missionaries. The captains and ministers form one half of the population; the third fourth is composed of common Kanakas and mercantile foreigners and their families, and the final fourth is made up of high officers of the Hawaiian Government. (Clemens 1866:42)

He sketched an occurrence where a stranger had addressed him as "reverence," but, finding that incorrect, as "captain." Then he tried "your Excellency," and on finding that equally inappropriate he suspected Twain of mischief. On being reassured that Twain was indeed unaffiliated in any of these callings, but rather a private traveler recently from America, he exclaimed:

> Ah, Heaven! it is too blissful to be true; alas, I do but dream. And yet that noble, honest countenance—those oblique, ingenuous eyes—that massive head, incapable of—of—anything; your hand; give me your hand, bright waif. Excuse these tears. For sixteen weary years I have yearned for a moment like this, and—Here his feelings were too much for him, and he swooned away. (p. 43)

Actually, the foreign community was somewhat richer occupationally than Twain's letter implied. The Honolulu paper *The Friend,* on January 15, 1847, presented a survey of the names, occupations, and naturalization status of resident foreigners. Of the 331 names listed, 50 were one kind of carpenter or another, a category of skill in great demand in the rapidly Westernizing nation which, in 1847, was in the midst of a building boom as private residences and government buildings multiplied. The next largest group consisted of 32 clerks or bookkeepers, and they, along with 10 printers, obviously supplied the documentation and record-keeping needs to which the emerging bureaucratic and literary culture of the new settlers was committed, and to which the Hawaiians were fast becoming acculturated. As trading and catering to the transitory population were the main industries of the fast-growing town, it is not surprising that 22 were merchants, 19 storekeepers, 17 hotel keepers, 8 tailors, and 6 spirit merchants. There were 11 government officials, 9 missionaries or missionary agents, 7 teachers, and 7 consuls or commissioners. All comprised a group which, no doubt, considered itself the guardian of appropriate acculturation. Beyond this, there were a sprinkling of the kinds of occupations one might expect of a small rural town.[7]

In a report from the Minister of the Interior, read before the king on April 30, 1847, it appeared that there were 453 males, 60 females, and 114 children among the foreign population of the Islands. The Ministry of the Interior reported in March, 1850, that the numbers of naturalized foreigners were distributed as follows: United States, 362; British (including Canadians), 147; other Polynesian Islands, 42; Portuguese, 37; German and French, 18 each; Chinese, 17; and others in far fewer numbers. The growing governmental, commercial, and landholding ascendancy of the United States had, by now, firmly established itself. A New Englander observed in 1848:

> There are many more Americans engaged in mercantile pursuits than any other nation. There are five American importing houses, two English, one French, and one Chilean, and between 20 and 30 retail establishments which are also mostly American—By far the greater proportion of the goods imported are American in American vessels . . . The residences of this Class are among the most genteel and handsome of the city and are fitted up with great luxuriousness—and taste. (Gilman 1970:145)

In 1853 the resident white population of the island was 1,687 of whom 1,013 lived in the city of Honolulu, the total population of which was 11,455 (Lind 1980:34, 50). This did not include the 200 to 500 sailors who roamed the streets each day when the whalers were in port. The white population soon constituted an elite, and the term *haole*[8] became almost synonymous with high status. Their separation from the Hawaiians had a caste-like flavor. It was clear that despite any individual feelings toward them, *haoles* considered the native Hawaiian a distinctly lower order. The words "poor native" or "ignorant *kanaka*" and far less sympathetic epithets crossed the pages of journals and the conversations of white men.

The white community was further divided into national groups. The interactions between the French and the Americans, the Germans and the Americans, or the Scandinavians and the Americans were limited mainly to the work place and, there, controlled by the status of their various pursuits. The Germans, Norwegians, and other Europeans most often began as plantation laborers, or in service occupations, but rose to the status of overseers fairly rapidly. The interaction between the English and the Americans was more regularized, even if periodically strained by nationalistic pride and competing desires for domination of the Islands.

Even within the American community, status divisions soon arose. The long-time residents, government officials, merchants, captains, and others of influence constituted an interactional nexus to which, occasionally, British elites were admitted. It was a group which Hawaiian royalty favored. Indeed, the marriages made by this group were often to Hawaiian *alii*. The journal of Stephen Reynolds provides occasional glimpses of how social organization worked among this favored elite. Present at one party, he writes, were some forty persons, including the king and several of his suite, some captains and English ship masters. This group "with a pretty general turnout of Yankees—went up to Haalilio's house in the Manoa Valley—where there was a very good luow [sic] and other eatables—with a plenty of good drinkables got down about sundown" (Reynolds: July 4, 1840).

Fayerweather also writes reassuring letters to his family, indicating that he boards at a respectable house in the village where "we have at the table merchants, clerks, shipmasters, physician, supercargos and others of the same class" (May 1, 1837). It is clear from Reynolds' journals as well that Fayerweather is often one of the persons in his social circle.

Although equal in terms of dominance in the emerging society, a distinct rift occurred between the white elites and the missionaries. The head of the latter group was Hiram Bingham, known as Brother Bingham to his colleagues and King Bingham to the adversaries who derided him for his authoritarianism, self-righteousness, and ascetic life-style, as well as the open disapproval he himself directed toward large sectors of the white community. Not only was this a matter of calling and unwavering moral righteousness, but the missionaries suspected other whites to be working against missionary teachings. They believed them to want to "have the reign of darkness continue" and to hasten the increasing depravity of the king. They thought them malicious and troublesome, and suspected that they spread the report that missionaries were spies, that their aim was to take over the islands, and that they were storing firearms and ammunition to that end (Thurston 1882:58).

About the same time, the men of the cloth were engaged in their own disputes. There was a severe conflict between the Calvinistic New Englanders and the few Catholic priests who ventured to those shores. In 1827, French Catholic missionaries arrived; and, in 1831, they were forced to board ship to sail away again. With some tenacity, however, a small Catholic outpost held on, although their mission was out of favor with the government. It was by no means an easy task for natives who came to their mission or school, for they were set to hard labor by officials as punishment for such transgression.

Most of the whites with some presumed status viewed the missionaries as distinctly lacking in humor and conviviality and, despite their obvious good intentions, among the most morbid and colorless of human beings. Fayerweather thought them to be without any redeeming social graces: "They mostly appear ignorant of the forms and manners of refinement and of course are rather insipid company—Those I have seen I like very well so far as respects kind feelings, but they *appear to have been brought up in the bush*" (Fayerweather, March 12, 1838, underlining his).

Two old women at Kalihi who had been to the Catholic school were ordered to the Fort—sentenced to hard labor—one said she was old and would not work and that they might kill her. Kinau ordered she should be rolled in excrement and then rubbed all over which was

done!!! Natives all said it was Mr. Bingham was to blame. He told
Kinau it was bad for her to allow her people to use the Catholic
forms of religion. (Reynolds: August 4, 1835)

The Protestant missionaries constituted an elite corps of
their own and one that has survived to contemporary Hawaii to
become a notable part of what can be called the white hegemony.
The descendants of missionary families, or those related to them
by marriage, have found their way into landholding and commercial
influence and figure prominently in the white corporate circles of
the "Big Five" (Gray 1973:39). This refers to the shipping, investment, sugar, and pineapple industries which came to influence much
of the Islands' business and corporate life. The Big Five are Castle
& Cooke, Alexander & Baldwin, Theo H. Davies, C. Brewer, and
Amfac. It is widely held in Island folklore that white power is invested
in the hands of some one hundred *haoles,* who are known to be
descendants of the original missionaries.

With the growth of enterprise and industry the white
community was in difficulties as to how to provide the labor to
make the industries successful. By the early 1870s, even though 50
percent of the Hawaiian male population was employed in white
enterprises, the industrial burgeoning was of such dimensions that
this labor pool proved insufficient to the demand. The dream was
to replicate similar experience elsewhere and import East Indian
labor. As Britain refused to permit this, the planters turned their
eyes to other Pacific Islands. They rationalized that this would permit
the indigenous population, which had declined alarmingly, to be
replaced by people racially and culturally akin.

The decline of the Hawaiian population is well known.
From a possible 242,000 to 500,000 persons estimated at the time
of Cook, the population had dwindled to 70,000 by 1852, 49,000
by 1872, 34,000 by 1890, 23,000 by 1920, 14,000 by 1940, and
to 10,000 by 1961 (Lind 1980:34). For most scholars this represents
a more optimistic figure than they would themselves be willing to
provide. The diseases of whites, such as venereal disease left by
Cook's crew and, later, the plague of 1804 (bubonic or perhaps
cholera), supposedly carried away half of the population. They were
followed by measles, scarlet fever, whooping cough, typhoid, chol-

era, yellow fever, tuberculosis, and other ills of the foreigners (Schmitt 1968b:18–24). Finally, the state census figures of 1970 show 7,697 pure Hawaiians, one percent of the population, and 125,224 or 16.2 percent who thought of themselves as part Hawaiian.

In the 1870s and 1880s, however, the concern was only superficially a humanitarian one. Rather, the trouble was the great need for more labor on the plantations. The people of the New Hebrides (now Vanuatu), those of the Solomons and the Rotumans seemed the most promising, and the *Stormbird* in 1878 brought 86 immigrants, mainly Gilbertese (Kiribatise), but also some from Rotuma (Bennett 1976:5). In the following ten years about 2,400 immigrants were introduced from the Gilberts and New Hebrides with a few also from the Ellice Islands (Tuvalu), Rotuma, Samoa, the Tokelaus, Marshalls, Santa Cruz, New Ireland, and Bougainville. They dwindled quickly, however. Dysentery, pulmonary diseases, and influenza were the enemies they met in Hawaii, and the majority of the survivors wished to return home.

There was a reluctance on the part of the Americans, whose dominance in the Islands seemed assured, to recruit from areas where any British influence could journey to Hawaii with the contracted labor. Besides, Pacific recruiting was expensive. Thus it was that 300 Chinese laborers were introduced inexpensively in 1876. Between that date and 1885, and again between 1890 and 1897, more than 46,000 Chinese came to the Islands. From the Azores and Madeira Islands between 1878 and 1913 some 17,500 Portuguese were introduced. They brought some women with them and thus, unlike the Chinese, seemed likely to settle. Although their original population was much smaller than that of the Chinese, they had, by 1910 exceeded the latter (Lind 1980:32).[9]

The flirtation with Japanese immigration began in the 1860s. So large have been the numbers of Japanese migrants since then that Hawaii is termed not only an American Frontier, but also a Japanese frontier. By 1920, The Japanese constituted 42.7 percent of the population. A sense of Japanese threat, first demographic, then military, and, finally, economic hung over the Islands and by the latter part of the century, there appears to be a widespread feeling of dissatisfaction with what is seen as encroaching Japanese economic expansion. It is not the local Japanese population, which is assimilated and considered native to the Islands, but rather commercial interests from mainland Japan that are at issue. American encroachment and commercial interests have, of course, long had the same disquieting effects.

Other groups came: in 1901 about 6,000 Puerto Ricans; in 1904–05 about 8,000 Koreans; and, beginning in 1907, about 8,000 Spaniards, mainly from California. Finally, nearly 120,000 Filipinos came to labor on the plantations in the first three decades of this century.

The American *haole* population retained power and influence, although Chinese and Japanese merchants had their own routes to wealth and status. The population from the continental United States rose steadily, accelerated successively by annexation, World War II, and statehood. In 1878 they were 1,276 (2.2 percent of the population) in the Islands; by 1900 this figure had risen to 4,284 (2.8 percent); by 1920 to 10,957 (4.3 percent); by 1940 to 54,224 (12.8 percent); and by 1970 to 178,808 (23.9 percent).

There were among the American population some non-Caucasians, who came to constitute separate categories in census tables and in island life. Being few in number their stories lie in relative obscurity historically in the pages of old obituaries or minor items in newspapers and archives. One black American, Anthony Allen, a slave from Schenectady, appears in Hawaiian history as one of the early figures of note. He arrived in 1810, married a Hawaiian, had three children, and became a lifelong respected member of the Honolulu community. He kept a dairy farm near Waikiki and also ran a sailors' boarding house.

Indians, too, principally from the Northwest Coast, passed through the Islands either as mariners on British or American vessels, or as traders and members of troupes performing native Indian dances and songs. Fayerweather observed that he had seen such a group perform in September, 1831; the price was well within his means, but prohibitive to the Hawaiian. Similarly, an item in *The Friend* on February 1, 1848, noted that an American Indian belonging to the Gay Head Tribe died suddenly aboard the U.S. Frigate *Brandywine* and that his remains were buried in the Nuuanu cemetery on the Sabbath afternoon. The Indian population of contemporary Hawaii numbers almost two thousand. The histories of these minorities as mainland migrants, however, remain interesting, but elusive.

The various streams of migration including the military could be cumulatively viewed in the last figures compiled for the Hawaiian Islands as part of the United States 1980 census. They showed that Caucasians, including Portuguese, made up 33 percent of the population; Japanese 24.8 percent; Filipino 13.9 percent; Hawaiians 12 percent; Chinese 5.8 percent; Koreans 1.9 percent; blacks 1.8 percent; Samoans 1.5 percent; American Indians .3 percent; and others, such as Vietnamese, Guamanians, etc: 5 percent (Department of Planning and Economic Development 1981b:36).

One way to make sense of the present is to formulate a historical route along which we have traveled to arrive at it. That is, we construct a past which is meaningful in terms of present ideologies. This past then forms a backdrop against which present experiences can be understood with new clarity. Anthropology in particular sees a construction of the past as paramount to its interpretive endeavor. The rendering of white settlement and enterprise which I have constructed above thus plays a dual role. It gathers together the knowledge often produced to account for contemporary forms of life. As it is at the same time knowledge available to the *haoles* themselves, it is commonly evoked by them in justifying and accounting for their own experiences. At the same time it permits the rendering of anthropology which relies, by virtue of its epistemology and methods, on the presence of an appropriate "setting," a necessary facet of the anthropological perspective. Thus, it comes as no surprise to recognize a past for contemporary issues, a past that nurtured them and made them, if not inevitable, then at least possible.

In recent years a new version of the Hawaiian paradise has been offered. It depicts Hawaii as the capital of a new civilization which embraces the Pacific islands and the oceanic fringes of Southeast Asia, a "tropical oceania, a new civilization where living is pleasant" (*Honolulu Advertiser* 1978:B3). One of the cited advantages of this civilization is a life-style requiring little energy, with much of what is needed available from solar power. Jungle diseases, once a serious health problem in the Pacific, are now controlled. Communications have negated the isolation of the Pacific. The sense of a Pacific trade community has been developing for some centuries along peaceful lines and can be augmented with contemporary policies and commitments. Unlike other parts of the world, ethnic and cultural plurality claims a relatively peaceable existence. The sense of the Pacific as a new world, a new civilization and paradise, is often derived from a shared political shift from colonialism to independence, from reliance on a major industry common to all, namely tourism, and from a sense of unity in the face of the rest of the world.

Paradoxically, the contemporary scene is also depicted in terms of the contradictions that paradise has produced and which in turn threaten it. Foremost among these is one that speaks most directly to the ethos of anthropology. That is the matter of native Hawaiian activism. It involves land claims, reparation for social disenfranchisement, and a wish to be free of social impositions essentially foreign to Hawaiian culture (Tagupa 1977). A perusal of newspaper headlines augments this with the cliché, by now well-known—troubles in a racial paradise. Violence and discrimination in housing and employment are most frequently cited.

While airline trade magazines distribute articles on such tourist oriented items as "four scenic drives" or "Hawaii's little people: the menehune," the government, ecological agencies, and activists challenge and criticize growth, keep careful scrutiny of the per capita inches of shoreline suitable for swimming, and alert the population to the doubling of water consumption. They produce alarming statistics, such as the fact that in 1940 there were 100,000 automobiles, but in 1976 there were 500,000, or that the numbers of visitors staying overnight in 1960 were one-quarter million and in 1976 were three and one-quarter million. Others agitate for the protection of the Islands' natural beauty and ecological balance.

While some articles extol Hawaii's racial harmony and cultural variability, others produce alarming contrasts. They note the population pressures resulting from fresh immigrants from Southeast Asia, the problems of disease and unemployment. Alarming statistics are produced by which the 50,000 incoming residents of 1950 are compared to the 125,000 of 1970; in which the negligible social welfare costs of 1940 are compared to the $170 million of 1976; and in which the rapid climb in major crime is depicted.

While real estate advertisements depict expanding condominium and apartment opportunities, and the commercial sections of newspapers announce the opening of another convention or hotel center, others pose vehement questions about the inconsolable polarities of development versus quality of life. Major challenges are laid to the nature of Hawaiian growth management and a folk version depicts the many building cranes on the skyline as the "native birds of Hawaii." While the business community seeks investment and diversification of industry, other segments of the economy become distinctly uneasy with the extent of foreign investment or with the nature of Japanese economic expansion.

The paradoxes of the Hawaii of the most recent quarter of a century reflect then the same profound tensions between ecological paradise and commercial instinct that have been implicit in every phase of its history. The uncertainties currently visited upon a once idyllic Pacific isle could be equated with the fall from grace, with the paradise lost. On the other hand, the commercial sense of progress and development, historically worked out and now amply manifested, suggest the ascending and evolving view of human destiny. Perhaps most ironically, Western understanding is the origin of both the inclinations and tensions they inevitably produce. Hawaii thus stands as the remnant of past events, and the outcome of European consciousness, American commerce, and Pacific migration. The rest of the book deals with the present that has emerged from that past and frequently shows how present understandings make use of past events. It deals with the experience of the contemporary *haole* in the environment of present-day Hawaii.

The encounter with Hawaii is through and through an encounter with a set of ideas. In that Europe claimed to discover Hawaii, it translated that discovery into recognizable ecological terms. These terms posed, on the one hand, an invitation to enterprise and, on the other, an invitation to hope. It left in its wake a Hawaii that the *haole* built, poised uneasily between paradigmatic tensions. At the same time an era was opened, an era of ecological hegemony which was to affect the Islands for two centuries. It might be argued that some of the problems manifested in the Hawaiian Islands are the inevitable progeny of the Western view of nature. They constitute a paradox, for the Hawaii of experience is not the Hawaii of imagination, and a world of meaning separates the distant dreamer from the present knower. An epistemological puzzle emerges, it begs the question of what it is to know a place.

Above: The retinue of Queen Liliuokalani, center, circa 1916, about a year before her death. Many a white person found his way into high office as an adviser to the monarchy, an official of the government, or by marriage to Hawaiian aristocracy. R. J. Baker, Bishop Museum.

Below: A privileged group at the sugar plantation, Spreckelsville, Maui, circa 1898. In the rear Mr. W. Taylor, Mrs. George Boote. On the chairs, left to right: Dr. Boote, Mac Sanborn, Mr. Norman, Cora Sanborn, head *luna* Copp. On the ground: Mr. J. Smith, Mrs. Griffith, Mr. P. Scales, Mrs. Ida Taylor, Manager George Boote. Bishop Museum.

CHAPTER TWO

Discovering the *Haole*: The Grammar of the Fieldwork Encounter

If we imagine the philosophical discussion of the modern period reconstructed as a judicial hearing, it would be deciding a single question: how is reliable knowledge (Erkenntnis) *possible?*

Habermas (1968:3)

Fieldwork is a passionate encounter. It means for the anthropologist an intellectual and emotional confrontation with the culture in which the work is to be done. She is expected to come to "know" this culture by living it. It is as if a formal methodology were derived from the old folk adage: "experience is the best teacher." Fieldwork seems to rely on this old assertion. Bertrand Russell, who makes the distinction between knowledge by description and knowledge by acquaintance, suggests that only through experience or acquaintance is reliable knowledge possible.

Fieldwork offers a unique vantage point. Not only is the culture observed at close range, but the cultural meanings to be recorded are also crucial to the anthropologist's own everyday life. Only by grasping these meanings can she be a competent member of the culture, and this very competence is crucial to the work. There is a curious paradox here, one on which the discipline of anthropology must rely. It is believed that anthropology is accomplished through the eyes of the stranger in a strange land. Yet, even though the learner's position must somehow be self-consciously retained to make anthropological awareness possible, it becomes an uncomfortable and even ludicrous stand after a certain period of time. Some things have to be taken for granted. Even in the most distant and obscure of cultures one is expected to learn *some* rudimentary things and practice them unself-consciously. A continually questioning and incredulous anthropologist could only be an oddity, an impaired intellect, or, at the most generous, a social nuisance. In some sense, what one learns in the field is immediately accountable in everyday life among sensible people who develop reasonable expectations about someone in their midst.

So what does one do in order to do fieldwork? Perhaps as a beginning observation it might be noted that fieldwork replicates everyday life. Life is fieldwork; fieldwork is life. It is in the very processes of mundane daily living, the daily interpretations of experience, in socialization itself, that the fieldwork dialectic is learned.[1] As we have essentially been fieldworkers all our lives, what we do in the field has a mundane familiarity about it. Just as everyday life involves, in Goffman's phrase, "a presentation of self" (1959), it involves too a presentation of everyday life to one's self. The basic familiarity is there, despite the many trials in that brand of living called anthropological fieldwork. The trials are, of course, legion. They are created by the extreme foreignness of a field, by its apparent perversity, by the embarrassing and inhibiting self-consciousness of "doing fieldwork," of "being on one's toes," of "not missing anything," or by one of the numerous other hardships that fieldworkers find to be their lot.

It is not only fieldwork as socialization, but also its more profound demands that make it both a painful and an exhilirating encounter. Its excruciating and continuous self-reflection leads some, like John Seeley, to define it as a "shattering encounter," others as a Maslow-like "peak experience." It is characterized by a continuous struggle to understand—to intuit the other's system of sense, to treat it with charity, to recreate it in one's self, and to render it into an anthropological idiom. These are its ongoing moral engagements. They alternately invite and threaten, at times creating excitement about a discipline that sees the importance of the procedure, at others inducing doubts about the process and about anthropology itself. These reflections are as much a part of the anthropological consciousness as are the concerns with the reliability of the knowledge the process produces. They are undeniably a part of the very experience that eventually becomes invisible in the finished ethnography.

As well as all those challenges to us as persons, fieldwork is through and through the anthropological method. Contemporary anthropology, therefore, makes a tacit recognition of the very human and rather "unscientific" procedures which make ethnographic experience into documented reality. A "methods" chapter, or in some cases an appendix, is fast becoming a requirement. In acknowledgment of this demand for form and of the sociology of knowledge that informs this work, it is my intention to sketch a reflective methodological frame for my ethnography.

Who Is the Informant? The Emergent *Haole*

To experience and to know may well be the aim of fieldwork, but these very simple expectations demand deliberate management and self-conscious performance. I spent my first weeks in Honolulu continually reminded of those accolades of successful fieldwork: "gaining entrée," "establishing rapport," "singling out informants," "establishing meaningful relationships," and "keeping careful fieldnotes." I was searching for mainland expatriates—the initial classification I had for the population I later came to call the mainland *haole*. Did they have distinctive physical characteristics? Where was I to find them? I recalled most of the advice I had ever been given about permitting the data to "emerge," but continued to be burdened by romantic notions that expatriates must be itinerant intellectuals under trees. "Find an appropriate bar and go there every day," I had been told. This would presumably foster consistency and rigor. The bars of Waikiki seemed at first glance to be resurrections of Wisconsin, Alberta, and California with added touches of *hapa haole* (half *haole*) music, Mai Tais, Don Ho, and a palm or two. The bars around the Manoa campus of the university suggested the coffee shops on Telegraph Avenue. I knew about those, but doubted whether they were full of the people I wished to meet. The bars on King Street were a different matter, but they demanded more bravado than I could muster. Even though I was convinced that in those dim recesses I would find many a liquor-saturated expatriate, I decided to avoid them until I had seasoned myself a little more. Never had I felt more middle class and straight as I did when I hovered in their doorways. Those bars with their dark and silent interiors and uninviting entrances made me privately doubt almost every tale of anthropological boy-scouting and dare-devilling I had ever heard.

So the necessary osmosis was not happening. No Gauguins or Stevensons, not even a single derelict on welfare could I contrive to meet. Occasionally I became elated over distant glimpses of people who seemed to fit my categories. Such labels seemed strangely important at that early time. I rehearsed various opening gambits which were to accompany casual encountering and inadvertent engagement. Just as often my own grasp of niceties informed me of the ridiculous posturing of "just happening by" or "casually striking up a conversation." The sense of inauthenticity was particularly poignant when it involved reaching some bedraggled, bearded—and therefore for me, promising—character over hundreds of yards of volcanic sea rock. How does one "happen by" after scrambling on hands and knees, scratching limb and ego? Undoubtedly such "natural scenes" could be contrived, and I have often resorted to them in past fieldwork. Even in those salad days, nourished by youthful brashness, I could not help but feel the inherent deception of it, and be uneasy about the outcome.

On several occasions I approached some likely person only to discover that my abilities to discriminate identity were far from perfect. People revealed themselves either as tourist or as *kamaaina,* native born to the Islands. The recognition of tourists, which is made with facile promptness by most Hawaiians, was an ability that even I perfected rather quickly. The *kamaaina* distinction is much more difficult, although I have talked with many who claimed to be able to distinguish _kamaaina haoles_ from mainland _haoles_. They assured me that in most cases the differences are obvious to them, although they were not able to articulate them sufficiently for me to glean from their descriptions more than that clothing, locale, and the activity in which the person was engaged seemed to be the indicators. There was also a more amorphous set of cues such as a disinterested self-assurance and a seemingly unperturbed familiarity with ensuing events. "The mainland types are more likely to ogle this or that" I was told.

Often, assuming a confidence that I hardly felt, I casually engaged one person or another in conversation only to be treated with bewilderment, sometimes bordering on suspicion. One conversation in the International Market Place in particular brought to my attention something that had eluded me to that time, namely the very delicacy of some of these encounters. The man I had engaged in conversation responded without undue wariness, seemingly oblivious to any unusual demands in the interaction. Paranoically it suddenly became clear to me that he was probably silently estimating how much all this would cost him. Perhaps he thought that claims to being an anthropologist constituted a new and creative approach. All in all I decided I was learning more about the way people make sense of drifting and apparently vagrant females of uncertain age and seemingly respectable appearance than I was about expatriates.

One day during the formless meanderings of those early confused weeks I surrendered to the obvious conclusion I had heretofore assiduously avoided. A casual encounter with a housewife at a supermarket check-out stand produced for my attention, not the intriguing tale of ideological discontent and self-banishment, but a slice of the everyday: "I hope I never have to live on the mainland again," she observed to me. It was a shattering encounter of a different kind. It confronted me with my own romantic illusions. I had been compulsively overlooking the obvious solution, that the ordinary and the familiar deserve their place in the sun. What kind of an epistemology directs any social scientist to ignore and demean obviousness? Why is the everyday to be outside anthropological attention?

Having once adjusted my anthropological focus, and rediscovered, as it were, my moral and ideological commitments, I was relieved to discover that "expatriates" were everywhere. Suddenly, instead of having no likely candidates, I had too many. I had expected a population modeled on American émigrés to Paris in the 1920s, where a distinctive community etched not only cultural boundaries, but physical ones as well. Tacit images of refugees in relocation campus, Hindus in Fiji, war resisters in Canada, the British who stayed in India, had informed my search. I had fallen heir to a classical labeling dilemma, a dilemma like Moerman's about ethnic identification devices (1965). True to a positivist tradition, I had gone to the field armed with elaborate, developed, undauntingly rigid—and later embarrassing—perceptions about a prospective population.

This particular liberation and others like it has forced me to consider repeatedly the nature of the transformations, the premises that operate in turning fieldwork into acceptable ethnography. It has made me consider how routine anthropological methods and theories influence and become silent mentors in the doing of fieldwork. The notion of an epistemological disjuncture is a way of describing an anthropologist's dual commitment to abstractions on the one hand, and to raw experience and human interaction on the other—to theories and to actual fieldwork (Whittaker 1981a). In the everyday practice of anthropology this is not, however, perceived as an impediment. Anthropologists go to the field with definite questions for which they seek answers, and for which they invariably find answers. This is the investigative style of positivism. Yet fieldwork seems to recommend itself as the very embodiment of nonpositivism. In fieldwork, the field and not the anthropologist decrees both questions and answers, relevancies and interpretations.

It was in the field that I learned that I was a *haole*. Sensitized by mainland ethnic tensions, with a conscience alert to racial slurs and an ear tuned for subleties of meaning and intent in designators and markers, I had felt myself adequately prepared for a multi-ethnic society. I was equally convinced that the elusive nuances of inter-ethnic interaction would initially, inevitably, escape me. Guardedness, previous sensitizing, and good will, I hoped, would save me from transgressing. Within a day of my arrival, the term *haole* was openly applied to me by a department store clerk, whom I, at that uninformed time, viewed as an "oriental." The clerk's manner was noncommittal, her voice matter-of-fact and without intonation. I knew *haole* meant white and I had embroidered upon it pejorative connotations like "whitey" or even "gringo." A day later I was offered yet another example by a mother at my child's school: "Our kids are among the only half dozen *haole* kids in the class." With such an obvious self-referrent it was crashingly obvious that I too was a *haole*. Moreover, it was clear that the intent was not to insult or disparage, but rather an acceptable, and even appropriate, way to talk of Caucasians. Since then I have become aware that the term has a history, can be endowed with varying subtle, and not so subtle, nuances, and is now subject to proposed changes. It is frequently now viewed, by whites themselves, as pejorative. Professors at the university, themselves of varying ethnic origins and political persuasions, who claim to have used the word consistently for decades and who have even incorporated it in their published works, report that in recent times some white students are objecting to the term in classroom use. The majority of Hawaiians of all ethnic origins, however, continue to use it as the appropriate designation for whites. They add resentment and anger with the addition of intonation or a chosen adjective: "God damn *haole,*" "stupid *haole,*" or even "fuckin' lazy *haole.*"

The discovery of one's *haoleness* is an experience common to all whites who migrate to the Islands. People who have previously thought of themselves as rather ordinary, average North Americans, who have learned to distinguish themselves by their occupation, city of origin, or their political affiliation, are now surprised to discover themselves to be *haoles*. It is a strange existential shift for those who have always thought of others as ethnics, themselves as Americans. They are placed in the position of learning, often embarrassingly or painfully, of their own ethnicity, their own minority status.

The notion of emerging *haole*ness, a new existential awareness, the recognition of new constituent implications about one's color, origin, or ethnicity, is not relegated to Caucasians alone. Persons of other ethnic origins, who have found their way to Hawaii, encounter parallel experiences. Other migrants who bring mainland culture with them, like blacks or Japanese, learn to think of their ethnicity in quite unexpected ways. Blacks report a poignantly different discrimination. The Japanese are surprised to find that a common ethnic origin does not necessarily ensure a smooth passage into island Japanese culture, but rather exposes them to new ethnic differentiation, namely *kotonk,* the designation for mainland Japanese.

With the discovery of the ubiquity of the mundane *haole,* a rather massive population, I began to be burdened with remnants of social scientific propriety. Should I think about samples? What kinds of measures should I adopt about representation and generalization? How could I produce reliability? Indeed, what occupied me throughout the fieldwork were the ghosts of researchers past who had crafted their methodology into a fine instrument of undisputed reputation.

The Positivist Over My Shoulder

Some concerns must be obvious to all fieldworkers, and indeed to all who have ever been strangers.[2] It is the eternal puzzle common to all ethnography. How is one to tell the story of the people studied? What kind of knowledge makes an appropriate ethnographic study? Indeed, which story of the many possible stories should be told? In traditional ethnographic works, chapters such as this are destined to explain the route the ethnography took, what "theories" and "methods" informed the process.

In the ideal world in which the research is initially constructed, usually in the safety of academia, these issues appear crystal clear and often bear the stamp of approval that accompanies the decisions of granting agencies. To transfer these notions into a chapter later on is not problematic. There, theories and methods again make their appearance—pristine and understandable. They are a perfect documentation of the abstract and conceptual discourse that moves the discipline forward. They reside in opening chapters of ethnographies like some methodological Genesis giving divine legitimacy to what is to follow. A perplexing juxtaposition, however, occurs. One part of the work is an ethnography of the people studied, but the first chapters on methods and theories which stand for the world view and assumptions of the fieldworker, seldom fulfill this avowed purpose.

In some kind of attempt to redress this seemingly awkward welding together of the culture of the discipline and the actual culture studied, anthropologists, in particular, have taken to attempting some ethnography of their own fieldwork. Presumably their intent is twofold: to remind the reader that the ensuing discourse is, after all, only possible through the field experience of a human instrument; and to satisfy the pervasive demands of the social and human sciences that "method" be an integral part of constituting what is ultimately consumed as knowledge. Yet while some parts of the anthropological community have come to demand it, other parts tend to view it with barely suppressed irritation and speak disparagingly of "confessionals." The former have come to see anthropology as an interpretive, hermeneutic, or phenomenological enterprise (Castaneda 1968; Geertz 1973, 1976; Rabinow 1977; Dumont 1978), the latter cling to positivistic traditions dependent on the objective reporting of facts, a process which for them has no bias or point of view. Perhaps the critics of "confessionals" are not entirely amiss, although for entirely different reasons. All too often reflexivity is presented as "a thing in itself," merely illuminating and reporting that the ethnographer is gifted with self-knowledge (Marcus 1980). Rarely do its critical awarenesses filter into or affect the nature or constituent parts of the ethnography itself. Clearly such confessionals serve as reassurance that the ethnographer is a sensitive fieldworker and, by implication, that the knowledge is more reliable.

There are, then, a number of questions pertaining to reliability that reverberate through an ethnography. How did I, the anthropologist, come by the knowledge I turn into text? Why should fieldwork be trustworthy? How does the reader know the knowledge is "right"?[3] These are all questions of reliability and there is great temptation to try to answer them as a positivist might. After all, this is the tried and true way, not only of anthropological tradition, but of Western knowledge generally.

The traditional route to claiming reliability in ethnography is clear enough. Commonsensically we associate a certain amount of time as necessary "to know the place." In anthropology, tradition seems to decree that this should be at least a year and a half. This is the amount of time expected of fledgling anthropologists. The "fieldwork-is-life" notion informs such estimates, and also assures the reader that some understandings ought to have been grasped by then. Thus my two years and three extra summers constitute an anthropologically recognized claim to a kind of reliability.

Anthropological tradition also makes some evaluations about reliability on the basis of the size of the community studied. The silent assumption is that the smaller the community the better the anthropologist ought to know it. Small villages are thus more knowable than "complex, literate" societies. The relationship among complexity, size, and difficulties-in-knowing adequately reflects the main methodological standards of the discipline, namely the reliance on face-to-face acquaintance. Size also indicates certain expectations about holism. It is believed that with smallness holism is closer to being achieved. Holism is still, after all, a silent standard. Naturally the size of the community involves all kinds of pragmatic considerations. For example, can official census figures be used? Is formal documentation available? Or does the anthropologist supply her own? Can the anthropologist become familiar with each household? A notion of community is central to the anthropologist's conceptualization, and its absence or its unclear boundaries are disquietening, and make one wonder if one is doing legitimate anthropology.

I had no recognizable community, but merely networks of individuals, distinguished only by similar geographical origins and some common experiences. I did fieldwork everyday, everywhere, both in pursuing my own life, as well as in purposeful observations and participation in the approved anthropological manner. I was continually cognizant of the fact that I myself was one of the population to be studied (Riemer 1977).

The enforced self-reflection, part of my own everyday life as a *haole*, made several things clear to me. One was that fieldwork itself, wherever it was performed, was in some senses the same as my reflection on my own daily existence as a stranger.

Essentially, field data are the experiences of the ethnographer, consciously reconstructed. Though it has a particular form, it is as if a kind of autobiography were being continually formulated. One is aware of the external cultural constraints that manage and produce meanings, and one becomes equally aware of how the internal order responds. One transforms them according to anthropological ideology. This ideology constituted for me a shadow fieldworker, a super-ego, judging and cajoling, pushing and prohibiting—the positivist over my shoulder.

Although I went to the field with my head full of non-positivistic theoretical intentions, I constantly felt the demanding incantations of positivism. At this safe psychological distance I can recreate my own innocence almost a decade ago, and note that my epistemological liberation was superficial indeed. With the subdued zeal engendered only in the recently converted, I was a lively advocate of phenomenological interpretation. Such interpretations permitted new and useful critiques. The shift to interpretive anthropology allowed a clearer view of the traditional ideology of anthropology and of the other paradigms the discipline affected. The phenomenological view seemed to provide for a liberal, noncolonial perspective in making it possible for each person, by being the narrator of the experiences, to be his or her own anthropologist. The possibility was there to have personal politics converge with theoretical preference.[4] I wanted to do an ethnography that was true to these convictions. Yet this proved more troublesome than I had expected. Sometimes I acted and made decisions that seemed designed for the sole purpose of meeting, in fantasy, the piercing comments and embarrassing questions hurled at me by an unsympathetic positivist. I came to think of it as positivist guilt, a puritanical moral correctness that a mere exhortation of alternatives could not appease.

Anthropological Ideology as Superego

My fieldwork was conducted somewhere in the period during which I was working out a paradigm change. Some of the understanding that I attempted to weave into my work, such as what kinds of data to collect, what to abstract from it, were informed by a phenomenological perspective. Yet the fact that I was "collecting," that it was to be viewed as "data," that it had to undergo transformation, and that I wanted to turn present appearances into future ethnography, was an acknowledgment of the moral force of positivism and of the anthropological ideology current at that time. I did, of course, anticipate a return to the anthropological community. Perhaps pure phenomenology or unadulterated nonpositivism can never be possible. It is certainly inadvisable if one wants to retain claims to doing anthropology, and to have one's work make sense to anthropology.

This was most clearly revealed in my fantasies about doing the phenomenological work that would honour Natanson's suggestion to attend to "the descriptive delineation of what presents itself to consciousness as it presents itself and in so far as it presents itself" (Natanson 1967:7). While in itself this continued to be desirable, ironically, by itself it was inconclusive and not completely satisfying. Anthropological ideology, if not common sense, led me to collect some data that would appease anthropological sensibilities. Should phenomenological rigor prevail in a later writing, I reasoned, these materials could, after all, be omitted. Thus I did not find my feet adequately, nor make sense of the culture for myself, until I had examined the rather commendable statistical demography put out by the state, read several histories, developed a cognitive map of the city and the Islands, noted ethnic and other communities, examined traditional and contemporary land use patterns, considered ecology and technology, and perused the economic analyses produced by the government, the Bank of Hawaii, and the newspapers. In making sense of the ethnic plurality that whirled around me daily, I developed every tool that physical anthropology ever taught me. In the interests of some residual holism, sheltered behind a touristic curiosity, I visited every island and became acquainted with denominational, ethnic, and educational institutions. I constructed a history of Hawaii and of the Pacific, and attended to the rudiments of writings on prehistory. Part of this traditional ethnographic preparation consisted of collections of Hawaiian and pidgin vocabularies, of names of flora and fauna, of ethnic histories, labor organizations, government policy documents, and of folklore and mythology. Clearly such attempts at holism are anthropological. Had I been a sociologist or psychologist much of this would have been considered irrelevant and relegated to private pursuits.

Driven by positivistic notions of rigor, I scheduled over a hundred formal interviews. I approached each with a roster of questions and taped them. Somehow these taped records promised accountability, replicability, generalizability, and reliability. They seemed to assure a composite portrait of the *haole*. When I later attempted to work with the results, however, they gave me little satisfaction, hovering on the borders of banality. They seemed to have been robbed of individual sentiment and experience. Nevertheless, at the time, the security of being able to demonstrate consensus and conventional rigor fortified me.

Apart from all that, I made it my business to evoke the commonsense categories, solidly adopted in anthropology, and tried to cover the usual age, class, sex, occupation, place of birth variables. Thus I talked to Caucasians of varying ages, to long-time residents and relative newcomers, to males and females, to people of different socioeconomic statuses, to the married and the single, urban people and rural people, to business executives and to hippies.[5] These conventional biographical details seemed an important part of reliability.

It eventually dawned on me that even I was willing to forgo the recognizable categories, to hold them suspended. In the final analysis, however, I realized that I was still bowing to the conventions of my discipline. For, after all, was I not making a study of race and ethnic relations? Did I not take the trouble to construct a history and a setting? Was I not concerned with cultural ecology, the relation of *haoles* to nature? And did not the notions of colonialism, its dying hold on Hawaiian life, its seeming re-creation in mainland migrants, inform my work? It is clear that in order to write anthropology, one cannot but do some form of positivism.[6]

As part of the positivist appeasement, I developed an account for the ways in which I met informants. Obviously, there was no community and thus no boundaries to be recognized. I depended upon an interactional network, where each person I met or interviewed readily gave me an introduction to several others. This method of finding informants had much to commend it. As each prospective informant was first solicited by a person who already knew me, I was never in the position of having to hurl myself at unwilling strangers. I was thus relieved of certain ethical dilemmas about which I was very sensitive at that particular period of anthropological history, and I virtually eliminated the theatrical staging of chance encounters. Happily no one appeared to merely tolerate me with patient endurance or suppressed annoyance. All I had to give up for this rather comfortable state of affairs was whatever mysterious "negative views" or "secretly guarded positions" are supposed to exist in those who refuse to speak to anthropologists. I was able to avoid the embarrassed, self-abnegating, and apologetic approaches which fieldworkers affect and at the same time find so distasteful (Whittaker 1978). Nor was I required to make the elaborate justifications that some anthropologists have been called upon to make. No grandiose projections about the ultimate worth of my work was required, although most people asked what I planned to do with the information.

It eventually came to my attention that my method of meeting informants was one recognized and used by social scientists working in such sensitive areas as black neighborhoods. I had thus acquired the methodological justification I needed. It was apparently called, simply and obviously enough, the snowball technique, and its reputation was accredited.[7]

Suddenly there were too many mainland *haoles* for me to meet, let alone interview. The multiplication was exponential for, not only did I meet persons in the orbits of my daily life, but each person I interviewed introduced me to three or four others. For example, while exercising my curiosity at a downtown art gallery, I asked the curator about the prints being shown. During the ensuing conversation I was introduced to one of the artists who chanced by to check on the progress of his exhibit. Both readily consented to talk with me, while expressing curiosity ("Why would anyone want to ask me?") and amusement ("Surely we could not say anything of interest to an anthropologist?"). The curator quickly put me in touch with five other mainland migrants—the architect who built her house in Hawaii Kai, a man who worked in an office in the neighborhood, a girlhood friend who had moved to Honolulu a couple of years ago, her sister, and a boutique clerk in Kahala Mall.

This network finally reached well beyond Honolulu and Oahu and I seemed to have almost infinite choice.

What I was finding was not a white community in the nineteenth-century style where daily interaction and cognizance of each other's concerns were the norm. The 1970s and '80s were characterized more by amorphous subgoups distinguishable by life-style—surfing zealots at Sunset Beach, retired condominium-dwellers on the fringes of Waikiki, international jet-setters in sheltered enclaves, comfortable suburban householders at Koko Head or Kahala, university faculty, commune-dwellers at Taylor Camp on Kauai or in Manoa Valley. Every now and again the network paths cut across each other, the same person being referred from different quarters. Characteristically all referrals came with attendant recommendations. They carried with them interpretations of my interests and intentions, plus the person's own notions of the issues to be researched. "Talk to her, she has an interesting story to tell." "He can really tell you what it's like to be black in the islands." "He's moved back and forth between here and the mainland more times than he cares to remember." Referrals occasionally converged on relatively public figures—a psychologist who conducted encounter groups, an island artist, a college professor, the owner of a well-known health food store, a radical clergyman.

In time the whole business of following up informants through referrals seemed too facile. Should informants be so easy to come by? Should data fall so readily into my lap? The only reference I had was previous fieldwork I had conducted in a hospital, the hardships of which were legion. The unwritten folklore of anthropology, too, seemed scattered with what Louch calls "traveller's tales" (1966:160; Marcus 1980:508). There are tales of exotic adventures, of unforeseen threats brought about by customs stranger than the imagination, or of the unusual tribulations involved when anthropological innocence is transformed to knowingness. The unspoken demand seemed to be there: true anthropology involves trials and some anguish, if not of the bodily ilk, then at least of the mental variety. I was also the anything-but-pleased recipient of the inevitable teasing that is one's due if one works not only in the South Seas, but in the midst of modern Western amenities. "Field-work, eh?" "*Some* people, you know, trek into the New Guinea highlands for two weeks before they come to *their* people." Sometimes a giggle or a guffaw was all that was needed. Much of the time I emerged from these encounters, unwillingly constructed as a sort of Stephen Potter character, drowning in the self-indulgent creature comfort of beaches, alcoholic beverages, indolent music. The implications of gamesmanship were presumably evoked by my claim that what I did was anthropology.

My response to all this was as unsubtle as the criticism. I produced the moral ideology current at the time, that condemned research on the less privileged as exploitative—"Just studying my own, you know." Sometimes I drew from my own developing repertoire of horror and hardship tales, heavy with cultural incongruities, threats to limb or dignity, and dietary violence. I managed to produce quite a few anthropological parables about hiking to hermit huts in remote parts of the Islands, interviewing a marijuana distributor in a public place while he transacted several thousand dollars worth of business, managing body and self in semi-nude living at Taylor Camp.

The Ideal World
of Truth and Objectivity

In some sense we all live our lives as positivists. Positivism is as much a precept in the commonsense world as it is for those who produce knowledge. Everyday interaction depends on this kind of certainty. It is clearly revealed in the devices we use to ensure conformity: be logical, tell it as it is, talk straight, lay it on the line, make sense, and so forth. There are also constraints on being devious, daft, and crazy. Such shared beliefs are treated as adhering to reality and to objective standards, which in themselves are seen as obvious. Any apparent disregard for objectivity is suspect, either as subjectivity, and hence unreliable, or as lacking in certainty: muddleheaded, absentminded, unpredictable, and "out to lunch." Certainty becomes a necessity of interaction. Into the notion called objectivity, for better or worse, are packed a collection of cultural absolutes and rules.

It is expected in anthropology, as in science, that the presence of this prized entity called objectivity be demonstrated. Objectivity is, after all, a recognized mark of credibility, showing rigor in methods. It separates the knowledge from the most suspicious data of all, the "merely subjective" (Dowling 1975). The knowledge I had chosen was, by and large, of the subjective variety. This is not the culturally acceptable route to truth. The presumed superiority of objective knowledge, in contrast, relies on one assumption that there is a world "as it actually and truly is," and moreover, that it can be discovered. Moreover, objectivity works. It fits. Further, it makes other knowledge possible.

With such responsibilities given to it, objectivity is not a status readily conferred. It must be earned by trial and error, by rigorous experimentation, and by continuing evaluations. Unworthy candidates are eliminated. Once conferred, however, it is imbued with truth. This was the general belief about objectivity and reliability that I felt I, in some sense, faced with colleagues in anthropology, but also, more generally, with those from outside the academic community. My task, it seemed to me, was to present the mainland *haole* in a subjective way and yet to make the portrait believable and reliable.

Fieldwork traditionally treats the problem of objectivity in two ways. First, it assumes that there are things out there that could be called "actualities." Second, it assumes that the reporting of these is an objectifying act. Actualities imply that events take place, objects exist, people act in various ways, and that all of these are visible as unambiguous facts, even "brute facts" (Searle 1970:50). They are immutable and not open to debate or interpretation. Thus, if I described one of my informants as living on a houseboat in Ilikai yacht harbor, presumably this has the appearance of objective fact that anyone in the discipline could verify. Initially it is a mere subjective observation on my part, a facet of my fieldwork experience. That it can achieve objective status when I write it in a text can be quite deceptive because it involves, of course, a necessary interpretation. No one would agree to a description that what is really there is some wood, paint, metal, furniture, food, and a human body floating in the Pacific Ocean. The objectivity is a commonsense one, interpreted culturally. The fieldworker can assume that facts are inevitably present in the field and can be gathered and authoritatively claimed. The assumption must also be made that only one adequate interpretation is possible. "Although theoretical frameworks have become increasingly elaborate and sophisticated, ethnographic data continue to be treated as in itself unproblematic . . . There is seldom any disagreement about the *a priori* existence of facts as essentially knowable aspects of reality" (Ennew 1976:43).

If the situation becomes more complex, the interpretation less commonsensically obvious, some of the taken-for-granted knowledge of anthropology itself becomes activated. Movements are interpretable as "dance," organization of words and meanings as "prayer," and particular cohabitation customs as "cross-cousin marriage." The objectivity of such observations is the product of a presumed "disinterested anthropological observer." Thus, as in all "objectified" description, selections are made as to what the "facts" are. These selections are informed by our already existing knowledge. Only traumatic discovery and revelation could alter this existing knowledge. Whitehead has written, one may clear up common sense, surprise it, or alter its details, but somehow ultimately one is forced to satisfy it (1932:160; Ford 1975:6).

If one wants to tell the ethnographic story in a new way, the objectivity advanced by science may not be applicable. Within the scientific paradigm objectivity "is the sought virtue of those who claim to have transcended the normal limits on truth in everyday life" (Gouldner 1976:10). The very notion of science is predicated on this ability to transcend. Anthropology too claims for itself a clarity that transcends the ordinary. Other knowledge is quickly relegated to second-class status and categorized as "mere" opinion or "only" subjectivity. There it resides as unreliable. The implication is that opinion or subjective data might stimulate some researcher to apply the appropriate methodology or objectify it.

Objectivity Without Rank
The "Native's Point of View"

There is an undeniable reasonableness to the demand for objectivity. The everyday world is everyman's objective reality. There is a fundamental discrepancy, however, in the ultimate hope of the scientist and that of the anthropologist. Surely both strive for objectivity. Science makes efforts to develop a unity, an agreed-upon standard of understanding to be shared and developed and by which the world can be safely viewed. Unity and certainty are its keywords. Anthropology, by contrast and self-proclamation, attempts to describe the variety of truths on which the width of human understandings are based. For anthropology the preservation of "the native's point of view" is a sacred duty. Malinowski advocated that anthropologists "grasp the native's point of view, his relation to life, to realize *his* vision of *his* world" (1961:25). This, from the theoretical perspective of anthropology, is the ultimate reality. It permits everyone to be his or her own anthropologist in that it permits self-description. Thus what anthropology tries to capture is an *existential* objectivity not a scientific one. The *haole* encounter with Hawaii, therefore, as they experience it, and relate that experience to me, is their particular objective truth.

How can this be captured? One may argue that what needs to be captured is the presentation of self in the language in which it is done, the explanations given as they appear in the discourse. This would be true in a radical empiric sense. "What presents itself to consciousness," to borrow Natanson's phrase, "how it presents itself," would then constitute the data. Perhaps it could constitute the whole work. Castaneda, adhering faithfully to certain facets of phenomenological philosophy, advocates the suspension of judgment. In attempting to make sense of Yaqui sorcery he notes:

> any event that occurred within this alien system of sensible interpretation could be explained or understood only in terms of the units of meaning proper to that system . . . The system I recorded was incomprehensible to me, thus the pretense to anything other than reporting about it would be misleading and impertinent. In this respect I have adopted the phenomenological method and have striven to deal with sorcery solely as phenomena that were presented to me. I, as the perceiver, recorded what I perceived, and at the moment of recording I endeavoured to suspend judgment. (1971:25)

The spirit of the endeavor and Castaneda's suggestion is that other minds and other consciousnesses remain essentially elusive. What an anthropologist can know, however, through the medium of interaction and language, is how experience is sorted and classified, and cultural knowledge constituted.

The Interactive Imperative:
Telling It

Therefore, ethnography depends on the actual language, captured perhaps *in toto*, but made initially possible by the interactive imperative introduced by the presence of the questioning anthropologist. It involves "trying to rescue the 'said' of such discourse from its perishing occasions" and fixing it "in perusable terms" (Geertz 1973:20). Yet there is still more to the telling than this. The "native's point of view" is a mediated truth. There is surely nothing learned by the anthropologist in the field that is innocent of her presence. Her questions, her supposed right to ask them, the identity categories assigned to her, the apparent underlying morality of the issues investigated, and many other situation-relevant matters are part of the grammar of the exchange.

The matter of being categorized by informants is obvious in the responses given me. When I approached a prospective mainland *haole* it was never as a nonentity. Although anthropology was a label I claimed when I introduced the nature of my work, a more commonplace categorization was obviously in evidence. Either I was a shopper at a store, a mother at a school concert, the friend of the host at a party. The legitimating facets of such encounters spoke on my behalf to enhance my credibility. Further immediate knowledge was transmitted by the contents of grocery baskets, child socialization language ("Don't throw sand," "Don't swim out beyond the reef," "You have to spit in your face mask first"), and other general attributes. Parenthood in particular, in my experience, seemed to alleviate any glimmering tendency to attribute malevolence to me. Moreover it provided almost immediate material for conversation. Importantly, each such encounter led, with no apparent display of reluctance, to an interview or at least to a lengthy exchange. In some instances the individual prospective informant even made the offer to talk about his or her experiences.

People were often puzzled. The notion of anthropology was the primary fulcrum around which the introductions and agreements were made. Usually I was called upon, either by a direct request, or in response to apparent uneasiness on the part of the new person, to provide an autobiography, an adequate explanation of how I came to do this kind of work instead of investigating "stones and bones," a common interpretation of what anthropologists do.

The manner in which one informant introduced me to another, either in my presence or privately before my telephone call, was pregnant with the overtones of inferred identity and implied notions of the enterprise. The conceptualizations were most noticeable in the descriptions offered about the prospective informants brought to my attention. "Jim Dunlap loves to talk. And he's had some pretty interesting experiences." "She's my friend from the mainland, and she's at home every day with nothing to do." "You should talk to Walter Smith. Do you know who he is? He can tell you a lot about *haoles* on this island. I can't think of anyone who knows more about them. He has to deal with them in his work of course." "I know someone you'd enjoy—this old lady in the green and white house around the corner. She used to have a lot of money. Would you like to talk to her?" "I mentioned you to Jeff Withers. He wants to talk to you. He's my dentist. He's from Ohio." "She's a real weirdo . . . but interesting!" "His wife has been to Midway and the New Hebrides. They could probably make some interesting comparisons for you. Would you find that worthwhile?" Each suggested introduction represented an assessment of what I was about or, conversely, should be about.

Sometimes the assumptions made about anthropological rights and privileges were very obviously woven into contemplations around possible introductions. "My neighbor would have very interesting things to say. He's a man with an important job, and may be too busy to talk with you." The implication here is obvious, if not more than a little disconcerting, about my being either a woman or an anthropologist. Happily this neighbor was by no means too busy to talk, expressed himself as "only too pleased" and "looking forward to it," and ultimately thanked me for choosing him. In contrast, the following comment imbued me with more authority and status than I would have wished. "I know Dr. Stanton would enjoy talking with you. He seemed eager to do so. Besides he is an authority on the matter. So if you think he might have something to offer and you have the time, call him up."

Inherent in much of the categorizing to which I was subjected, and which had an influence on the knowledge that grew out of the encounters, were notions of status and power, of social worth and importance. At times my social importance was placed embarrassingly out of focus and I arrived to find special meals prepared, special china and cutlery brought out, or the house especially cleaned and ordered. At times there were other deferential acts showing undue concern, addressing my supposed convenience and requests. Occasionally, by contrast, my importance seemed completely undermined and I had to resort to constructing it on arrival to permit a successful and appropriate conversation.

One particular fieldwork encounter made this very clear, but also reflected current concerns about depersonalizing information and retrieval systems. I had been referred to a physician by a man who claimed to be his friend and described him as "an awfully nice person . . . one who would be pleased to talk with you." The consent of the prospective informant was duly solicited, accorded, and arrangements for a meeting made. My previous year of fieldwork experience, however, had not prepared me for the rigorous questioning I was to receive on the moral worth of my endeavor, of anthropology in general, and of information gathering and retrieval in Western society as a whole. The man engaged me in a rapid debate about the moral worth of social scientific studies of any kind and wanted evidence of successful ventures in the area— "for example history, sociology, psychology . . . and your field . . . I don't feel that way about economics." The comfortable intellectual-in-residence status provided for academics and anthropologists overseas was not about to be evoked in this situation. Rather the analogy was illegal power through information control. The invasion of privacy by government wiretapping, the easy access to credit card information and to mailing lists, and the infinite polls exploiting the individual were introduced for discussion. By implication anthropology, or any study, could be classified with these, any form of intrusion for information was a violation of the ethic of privacy. We were successful in keeping the discourse within realms of politeness, arguing about assumptions and logic, and about ultimate implications rather than my presence specifically. After a couple of hours we turned to my interests and took care of the rudiments of my questions. I was sufficiently demoralized, however, to keep the conversation at a very superficial level and to omit the use of the tape recorder.

Monitoring and Establishing Experiences

In short I am implying what is already well-known to all those who do fieldwork. The grammar of the field encounter, made up of such considerations as the quality of the interaction, its perceived intentions, and innumerable other factors, shapes the knowledge produced. Not only the matter of who *I* was, or who *they* were, affects the knowledge, but experience and memory are themselves contingent and emerging. They are not pristine, adamantine entities, but rather formless, uncoded possibilities. They must be exposed to cultural monitoring. Thus experience and memory are not crystalline events, but organized interpretations. Clearly then I propose that the fieldworker and the person interviewed come together with some memories and experiences clearly established, and some that are given form only in the interaction. Some matters have no previous history but become formulated in the here and now of the encounter. There they are somewhat stabilized as "what actually happened" or "the way I felt at that time" or "the way things were." The flow of the conversation, the cognizance of changing interpretations, the continually shifting realities all play a part in this stabilization. As the parameters of the acceptable discourse change and become clear, so the interpretive mode for past experience becomes increasingly distinguishable. It is perhaps no wonder then that this emerging clarity and consensus is usually recognized and termed "growing rapport."

It could be argued that emerging realities offer new contexts for viewing and understanding experiences. Meanings are continually under mutual construction. The ethnographer and the person interacting with her conspire, in a sense, to make this possible. George Herbert Mead observes: "It is of course evident that the materials out of which the past is constructed lie in the present. . . any interpretation of the picture we form of the past will be found in the present, and will be judged by the logical and evidential characters which such data possess in a present" (1959: 29).

The sense of what I am trying to argue about the shaping of knowledge can best be captured through a series of encounters in my fieldwork. Perhaps the most obvious examples of the monitering of experience, or the creation of a common reality about the past, occurred when I interviewed groups or a husband and wife together. In some cases, of course, a reality about the past had at a past time been established and either partner could be charged with its presentation. In other cases all three of us were involved in the construction of the experience:

> WIFE: . . . plus, out here, there's no telephone. It's very social. And, I sincerely don't remember the time George and I had had dinner alone last.
> HUSBAND: Yeah. Every night we have dinner with somebody.
> WIFE: Yes. . . this house is the gathering place. Oahu is the gathering island, and this place the gathering place for the whole North Shore. They all come here. . .
> HUSBAND: (*with some irritation*): Oh, that's not so. You make it sound as if everyone on the North Shore comes here. Just a few friends come here. . .just friends. . .
> WIFE: What do you mean, just friends? Look at all those people last night. I wouldn't call all of them friends, but they were here, eating and drinking.
> HUSBAND: They may not be "friends" in the sense you mean; but we knew them all. . .you go overboard sometimes.
> ANTHROPOLOGIST: Do you mean that a lot of people come here, rather than your going to their place?
> WIFE and HUSBAND (*in unison*): Yeah, yeah. That's it.

Later references in the same conversation indicated that this particular reality had been adopted as some kind of consensus. Both spouses elaborated on their sense of exploitation at the continual use of their house by friends and even complete strangers. By contrast others in group conversations recognized the authenticity of multiple views and experiences. They noted, for example, "That's Fred's view of what happened. This is mine . . ."

Fieldworkers often experience responses to some of their questions that clearly demonstrate that the person being questioned does not have an organized interpretation. Indeed, as the following case implies, the very experience has not been previously developed but is constructed within the frame of the interaction:

ANTHROPOLOGIST: Did you consider any alternatives when you came here?

INFORMANT: Well . . . I don't know . . . I just wanted to come here.

ANTHROPOLOGIST: I see, you didn't consider doing anything else?

INFORMANT: Hmm . . . No, I don't think so, I guess I just . . . well . . . (_uncomfortable silence ensues_).

ANTHROPOLOGIST: Well, I wondered because, quite often, people tell me that they have thought of going elsewhere. Some say Australia or New Zealand. Others talk of New England or the Sierra Nevada. You know. They have had other possibilities.

INFORMANT: Oh, I see. Well, yes, I did think of other places, but I wanted to be somewhere I could surf. On the other hand, I would have almost gone anywhere as I haven't been anywhere . . . Still, there's something about Hawaii that appeals to me most of all . . . (_somewhat later in the conversation_) . . . I thought of staying somewhere in Southern California, but I wanted to get as far as I could from my draft board . . . Tahiti was a little too far away . . . too foreign.[8]

Obviously in terms of the interactional construction of experience out of mere possibility, this is a case where the informant had not created any recallable reality. The interactional demand implied the appropriateness of such a response. Consequently, interpretations and memories were organized to produce it. In other words, each individual "must, essentially, be able to point to what he means in the presence of some second person who, thus sharing his 'discovery of meaning,' develops the same 'map' as our first observer" (Holzner 1972:23).

Another variant of the monitoring of experience is the enriching of accounts provided by the informant with his or her increasing awareness of the nature of the parameters of permissibility set in the interaction with the ethnographer. Again, this is conventionally referred to as "rapport." In the following case the shaping of knowledge, its shifting nature and essential drift, can be captured in the recounting of a series of encounters with a young man attempting to describe his decision to move to Hawaii. Each response was bound in a somewhat different context in the interaction. Thus, each time a slightly different version of the past emerged. The contexts imbued each version with authenticity. It is not a matter of not telling something we call "the truth," or of increased trust in the person of the anthropologist. Rather it is the infinitely rich possibilities of experience and the many faces that the past presents for interpretation. Speaking of his decision to migrate the informant offers:

> When I was still back in Laguna, he [a friend] wrote to me and said, "Well, I'd like you to come over and visit this place. It's just so amazing, it'll blow your mind." ... At the same time, my grandmother was over on Oahu. So, I was invited by her to come and spend some time. And I had wanted to come and visit the Islands for several years, but I didn't want to come unless I had a place to stay outside of all the tourist spots . . .

After another five minutes of conversation, within a different context, he produced the following version:

> I'd always wanted to live in a communal-type scene, and this was such a place. It's an experience that I really wanted to have—living close to the land and having your own garden, knowing that I'd be able to build my own house, and that was tempting . . . The smog was closing in on Laguna [where he lived on the mainland] and it's very hectic living there with the city all closing in on you . . .

On another day of conversation, speaking again about his life in California and implying his decision to move, he noted:

> The cops started coming and giving me a lot of trouble all the time. They would come right into the store and try to scare me and things like that. They're always trying to smell if they can—to see if they can smell marijuana or something. We didn't keep it around, it's too risky. And, not only me, but a lot of my friends in town, were always hassled by them. I had a part-time job while I was going to school. One time, I was coming home at two in the morning from the job— it happened several times—they would stop me on the street, phone in the station, and ask if I was a wanderer, and they'd just go through this big, big hassle with me every time.

Later the conversation moved to matching stories about the work of police in places like Berkeley and Laguna Beach. The parameters had expanded again and made possible the following:

I said it [fuck] under my breath, but they still heard me, and made me put my hands behind my back and hustled me into the car. What was so maddening is that I heard one of them say the very same word on the way to the station. Anyway, I had to go before a judge for using that word, so I gave a false name . . . Anyway, after my dog had been picked up three times, and I had picked him up at the pound, I had to go before the Court for my dog. So, two days before I had to appear, I moved to Hawaii because I appeared before under a false name. And now, I would have to appear before the same judge under my real name . . . So I came.

In this chapter I have argued that knowledge is contingent. More strongly I am persuaded that contingency is characteristic of all knowledge. It can be demonstrated for the knowledge of the "exact sciences" as well as that produced in fieldwork in the social sciences. The determining conditions are such matters as purpose, selection, identity awarded to and claimed by the researcher, the interactional process, and the dogmas of adequate data and analysis. Such observations, of course, are not novel. A continual reaffirmation of them, however, together with the presentation of any ethnography produced from them, seem to me to be an intellectual imperative. An appreciation of the data surely involves an appreciation of its production.

Empirical purists and whole-hearted positivists would view such displays as tiresome indeterminancy, or worse, as "putting ideas into the informant's head," a synonym for illegitimate and improper. There is only one answer to that. It is to remind ourselves that objectivity, scientific accuracy, and logical precision are themselves, after all, cherished myths. As myths they make our knowledge world go round.

Even further, and particularly in the case of anthropology, perhaps all that can ever be studied are the parameters of cultural possibility, and not definitively etched and individualized facts. Anything beyond such cultural boundaries would lie foreign and unanswerable. No comfort can be found in the thereness and absoluteness, or the uniqueness of cultural experiences and events. Perhaps what we construct, over and over, are varying contours of a shared cultural universe.

A continuous stream of the famous has sought out the legendary isles to partake of offered pleasures and to perpetuate the imagery by putting the islands into poetry and prose or posing among the symbols. Mark Twain, Robert Louis Stevenson, and Jack London were among the early visitors. Right: Jack London poses with his wife Charmian and her cousin, Beth Wiley at a Waikiki Beach Walk cottage in 1915. R. J. Baker, Bishop Museum.

Above: The Prince of Wales, later the abdicated Duke of Windsor, at Waikiki Beach in 1920, enroute to Australia. He was honored at a ball at the British Club. P.M.C.

Right: A familiar figure from the middle 1930s, Shirley Temple, attracts a group of children at Waikiki. Photographs such as these helped disseminate visions of the Hawaii that tourism built. Hawaii State Archives.

CHAPTER THREE

The Migration Story: Organizing the Past

. . . the import being not whether the past occurred as depicted but how it is called forth to make the present meaningful.

McHugh (1968:25)

For every migrant to Hawaii there is a migration story. Each story tells how Hawaii was discovered and how imagination made it into a possible home. Each depicts how optimism made Hawaii an attractive answer to discontent, and, finally, how determination made it an actuality. The stories show how experience and knowledge converge to bring people to the Islands.

The narrations reveal much more than an answer to the crucial question "how did you get here?" They are more than a passport to understanding, more than a legitimation of presence. Past experience is effectively organized so that it links itself to present motivations and accommodates the expectations of the listener. This ordering is neither manipulative nor conscious, yet it provides an appropriate and necessary background history to the matters under discussion. A person's experience, as I have already suggested and the stories support, is full of tacit, raw knowledge awaiting a situation for which it can be ordered and revealed.

The stories depict the nature of people's dilemmas, how they reason about these dilemmas, how they were advised by others, and the events leading up to a final decision. Diverse experiences are arranged into a situationally proper account. Implicit in the stories are visions of a future good life, and this tacit future becomes a strong undercurrent in the discourse. Part of each complaint about a life that existed is an unspoken declaration about a vision of an ideal life. In each spirited attack on smog or winter, there is an obvious yearning for atmospheric purity and summer. In each deprivation there are the contours of what could, or ought to, be. The migrant places into the very fabric of his or her story a kind of moral claim about what a rightful expectation about the future might be, and a rationale of how Hawaii fitted that orientation.

Western philosophers frequently note that past, future, and present are inextricably part of each other and that their content is a mediated matter (Luhmann 1976; Mead 1959). In other words, while the past determines the present, quite obviously the present also defines and creates the past. Thus the present is as it appears because of the very nature of past events. The past, however, is always in change, brought forth again by succeeding generations and articulated in the light of new understandings. Similarly, the future resonates with the present and the past. Such temporal connectedness, we know from anthropological depictions of time in varying societies, is not a universal matter. An analysis of folk knowledge and linguistic usage has shown that North Americans have a clearly discernible future orientation (Dundes 1969). While this seems evident enough, it would be just as convincing to argue that these same people had a profound engagement with the past. Any request for identity, for example, usually involves a selective recounting of the past, a kind of personalized history. Such personal histories are integral to the migration story. The decision to move becomes, for the listener as well as the narrator, the inevitable outcome of the events provided in the history. Such certainty results from a cultural competence about the structure of stories and their predestined endings. Indeed, stories become structured to fit this obvious conclusion, namely the move to Hawaii.

The stories themselves reveal their discernible structure. They begin with events that place the tale in location or time—"I was sitting in my kitchen one day . . ." or "After the kid next door got beat up . . ." This constitutes a beginning around which other events come to be placed, and from which the story is taken further back in time or brought forward to the present. Next there are indicators of the significance of these events in the whole narrative, exactly where beginnings to discontent are to be discerned and where various other decisions become obvious and imperative. "It all started with my suddenly being fed up with the crime and the traffic . . ." Other accounts indicate the amount of consensus, or conversely, lack of it, that their plans or thoughts encouraged, "My wife wouldn't even think about it . . ." The structures are thus familiar ones, part of cultural narratives as we know them (Polanyi 1979).

Another part of the organization of experience into narratives is to structure it according to recognizable folk theories about major changes in a life cycle or about what causes people to make radical changes in domicile. Thus it is credible to reason that one came to Hawaii "after I quit my job, there was nothing to keep me in Chicago, so I decided this was the time . . ." It would not be credible, for example, to expect a serious reception of "I really came here because our apple tree did not flower that spring," or "I was so sick of reactionary politics and wanted to sample true socialism, so I decided upon Hawaii."

Whether an account is culturally acceptable is as much a part of the way experience is organized and presented as it is of the actual content. Thus current ideology becomes a resource for the structure of the narrative. It reverberates back and forth with biography to make a coherent story. The whole set of migration narratives, in order to become acceptable knowledge, must somehow be in accord with what we, in a commonsense way, understand migration to be about.

Official Migration Narratives and Ideological Facts

The commonsense notion of what an appropriate rationale for migration should be is undoubtedly informed by what official versions consider it to be. The migration experiences and the migration stories of countless individuals are transformed into official knowledge, useful in areas where "correct" accounts need to be produced, decisions need to be made, and actions taken. The knowledge that is meaningful to various governmental agencies and others concerned with the burgeoning rate of migration is a positivistic knowledge shaped to fit their dominant concerns (Handelman and Leyton 1978; Wheeler 1969). Its categories are shaped to these concerns, analytically chosen from a commonsensical basis of understandings about why people move. There is as well the tacit acceptance that this is completely meaningful only in terms of tried and true categories such as age, sex, occupations, size of city from which the person migrated, and so on. The assumption appears to be that a workable enlightenment will come with the viewing of certain weighted categories and their relation to others. A certain kind of objectivity, and hence reliability, is worked into such accounts of migration. Thus discernible "facts" are produced to satisfy a special arranging process where data are chosen according to the requirements of norms recognized by bureaucratic agencies.

It is of paramount immediacy for Hawaiian officials to have reliable and verifiable knowledge about "*who* are the mainland migrants" and "*why* did they come here." This choice and coding of knowledge becomes important for officials, for they believe that it will permit them to understand the flow of population to the Islands and to seek remedies for the increasing hardships created by the flow. The state government, welfare officials, unemployment bureaus, health bureaucracies, ecologists, water resources management, and others produce versions of the migration narrative. While it is apparent that the figures and tables are not immediately and obviously narratives, they do tell a story of migration that is located in an epistemology different from the one employed by the migrants themselves. The official story is informed by an assumption that *why* people come is inextricably the result of *who* people are. In some socio-psychologically derived epistemology the answer to *why* lies in *who*, which in its turn is understandable in the basic census language of age, sex, former residence, and so forth. It does not seem plausible that the *who* can provide an adequate accounting of *why* migrants come, and further, disappointing that officialdom sees *who* in terms of such impoverished, skeletal descriptive features. Yet this is part of the cultural reasoning of official agencies, made valid by the promise of universal comparison.

The official migration narrative becomes constructed in response to what are perceived as the problems of economics, politics, and population that beset the state of Hawaii. These problems are defined as soluable through a process that begins with the study of the statistical picture of migration. This would then lead to official action in accord with formally developed perspectives as suggested in the Hawaii State Plan Program: "a structure for policy plan formulation and program plan coordination which will order the actions of all State and County agencies . . ." (Department of Planning and Economic Development 1977b:vi). The problem as it is posed for solution posits, on the one hand, a notion of "quality of life" with "images of equity, social justice and economic well-being" (p.x). On the other hand, this ideal condition is hampered by many factors, including the fact that since 1965 Hawaii has had the highest immigration rate of any state. It is believed that this problem can be addressed by trying to discover the identity of the migrants. This is attempted through using the impoverished categories of the national census, augmented by spotty data collected by the Hawaiian Visitors' Bureau through brief questionnaires distributed to travelers on carriers to the Islands.

One version of migration is available in historical statistics (Schmitt 1977:90-105). In 1970, for example, there were 178,531 persons, born on the mainland living in Hawaii. Of these 125,732 were living on the mainland five years previous to 1970, indicating a recent accelerated in-migration.[1] The number of residents moving from the mainland, excluding military personnel, numbered 13,544 in 1965, 24,383 in 1970, 18,340 in 1975 and 3,266 in 1980 (Department of Planning and Economic Development 1982:table 1).[2] In addition the record reveals a mean age of 24.4 in 1970 and 23.9 in 1980, showing that the early twenties is the age of migrants from 1965 to 1981 (table 2). Large percentages come from the states of California, Oregon, and Washington—42.8 percent in 1970—a trend that continued until 1980 when an unprecedented low of 22.5 percent came from the Western states. Traditionally there have been more males than females. In 1970 there were 118 males to 100 females, and in 1980 there were 135 males to 100 females. The incoming population has consistently been about two-thirds "high-status workers." In 1970, 65.6 percent were in this category, and in 1980, 72.8 percent were in it. "High-status" workers is used to classify professional, technical, business, managerial, or other official occupations (Department of Planning and Economic Development 1981a:table 10).

The implications are obvious. The *"who"* becomes sketched, if not with a wide and rich brush, at least with the rudiments necessary to make some sense and permit speculation. The migration story is told in a way that would permit "projections" for example. It becomes possible to project population growth against various rates of growth in the tourist industry against need and supply for jobs, and to do it for some decades in the past, and into some decades into the future (Department of Planning and Economic Development 1977a:14:48-49).

The *"who"* is visible and readily classifiable not only by government statistics but also by the observations of anthropologists (Maretzki and McDermott 1980). The *"who"* for the anthropologist who looks at Caucasians as a population category is to view them as parts of a wider Hawaiian ethnic social organization with ramifications for economic, political, and other orders. One recognizable category of Caucasian is the *kamaaina* who exercises political and economic power, is culturally a mixture of old New England and missionary values, has close association by marriage with Hawaiian nobility, and has become self-perpetuating as an endogamous clan. The ancestral heads of this clan are the early missionaries and Caucasians of high status. Their social relationships are, on the whole, limited to others of *kamaaina* status, and any acquaintance with the main body of mainland *haoles* is coincidental and transitory. Their social standing is an obvious example of American blue blood, social register, landed gentry, and now, even though increasingly some of them lack the extensive display of the material well-being of former times, they exude enduring gentility. Their influence is sustained in many cultural establishments, whose histories bear the mark of their powerful economic attention. While evoking images of established position, the term *kamaaina* is frequently used in its literal translation of "child of the land." Some Island residents self-righteously claim the term for all those born on

Hawaiian soil, whatever their ethnicity. Some Caucasians claim it after what they consider a lengthy residence in the Islands, mainly to distinguish themselves from the more recently arrived *malihini* (newcomer). Nevertheless I have heard the term applied to migrants as recent as pre- or post-World War II. Others bemoan the fact that the designation is denied to them when fifty years of residence are negated by the mere fact of mainland birth. It is the families of old wealth and elevated social status in the main, however, who are consistently seen as *kamaaina* (Hormann 1982).

The rest of the *haole* population is composed of categories readily recognizable by most Hawaiians who consult their own daily experience and the obvious suggestion in the official figures. One category is discernible as executives and technicians, who have either been transferred by their corporations from the mainland, or have purposely effected their own transfer in order to live in the Islands. Some have small businesses, restaurants and the like, operating on the fringes of the tourist world. Many of these act as carriers of mainland culture to Hawaiian shores; for example, the latest trends in popular restaurants, craft shops, leather stores, art galleries, and the like. Other whites make up a large proportion of the professional community, either as permanent residents with successful practices or as transitory professionals using their skill to permit a year or two of sojourn in Hawaii. There is a smattering of writers, artists, and performers, some of whom choose to live in the Islands although their reputation is developed and maintained elsewhere, while others have a purely Hawaiian prominence. Further, the colony of those who come to the Islands to spend their retirement continues to grow. Paradoxically, while this latter trend is well entrenched and has been in effect for most of the decades of this century, there seems to be a new pattern emerging. This is a direct result of the escalating cost of living in Hawaii. Many *haoles* who have lived in the Islands for decades indicate that they cannot afford to retire there and are being forced to move back to the mainland.

Since the 1960s and well into the 1970s there has been a proliferation of the young, many of them "counter-culture" adherents, seeking a place close to the land, endowed with a community of like-minded others. Whereas in the years prior to the

1960s the *haole* population found employment in the executive, technical, academic, and professional areas, there appears to have been a shift of these categories to other ethnic groups, and whites themselves have turned to other categories of employment. Partly as a result of some of the young who stayed on from the 1960s, there has been a growth of white participation in skilled labor and service occupations.

The military constitutes a special *haole* group, living in self-sufficient isolated enclaves in various parts of the islands, at Schofield Barracks, Pearl Harbor, Fort Shafter, and Hickam Air Force Base. From these protected and culturally homogeneous communities, young military recruits sally forth to seek entertainment at various tourist meccas. There they frequently occupy an uneasy position in confrontation with the young local population. After their terms of duty are over, however, significant numbers of the military remain to become part of the Islands' *haole* population. At this point they are exposed to all the forces of acculturation.[3] Previously their position had been one of divided affiliation; on the one hand, official direction and restraint from the military bureaucracy on the mainland, while on the other, they themselves were in daily contact with the Hawaiian way of life which they had to accommodate.

Last there are the tourists, relegated by their innocence and lack of experience to various "tourist ghettos" (Farrell 1974). In addition to weekly and two-weekly holiday-seekers, there are the annual sojourners. In a perpetual search for summer, they wait out the mainland winter, confined in their condominiums and rented apartments, and condemned to their inevitable marginality and non-involvement, recreating small communities of mainland culture on the more popular islands. From this mammoth transitory population the mainland *haole* migrant usually originates. Captured beyond recall by an idyllic couple of weeks in what they quickly fantasize into an incomparable paradise, they work to make this best of all worlds their everyday home.

These official accounts, therefore, though constructed according to the normative requirements of demography, economy, and employment, constitute only one kind of migration narrative. They are coded to formal ideologies and carry all the characteristics considered commonsensical to official world views. While the features deemed necessary to describe the migrant population are present, they remain obstinately silent in providing workable explanations about motivations. Various combinations of the given factors do reveal basic components about who the migrants are. They do not provide, however, an enlightening vision on why some people of these combinations of variables move, and others do not. Access to an adequate predictability is missing. A satisfying answer to the question "why" is not forthcoming. Authorities do attempt to weave some of the available descriptive features together with migration accounts produced by academics, or attach them to their own commonsense experience and everyday observations.

Commonsense understandings about motivation, available to all in Western cultures, also inform theorizing about migration. Such theories are in essence yet other versions of the migration narrative, formalized into a specific language. Much of the explanatory style which characterizes theories is to view the matter in deterministic frames such as "expulsion and attraction" (Haddon 1911) or "push and pull" (Rossi 1956). This basic paradigm, both commonsense and academic, pervasively underlies explanations of migration regardless of their disciplinary origins or theoretical thrust. No doubt it endures because it most satisfactorily supports commonsense understandings. It pervades the narratives I report and obviously structures how the mainland *haole* see their own behavior.

Determinism as official theorizing is revealed in the attention paid tacitly to "causes." Theories ponder on the significance of voluntary or involuntary migration, on the salience of age and education, and on the nature of limited resources and opportunities (Marty 1978; Ritchey 1976). The "push and pull" determinism seems to be there, whether cost-benefit analysis (Speare 1971), personality variables of risk-taking, optimism, and flexibility (Kemper 1973), or the attractions revealed in mental maps (Fuller and Chapman 1974) are the specific focus of the analysis. It informs the description of various adaptive strategies such as those suggested by Graves and Graves (1974). The Graves point to a foraging type of migration where temporary forays are made to a new area to supplement local resources (like tourism to Hawaii), to circular migration of more or less permanent ties between the two cultures (perhaps like the biannual sojourners), and to permanent emigration which approximates most mainland *haole* intentions. Interestingly, the deterministic underpinning does not seem to alter, though the deliberate evoking of this analytic, of the concept of "cause," is outside current social scientific fashion.

These are the expert explanations by those whose business it is to research such issues and produce bias-free, reliable knowledge. This coding of the experience of others is taken to be the "real reason," while those offered by migrants themselves are given the status of "anecdotes" or "opinions" or "claims." These offerings are then viewed as raw data, certainly not to be taken at face value, but subjected to analysis so that the "true" reasons can be revealed. These official analyses, therefore, produce yet another narrative.

The historical accounts of the migrants of the nineteenth century which I discussed in an earlier chapter can be profitably resurrected here. The migration narratives of contemporary Caucasians do not, in some fundamental sense, differ from the stories produced about their predecessors of the earlier century. The attractions of enterprise, economic advantage, and an expatriate sentiment continue to reappear.

Cultural Reasoning
and the Performance of Experience

As I have already shown, if experience is, in one sense at least, raw, unanalyzed, and unorganized, it does call for coding in order to have meaning. It needs a situation to stimulate the coding. The situation in which the migration stories were constructed was the context of my presence and the context of my fieldwork. In that sense one of the major features of the organization of experience was the understandings of what my work entailed, what was required from the narrator, and what could be given credit as legitimate reasoning. As these understandings are negotiated during fieldwork, the meanings and the stories are constructed as the acquaintance between anthropologist and informant proceeds. My questions, my explanations, and my responses were instrumental in shaping the knowledge. This resonance of consciousness and meaning is depicted in a comment attributed to Stravinsky: "My knowledge is activity, I discover it as I work, and I know it while I am discovering it, but only in a very different way before and after" (Gotschalk 1969:12). Thus the epistemological base of migration stories is twofold. First, and perhaps most demanding, is the situation of the telling. The tacit and the open request and their implications make a performance out of the narration. This performance is culturally tailored and situationally specified (Kirshenblatt-Gimblett 1975). Second, the amorphous beliefs and events, which constitute something we call experience, are coded and organized to meet the first demands of performance. One might suggest that "human action is an open work, the meaning of which is 'in suspense.' It is because it 'opens up' new references and receives fresh relevance for them, that human deeds are also waiting for fresh interpretations which decide their meaning" (Ricœur 1971:544).

The cultural knowledge that goes into the coding of experience is complex indeed (Whittaker 1981b). First, my informants had to make sense of what they were being asked, either directly by question, or indirectly by implication. The indirect implication is particularly elusive and requires the kind of cultural competence that can choose a reasonable meaning from a whole vocabulary of known motives (Mills 1940). Every question resides in a culture of understandings and has a vocabulary of possible answers. This exchange has to be known, and the knowing is far from straightforward.

In thinking back on the exchanges that produced the knowledge about which I came to write, I am astounded at the complexities and infinite nuances that are absorbed by a competent interactant and acted upon unconsciously. To mention them imbues them with a false clarity and simplicity. Briefly, however, each person questioned made a fast assessment as to who I must be, what I must want, and what answers must be deemed adequate. This is not a stationary assessment but changes continually in the ongoing interaction and in succeeding interactions. Thus the initial knowledge produced tends to be more cautious and more stereotypically appropriate, later knowledge more idiosyncratic and daring.

Such changing interpretations of context bring about

what ethnographers often refer to as initially disappointing fieldwork because they were given "the party line" or "just the cultural formula" or that "nothing new happened today." Ensuing situations in the field, however, mediated by the construction of a common reality, are seen as more fruitful. This more fruitful state of affairs is often reasoned to be "rapport" or "trust" or just "because we know each other better." It is frequently interpreted as "finally getting the true story." This is the fieldworker's lot wherever ethnography is done. The definitions of context, the interpretations of intent, and the cultural coding of experience in remote cultures must sometimes make the process very difficult indeed.

Given this imperative to understand, for the present, what is being asked and indeed *what* about the past is expected, experience reflects the present (Yarrow et al. 1970). As past experiences are so malleable and so infinitely flexible, it is "primarily in a person's efforts to comprehend his present experiences that his conceptions of both past and future are shaped. If, in his retrospections, he can find a sense of continuity and of orderly, predictable change which accounts for his current circumstances, he is likely to project into the future a sense of new possibilities" (Cottle and Klineberg 1974:12). Thus in establishing and confirming the realities of experience, in our culture we extrapolate from the known of the present to the unordered of the past and from that back again to the present.

The migration story is a giant metaphor which asks us to see the actual migration in terms of something else. The something else, the story, is culturally determined and therefore in some sense its reception is prejudged. As it is not preordained like the words of a ritual, it leaves scope for imagination, a well-tempered imagination. While the structure and content of the narrative have a grammar of their own, the competence of the teller and of the listener are displayed in the nature of the narrative (Agar 1980; Colby and Cole 1970:85). The story represents in some sense a confluence of memory, imagination, and ideology.

The question "why did you come?" places on the informant the responsibility to demonstrate competence. The narrative must be convincing, must show certain factors which we believe are warranted in deciding on a rather major change in domicile.

"Oh, I just came because I wanted to . . ." is inadequate in the extreme and is interpreted as a request to make the context clearer, the expectations more visible. Obviously at times like this I had to prompt the person with another question, and indeed in some cases the narrative was constructed, kernel by kernel, in the interaction, with the person clearly unwilling to offer either private speculations or fantasies.

> INFORMANT: Oh, I just came because I wanted to.
> E.W.: How long ago was that?
> INFORMANT: About ten years ago.
> E.W.: Where did you live at that time?
> INFORMANT: I lived in Burbank, California.
> E.W.: And you just decided to come.
> INFORMANT: Well, it's a long story. You see I was stationed here during the war. I liked it then. I liked the pace.

The story then continues to resemble in one way or another the narratives I had collected previously. I had introduced the themes that others had supplied and had essentially led the informant to a recognizable narrative structure. Obviously "and you just decided to come" was a discourse challenge, creating on the one hand a more discernible set of boundaries for the narrative, and on the other making it almost impossible to ignore the invitation and be seen as both an incompetent manager of one's own life (after all no one moves merely on a whim) as well as an incompetent conversationalist.

The first notable feature of the narrative is *referential*, orienting the listener to what is of obvious importance in migration. The feature is so obvious and frequent that it fades by its inevitability, but "its omission may be disturbing" (Colby and Peacock 1973:618). Time and place are inevitable. It is obvious that one of the organizing themes for experience has to do with place and what it is to live in one and to conceive of another. A contrast of imagery and meaningful juxtaposition embellish the explanation.

> I was living in Oregon. Eugene. I had been there for a few years. I was born in Texas, and I've lived in Minnesota and New York. I've tried them all, winters and summers. I'd been to the Caribbean and

to Hawaii on vacation. Then this past spring when I decided that I
had had enough of that particular job, I came here.

By contrasting different locations, by evaluating them ("I've tried
them all, winters and summers"), the reasonableness of the move
becomes apparent.

The time variable, the time of arrival on Hawaiian shores,
is an equally common referential and sense-making practice. The
time of discovery was of paramount importance for the declaration
of possession in earlier centuries, so it has added meanings in the
Hawaii of the 1980s. The obvious time differential in living in Hawaii
for two years or living there for twenty-two years acts as a classifier,
categorizer, and awards and denies status. A lengthy residence becomes assimilated in the minds of most Hawaiians with rights and
claims to that most treasured entity for the mainland *haole*, Hawaiian experience, and by implication, for being Hawaiian. To have
come before World War II carries with it all the implications of
discovering unknown, obscure places. It suggests acculturation, acceptance by local inhabitants, and innumerable other "rights," and
permits a proprietary and even condescending stance toward the
less fortunate recent arrival. It was common to have someone respond with "I've *only* been here three years," speaking to an assumed tacit understanding, presumably shared by all whites and
hence also by me, that the short stay implied certain kinds of ignorance, definite marginality, and, perhaps worse, merely prolonged
tourism. It also assumed that the person's intent needed to be ex-
plicated publicly, and made honorable. "But I plan to stay." The
notion of ownership and the inevitable resentment of the "recent
hordes of migration" is frequently apparent:

> I came twelve years ago. And if I'd had the gumption to make a
> decision I would have come much before that. Now look at this
> place, all those mainland people moving here in great hordes, using
> up resources, polluting. People from the east as well. But there they
> are, here from the mainland to settle, still running around like stupid
> tourists, trying to get a tan.

In some cases, of course, whatever the amount of time in the Islands,
it is far too long for them and the person readily claims marginality:

> I've been trying for almost all of the two years here to get transferred
> back to the mainland. I just don't like it here.

There is also an implicit time structure in the narrative, evoking the before-and-after theme understood in each migration. This is usually handled by presenting a description of the earlier time which culminated in decisions. The time succeeding is self-evident, sometimes introduced by an evaluation of the person's life in Hawaii, sometimes left implicit and presumably obvious, sometimes summarily dismissed with "and so I came here," or "here I am." This latter declaration has been termed the *coda*, a functional device for reasserting the present verbally at the end of the narrative (Labov and Waletzky 1967:39). The present in itself is, of course, the assumed answer to the objectionable past.

The narratives have a definite *sequencing*, using events to create ambience and inevitability. The events do not always have a linear structure, although this would be considered in some formal sense "correct," and some people make efforts to rearrange a previous telling in order to bring this about.

> I decided about my need to get away, to live somewhere else before the end of my schooling . . . or was it after my parents moved to Florida? Anyway, I decided.

Typically the migration narrative takes one of two kinds of organizing routes. One is the strict adherence to linear time sequencing when the narrator takes pains to relate events leading to the decision in some kind of chronological order:

> I had a bad car accident in 1947, and after that I came to the Islands. I wanted to get away from Seattle. I got married, but that didn't work out, so I returned to the mainland, to California. I fooled around there at one job or another and then I decided to set up business on my own. I came back here.

The other route uses sequencing as an elaboration of the story or as a description making other events more meaningful. Thus the story weaves back and forth between various events, introducing a nonlinear narrative similar to those found in Dorothy Lee's account of the Trobrianders (1959).

> I lived a short time in Florida. And even before that I had been to Hawaii. I was born in Southern California. When we finished college . . . we were already married by then . . . and Jean's father had been here during the war . . . we decided to find jobs here. We

came here for our honeymoon, and it seemed a good time to try living here.

Part of every narrative involves *paradox* and *discovery*. The noting of events, the sequencing of them, inevitably leads to what has been called an intensifier or "negotiating the point of the story" (Polanyi 1979:207). The story leads up by intensifying and complicating the prelude of events and inferences until the ultimate paradox is posed. It has a "final straw" quality, when the tension of the discourse has reached its intended peak. At this point what has been called both "evaluation" and "resolution" occur (Labov and Waletzky 1967:37–39). The migrant indicates that past events indeed have converged into a picture of discontent and culminates with "I just couldn't put up with it any more," or "that decided me." At this point the "discovery," already expected by implication, is brought forward, an insight is formally recognized in the telling, and the move to Hawaii is declared in the narrative.

> I came home one day and found my home robbed. I was not well at the time—I've had sieges of illness. I had had a cancer operation and, shortly after that, I came home one day and found my house robbed, our stereo gone, all my jewelry gone, my money, and my personal effects. They had entered my house by a back door. They had slashed a screen and just opened the door. Had I been upstairs and lying down, I could have been a statistic.

This narrative builds up to the posing of the dilemma, the notion that there comes a turning point, and that surely the evaluation to come is self-evident in terms of a common culture of motives and actions. Then the "discovery," the notion of the alternative or decision, is presented as an answer to the dilemma.

Clearly not all narratives, regardless of their location and intent, move to the same grammatical tune. They do not appear to be similar even though in the same culture, but rather suggest diversities along contextual and other lines. Children's stories apparently are structurally different in sequencing, referencing, highlighting "the point," and in the resolution (Pitcher and Prelinger 1963; Sacks 1972). Women in rap groups, on the other hand, project a different interactional style of narration, the use of "kernel" stories as initiatory strategies and reliance on the final narrative being produced by the group. This presumably is brought about by women's sense of powerlessness and their resolve to work together. They also employ a sequencing order which produces the punch line of a joke prior to the actual build-up (Kalčik 1975).

The narratives of other cultures clearly differ markedly from those of Western cultures. Barth notes that as the Baktaman, for example, have no adequate objectification of time, the present seems to dominate over a kaleidoscopic past and an unspecifiable future. Their referencing of narratives, therefore, is according to place, leaving time as a puzzle for the anthropologist (Barth 1975:135). Malinowski's data on the Trobrianders, as analyzed by Lee, reveals a narrative sequencing that is unintelligible to Western cultures (1959:105). The Kpelle of Liberia, when contrasted with American children on memory tests, do not recall as well, and hence present sparser narratives. Colby and Cole (1970:80) reason that certain processes in American society, with which the children are familiar, are the same as those in memory recall, and these processes are neither important, nor frequently used, by the Kpelle. A further example is one by Evans-Pritchard, who notes that for the Zande the idiom of expression in conversation is different from that of narration or description, thereby confusing the anthropologist. Further, adding to the confusion, the Zande have learned different codes from various missionaries and other officials (1963). Thus, from time to time anthropologists focus on how stories are transmitted and the grammar necessary, thereby reflecting on an important matter, namely how experience is coded for presentation.

Biography as Folk Explanation

Among the metaphoric possibilities through which my informants led me to appreciate their migration accounts as somehow valid was that of placing them in a mode commonly recognized by Western discourse. The mode is that of biography or, perhaps more appropriately, autobiography, presenting thoughts and actions in a particular order. This is not to imply that all experiences are not in some essential and ultimate sense biographical. Yet biography has about it an undeniable compulsion. It seems destined to etch out of undifferentiated encounters through time those features which contribute to a publicly presentable and correct version. Biography in one sense is a constructed micro-culture depicting how one is willing to be seen by the world, a kind of public monument to the self. It meets cultural assumptions about how a life should appear (Schwalm 1980; Gilmore 1978; Hart 1956).[4]

The contours and textures of a biography are a self-portrait guided by fashion and style, ideologically acceptable, and tempered only by the existence of relatively unbounded experience. Despite such fluidity and amorphous features, we tend to view biography as somehow immutably fixed, always available, and merely regulated by the individual's preferences for revealing it. Yet like any narrative it is interactionally performed, as much a product of the assembled others and their expectations, as of biographical fact. Sometimes, no doubt, biography presents features etched from the most elusive materials to satisfy present needs (Frank 1979:82). One's biography becomes a resource to be molded into creative explanation, to permit theorizing, or, as in the case at hand, to become part of migration narratives. It makes it possible for the migrant to produce sense out of the potentially unfamiliar, namely the act of migrating, by explaining it through a familiar content, that of biography.

The Whole Explains the Part

There appears to be an assumption that life history explains the present. It is as if migration could be meaningful only in terms of biography, as if motivation could be comprehended only through an individualized history. If a sum total of experience is suggested, perhaps merely by the act of evoking biography, the present part of the biography, the move to Hawaii, would be suffused with meaning and rendered credible. Often a life history was constructed for me by the suggestion of only salient parts of it, for example, where one was born, where schooled, whether married, and so on. Inherent in this, the telling tacitly suggests, is the major clue which should explain all. Biography is a vehicle which infers some features enduring through time, sometimes personality, sometimes characteristic responses to events. These features were the kernels which were made to do the work of explanation. As the following narrative reveals, some assemblages of biography are reminiscent of the salient features necessary for filling in application forms or providing thumbnail sketches. They have a classic linearity which builds up into the inevitabilities of explanation.

> I was born in Pittsburgh. My father was a senior partner in a law firm and insisted that I go to a good college; hence, I found myself in Boston, in Cambridge more exactly, enduring the dreary winters, studying a subject that I did not like, wishing I could be elsewhere. Anyway, I finally finished college and didn't have a job. So, my uncle invited me to Toronto to help him run that section of the business. By this time, I'd married and we were expecting a child. Once again, here I was in those terrible winters: but, even worse, I began to feel the pressure of crowding, the dreariness of urban life—it was ugly. Anyway, I kept at it . . . The kids were finally away . . . and, suddenly, I thought—"What for?"

From a linear beginning the narrative moves to reorder time to permit appropriate sequencing. The time associated with unpleasant periods in life—such as studying a subject he did not like, working at an unsatisfactory job, living in crowded conditions—is juxtaposed with the decision to come to Hawaii. But underlying it all was the notion—that the whole of biography must somehow explain a happenstance in it.

Explanation by Contrast and Comparison

Clearly in their recollections at the time of deciding to migrate, each person was the possessor of a vague conception of the Islands. While not a clearly articulated and graphic description, it appeared implicitly in their depiction of the mainland. Implication by contrast is a mode deeply embedded in Western consciousness, a mode that presumably made its initial appearance in Greek thought (Lloyd 1966). From the imagery constructed about the mainland, vividly and frustratedly chronicled, an unarticulated fantasy world of Hawaii appears.

> Every night, coming tired from work, I'd get in the car and, with literally thousands upon thousands of faceless other cars, in an impenetrable cloud of carbon monoxide that covered the sky, we'd head onto the New Jersey Turnpike. For an hour, I'd crawl past those rows of houses, each looking the same, under those dreadful murky skies. Jesus Christ, it was bleak—dreary—depressing! And, I thought to myself 'Man, you're just one of them. Surely, life means a little more than that.' So, as soon as the job thing happened and I was free, we packed up and came.

The implication is clear, the justification for migration explicit. What the East Coast and the turnpike did not offer, Hawaii did. Conversely, whatever was said about Hawaii was, by heavy implication, a presentation of the deprivations on the mainland.

> There is magic in the word, Hawaii—blue Hawaii. It just does something to you.

> I've always wanted to live in a warm climate—a place where I could get a lot of skin diving, sun, and beach.

> I guess I thought of hula girls, long black hair, grass shacks, and tropical nights.

> It was just all that wonderful romantic music, the idea of soft nights, guitars, water lapping, and nothing to worry about.

> Well, for one thing, I just wanted to be a connoisseur of good waves.

> My father used to tell me about all those marvelous things, about the lush greenery and all the water where you could go swimming. The Hawaiian Village was called "Don the Beachcomber's," and it was where he stayed. It was six thatched huts, and he said that flower petals were just all over, and there were no doors—just hanging beads—and the huts were around a pool—and I pictured that all my life.

The very core of romantic philosophy is woven into these descriptions, a familiar Western view of the South Seas. The Islands suggest a seductive nostalgia and hold out a promise for a life of simplicity, immediacy, licence, sensuality, warmth, mysticism, and unabashed sentiment. The mainland, in inevitable contrast, becomes lacking in magic and romance, anxiety-ridden and morally constipated.

The imagery presented is, on the whole, impressionistic, without detail, and in the main given to easily recognizable stereotypes. While the vision legitimizes their illusions and provides an almost osmotic sense of salvation from prevailing ills, few can claim any practical knowledge. They were notably silent on social and economic conditions, ethnic relations, political issues, possibilities for housing, employment, and so on. Thus an ambience of compensation for past sufferings and a surge of remedial promises hang over the new environment. It is an almost mystical notion, that the new place will permit and encourage one to be the person one would like to be, and to live the life fantasy holds out.

By chronicling the evils of technology and industrialized society, the migrant implies that Hawaii is free of them. By enumerating the burdens of encroaching ecological misfortunes, it is implied that Hawaii offers a more desirable relation to the natural environment. By stressing the banality and monotony of urban existence, it is suggested that Hawaii has avoided these problems. By complaining about the ever-present pressures of a growing population and the narrowing of life space, the impression is created that Hawaii has a utopian distribution of people to space. By railing against the forces of violence, impersonality, and moral laxity on the mainland, Hawaii emerges with a promise of moral inturpitude and personal responsibility. By bemoaning the swiftness and meaninglessness of temporal existence on the mainland, it is suggested that the Islands permit a savoring of time and a leisurely pacing of events.

The Language of Self;
or, The Self That Psychiatry Built

Even though my attention was captured early by the use of biography in the accounts, something else soon became obvious. There were two seemingly different ways not only of doing the biographical interpretations but also in the coding of experience. Some narratives seemed suffused with a special quality, where the very reflection which makes it possible to address experience became itself talked about as part of the story. It was as if my informants were attempting to perform the very process of reflection itself and to make clear how their knowledge became possible. At first I tended to interpret this as "just that some people are more open" or even "felt more comfortable with me." Later another interpretation struck me, as obvious matters sometimes embarrassingly tend to do, much later than I would have wished. The difference, it seemed, lay in erasing the hard edges of experience as brute fact, and suggesting that meanings were themselves attributed through "explorations of the self." There was a whole biography running in competition with the "factual" one tailored by our accepted ideas of actualities. This second biography seemed to eschew the straightforward recounting of a positivistic type of experience, and instead became a parody of surface facts, a kind of folk phenemonology. The two portions of narrative following deal with a substantially familiar biographical content, in that such details as career, place to live, drugs, and an unhappy love affair are raised. Yet the biographical events are very differently treated in each. One provides objective fact after objective fact, leaving it to our shared understanding to make whatever sense could be made of it. The other essentially provides an account of consciousness and motivation, mediation and reflection.

> That involves a great deal of story. I was born and raised in the San Francisco area. I didn't want to stay there; there was just too much stagnation. All my friends were either getting married, or they were just staying in little old Mill Valley and not seeing anything. I didn't have a job, so I decided I might as well go to school and get away from all this. My boy friend, at the time, was a lot into drugs and stuff, and I didn't want any part of this, and he lied to me—so I didn't want any part of it. So I decided to go to school on Maui.

The other, raising the same issues, said:

> I have a set of answers for how I started—synonymous with my career having sort of fallen apart, I thought then, temporarily—and no new job prospect on the horizon, the ending of my lease on the apartment—there happened a very emotionally packed breakup be-

tween myself and the girl I was living with. It really made me sit down and think about myself, about my life, what it all meant to me. I was also getting into enough dope that I was doing a great deal of questioning that I had never done before. In other words, I was taking time to question. But, nevertheless, all of these runs of chaos were happening at one time, which was a lot for me to handle, being the kind of person I was—so, I thought "Everything is happening immediately around me"—so I thought "This is the perfect time to go, the perfect time to get away"—thinking all the time "I would go temporarily for perhaps a month or two and then think it over again"—or, thinking, "If I like it I might stay permanently." I just couldn't stand the anxiety any longer.

This portrayal of meaning in terms of the language of self is even applied to explain the migration of others, filling in a possible reflection where it seemed motivationally appropriate. In the following such motives and self-examinations are attributed to a person who at the same time is depicted as someone unable to reflect himself:

For my father, it's the looseness and openness of the place, because he's a very tight person; he's a very miserly person at all levels, I think—kind of small, but he doesn't want to be, and the expression of big warmth [like Hawaiians]—it was something that appealed to him, that he didn't quite know how to do himself—where this could be a reality. He came from a strict, structured family and, though he insists on this strictness for himself and everyone else, he doesn't really like it.

The same differences in narrative style and biographical explanation are also apparent in other encounters with the informants. In describing the appeal of island imagery, the same differences emerged. One person produced linear facts and a commonly held imagery, the other introduced an individualized assemblage of reflections.

From the time I can recall, as a child, I've always wanted to come to Hawaii. In the 1930s, I can recall, I could hear Hawaiian music on the radio at two or three o'clock in the morning. I would stay up. I had heard about the beauty of the place, the kindness of the people, and the weather—this meant a lot in Nebraska.

Another Midwestern immigrant:

> It was a great opportunity to come to the Paradise of the Pacific of
> which I had thought from time to time . . . began to think that it
> was fantastic and "Wow, I'm really the envy of the block." I could
> place myself in a setting of waterfalls and native girls swimming in
> the lagoons—you know. And, I figured to myself, "This is out of
> sight" and "How could I go wrong?" There might have been an
> inclination in thinking about these Polynesian-type of chicks. We saw
> the *Hawaiians* and *Hawaii* . . . couldn't help but visualize myself as
> Charlton Heston—all those chicks, all this money, all this white man
> power, tropic shores—I could imagine all this for myself.[5]

In trying to understand what contributed to the difference in cognitive style I ran a few positivistic variables through the
data. These variables of age, sex, occupation, education, regional
culture, and so forth did not produce any recognizable analysis. On
reexamining the matter in the whole context of individual biogra-
phies, however, something usable did emerge. The reflective persons and those who used self as explanation had participated, in
one way or another, in encounter groups, sensitivity training, T-
groups, or had undergone some form of psychotherapy. They had
been socialized not only into a special way of interpreting the world,
but also to the use of self as an appropriate way of doing interpretations. Their commonsense world had been made over. I began
to think of it as the "self that psychiatry built."

Those who had not learned the language of self presented narratives with rationality, coherence, and consistency. They
portrayed events as devoid of human perplexity and contemplation.
Their thoughts seemed informed by the proposition that logical
positivism is not only a formal aspect of Western thought, but reverberates through the realm of common sense as well.

Those speaking in the language of the self were more
inclined to structure their knowledge, admitting ambivalence, ambiguity, anxiety, irrationality, indecision, stupidity, and other "very
human" traits as if their permissibility had suddenly been acknowledged. They seemed to adhere to the notion that their world was
structured with such thoughts and such thoughts were appropriate
to the discourse. Thus they readily interjected information about

adultery, homosexuality, drugs, financial manipulations, animosities, and prejudices.

An ideology of telling things "the way they really were" seemed to pervade their narratives. They reflected an awareness of the cultural difference by referring to others as "straight," "haven't got it together," "up-tight," or "square." The practical reasoning apparent in their discourse, compared to those not speaking the language of the self, was dependent on existential notions where events and actions were constructed in their heads instead of deterministically "out there." As adherents to this interpretive mode they were always in a process of becoming.

> I see my life as always changing. I feel as if I really haven't decided to stay yet. There is so much about the mainland that I want to keep as part of my life. I don't know yet how I can do it. I am always conscious of the fact that rose-covered cottages and the glories of autumn are part of my heritage and important to me; and, in time I'll go back and look at them again—but, also I see myself as a beach and lush foliage type. I just don't know—I'm here, but I might just as well go. I often discuss these things with myself, but I don't feel pressed to make a decision.

Carl Becker suggests that we are each our own historian. If so, then the two types of narrative, namely those that assert that the facts of their story exist out there in the world and can be rationally ordered, and those that view facts as somehow continually in creation and negotiation, can be viewed as Becker views two kinds of history. For him there are "the actual series of events that once occurred, and the ideal series that we affirm and hold in memory. The first is absolute and unchanged—it was what it was whatever we do or say about it; the second is relative, always changing in response to the increase or refinement of knowledge" (1932:222; Schwartz 1977).

Life Crisis as Justification

There are a number of ways of depicting biography. It can be organized according to some form of practical reasoning where events are selected so that the point being made becomes obvious, where existential dilemmas of life are posed in such a manner that they have meaning for all those whose interpretations of "what makes a life" are constructed by the same culture. The "life crisis" is such a notion. Using this as a justification for making a major move in one's life can only meet with approbation. In reviewing the work on migration, Bogue (1959:500) lists twenty-five "stimuli," among them are graduation, marriage, lack of marriage, offer of good employment, news of bonanzas, prolonged low income, sale of business, development of profession not marketable locally, retirement, onset of poor health, conviction for crime, oppression, invasion by others of different occupations, income or ethnicity, personal bonanza, acute personal maladjustment, and the desire to escape the responsibilities of adulthood.[6] Each suggests a life crisis.

Parenthetically I should note that the term "life crisis" essentially arose out of the data, being used by a few of the informants to describe their own state. In one rather intriguing case, no information was given which could be construed as belonging to the "life crisis" category. After knowing the person for some time, I mentioned that many mainland *haole* had mentioned a "life crisis" experience, and asked him what he thought of this as a possibility. "Hm. . . interesting," he replied. After reflecting for some moments, he added: "I guess what I did when I went in to tell the bosses that I was thinking of moving to Hawaii was to create my own crisis. Probably, I even did it for that reason." Not only is a life crisis immediately understandable, but it permits a deterministic view of the individual's life being steered by factors seemingly outside his own control. A comfortable mode of doing justification narratives is to depict the "cause" as imposed from the outside. Then the "decision," on the other hand, occurs by the will and impetus of the person. Such explanations adhere closely to a cultural code of reasoning.

Each crisis can be seen as representing a threat to everyday existence. It indicates license to deviate from established patterns, to forego some social responsibilities, to withdraw, to "escape," change, and ultimately to construct an alternate possibility. It suggests a culturally viable turning point, an opportunity to consciously restructure and redirect experience (Silverman 1967).

The following examples reflect the use of the life crisis account:

> The first time I came to the Islands was 1937. I had had a divorce and had wanted to get away from California and came here and worked for two years. Then, I had an unhappy love affair and returned to California and stayed there for eighteen years. Then, my mother passed away in 1955, and I sold the house and came here.

> Well, I had a bad experience in Florida with a hurricane. Basically, that's the reason. It wiped me out of business. I had a sign shop and it just wiped me right out.

> My father had just retired from the Army. He was quite depressed about that. As far as he could see, he wanted to get away as far as possible.

> The strongest and most important reason was because I was involved with a fellow whose faith was not at all approved of by my parents. They wanted to get me away from him and out of the Berkeley situation.

> I was mugged on the street one day. Got so that I was afraid to go out anymore.

In the cultural vocabulary of motives it was assumed that a life crisis was sufficient as a turning point. No other motives needed to be offered, it had an inalienable quality of moral correctness recognized by both informant and anthropologist. It had all the moral authority of folk theorizing (Ellul 1968).

The Dynamics of Cultural Reasoning

Every social scientist seems to suffer from an inherent impulse to generalize across cases, or to offer abstract truths that might speak of all possibilities. My impulse is to try and forgo these dictates and to offer variability. Ursula Le Guin suggests that: "The story is not all mine, nor told by me alone. Indeed I am not sure whose story it is; you can judge better. But it is all one, and if at moments the facts seem to alter with an altered voice, why then you can choose the fact you like best; yet none of them are false, and it is all one story" (1969:1–2). Perhaps the one story that is told by all is a story about the role of ideology. The narratives are constructed according to ideologies about the structure of discourse; the views expressed in them resonate with ideological issues shared in Occidental cultures. By inferring reasons for their migration, they make visible the ideology they hold. They are not concerned with the "whole truth," whatever that may look like, nor do they wish to arrive at "ultimate" causes. They merely wish to make sense, to produce an account that will be acknowledged.

Thus, those who come in the '60s, '70s, and '80s cite ideologies about the threat of the industrial climate, the plight of urban centers on the mainland with their overcrowding, slums, and crime. Foremost on all lips is the overriding problem of our ecology. If they are young they speak of the military-industrial complex, of the horrors of American domestic or foreign policy, or of the ugliness of mainland ambitions and inhumanity. They are prepared to find in Hawaii a palatable alternative. These people have all the trappings of expatriates or ideological nomads. They speak of the mainland United States in all the terms that sent previous generations of like-minded to Paris, or Spain, or Mexico.

Vast numbers still come to actualize an old virtue still much admired in the Western world. They come to seek their fortune. They come to be entrepreneurs, to take a higher position in some corporation. Some come to be released from various kinds of socially depressive situations, to seek a new life and to create a new self.

For those who came in the years before World War II, the justification evoked does not concern ideologies about technology or ecological issues, but rather nostalgia, enterprise, or hope for a better life. They came to escape mundane existence and to be saved from an unsatisfactory economic future.

They came by sea in those days, on a journey to a foreign land. One man sailed his own boat to the South Seas in "search of adventure," to make a discovery, and finally settled in Hawaii. Another, originating in New York of the 1920s, had all the progressive ideology so much a part of Western consciousness, pushing ever westward to a frontier which offered both paradise and opportunity. He was separated from it by yet another geographical barrier:

> Well, I think you'd classify this under romance, perhaps, or something. Something in Hawaiian music completely entranced me, and I knew that this was my destiny. At fourteen, I didn't put it in those words, but I had that feeling, and it began right there. My intent always was to come to, or go to, Hawaii. And it took me twenty-three years to get to go . . . I didn't have at that time all the lovely words you learn later on—karma and fate and . . . I now charge it up to this department—I just knew that, sooner or later, I would end up in Hawaii . . . I sprung out of New York at the flick of the age of twenty-one. This was the thing that—bingo—gave me freedom . . . I moved to Los Angeles . . . I lost my job and I was forced to go into business by myself, and I built that up to a real good thing. But, running a one-man business was a horribly depleting sort of thing for, when you're working for someone else, you work eight hours a day; but, when you own your own business, you work twenty-eight hours a day, sevens days a week. And this was getting me down, and the marriage was coming to an end, and so I just said, "To hell with it," and I just got up and walked out, and I left my home, automobiles, clothes, everything—and just said "Goodbye!" I kept enough money to buy a steamship ticket, and I think when I hit here, I had $50. And I started my life all over again, from the ground up . . . And looking back, I can see my life more plainly; I see it more concisely and more clearly. I had done all I could do in New York for that kind of life I was leading—a new country with all the opportunity of excitement, a new place, learning, and so on . . . I am now casting eyes towards the New Hebrides, but I'm too old.

In some sense the Hawaiian Islands still seem to hold out the same promise as they did in the nineteenth century. The hidden licentiousness, the license, and the puritanical zeal are still there in the stories told by Caucasians. They still come to seek their fortunes in commerce and trade. They are still drawn by the *terrae incognitae* and its possibilities. They are still expatriates and modern beachcombers, derelicts and drop-outs, constituting a living protest against a Western way of life. They do it in a place reasonably close to the amenities they have learned to enjoy and the language they know. Finally, there are still those, in awesome numbers, who are seeking a better life in the promised isles. The morality and motivations they espouse are public ones, elucidated in contexts where their reception is guaranteed. The values are culturally justified and well understood in the situation in which they emerge—two people of the same culture speaking with each other about the past.

"THE MELTING POT"
KAWAIAHAO SEMINARY
HONOLULU, T. H.

1—Hawaiian.	17—Hawaiian-Indian-American.
2—Ehu Hawaiian.	18—Hawaiian-Japanese-Portuguese.
3—Japanese.	19—Hawaiian-Portuguese-American.
4—Chinese.	20—Hawaiian-Spanish-American.
5—Korean.	21—Hawaiian-German-Irish.
6—Russian.	22—Hawaiian-Chinese-German.
7—Filipino.	23—Hawaiian-Chinese-American.
8—Portuguese.	24—Hawaiian-Portuguese-Irish.
9—Polish Russian.	25—Hawaiian-Japanese-Indian.
10—Hawaiian-German.	26—Hawaiian-Portuguese-Chinese-English.
11—Hawaiian-Chinese.	27—Hawaiian-Chinese-German-Norwegian-Irish.
12—Hawaiian-Russian.	28—South Sea (Nauru)-Norwegian.
13—Hawaiian-American.	29—African-French-Irish.
14—Hawaiian-French.	30—Spanish-Porto Rican.
15—Hawaiian-Portuguese.	31—Guam-Mexican-French.
16—Hawaiian-Filipino-Chinese.	32—Samoan-Tahitian.

Part of the white dream is the much-admired notion of a racial paradise. The young women of the Kawaiahao Seminary are posed in a 1918 photograph to reflect an early version of the "melting pot" which honored ethnic pluralism and promoted ideas of ethnic compatibility. The picture also displays the ethnic categorization commonly used in Hawaii to account for identity. Bishop Museum.

Western fantasies about the Hawaiian isles with their promise of leisure and licence. Right: A post card of the first decade of the twentieth century entitled "Hawaiian Islands Beauty." It reflects, perhaps, how a male culture has structured Hawaiian symbols. Women, inviting, sensuous, and removed from mainland constraints have long been associated with the South Seas. The card shows all the accoutrements of femininity, such as long hair, flowers, a lei, soft rotund flesh, and a welcoming smile. Particularly intersesting is the rather westernized ethnicity of the woman. Hawaiian Historical Society.

Below: The retirement dream. Hawaii, or some other place, becomes the focus of a Western preoccupation with the South Seas. Pat Leong.

Right: A photograph from the 1950s displays the male fantasy directly. The participants pose as if fully cognizant of the parody they are enacting—male and female, brawn and beauty, white strangers and island women. Tai Sing Loo, Bishop Museum.

Above: A post card dated 1951 informs the receiver that "lovely hula girls posed on sparkling beach sands exemplify the Island youth." Hawaiian Historical Society.

Below: An early settler photographed among a bevy of beauties reenacts the classic pose suggested by the post card. Hawaii State Archives.

Right: An early *luau* in the Waihu Valley, Maui. The newcomers have adopted the feast pattern common to the Islands. A colonial type segregation is evident, with the whites seated at the meal, the local people standing in attendance in the background. Hawaii State Archives.

Below: Another century, another ideology, and another *luau*——from colonial supremacy to ethnic harmony. A very congenial feast of the late 1940s or early 1950s. The only protest registered seems to be against the privileges of age. Tai Sing Loo, Bishop Museum.

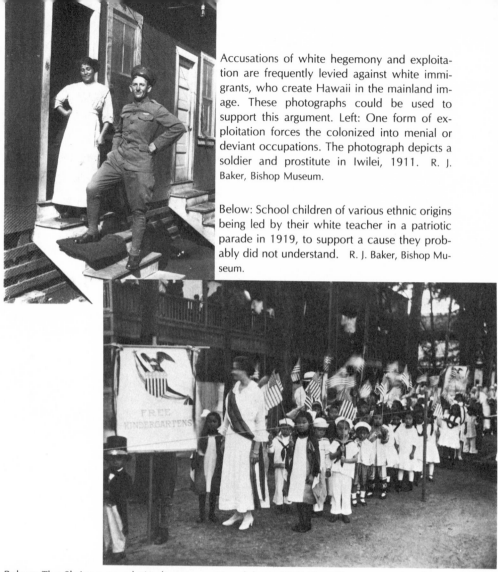

Accusations of white hegemony and exploitation are frequently levied against white immigrants, who create Hawaii in the mainland image. These photographs could be used to support this argument. Left: One form of exploitation forces the colonized into menial or deviant occupations. The photograph depicts a soldier and prostitute in Iwilei, 1911. R. J. Baker, Bishop Museum.

Below: School children of various ethnic origins being led by their white teacher in a patriotic parade in 1919, to support a cause they probably did not understand. R. J. Baker, Bishop Museum.

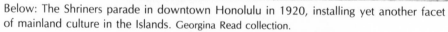

Below: The Shriners parade in downtown Honolulu in 1920, installing yet another facet of mainland culture in the Islands. Georgina Read collection.

Through puritanical zeal many *haoles* made considerable fortunes in sugar, pineapple and cattle. Above: Cattle round-up at Dowsett Ranch, Leleihua, now the site of Schofield Barracks. Hawaii State Archives.

Below: Awaiting orders—a *haole luna* with local people standing at attention during an epidemic of the bubonic plague in January 1900. Some *haoles* did not make large personal fortunes, but were readily placed in supervisory and managerial positions. Hawaii State Archives.

Others became merchants. A cigar store operated by David Lawrence and Co. Ltd. in the Alex Young Hotel Building in Honolulu. Edgeworth collection, Bishop Museum.

Not every white migrant made a fortune or was destined for a life of privilege. Above: A typewriting class at McKinley High School in 1911. Edgeworth collection, Bishop Museum.

Below: Pedi-cab operators on the streets of Waikiki in the 1980s. This work seems to be done mainly by young men from the mainland and they reflect the shifting division of labor among ethnic groups in contemporary Hawaii. Pat Leong.

Part of the promise of the South Seas is a particular life-style. Above: The Ahfong house on Nuuanu, the kind of house desired by those who went to the Islands in the 19th century to seek their fortune. Ahfong was the wealthy husband of Julia, the daughter of Abraham Fayerweather. Hawaii State Archives.

Tree-houses on the beach at the commune of Taylor Camp on the island of Kauai in 1972. These are the dwellings of self-proclaimed expatriates who recreated for themselves a mythic life modeled on the romantic isolation of the Swiss Family Robinson. Author's collection.

The interior of a tree-house at Taylor Camp. This is the traditional anthropological "I was there" photograph. Walter Waik.

Conquering and subduing nature is a theme in the Western consciousness. Below: A group of hikers of the Trail and Mountain Club have mastered the mountain and look into the crater of Haleakala, Maui in 1924. R. J. Baker, Bishop Museum.

Above: Surveying is one way in which landscapes are transformed into the Western idiom. The Hawaiian Government Survey on the island of Hawaii about 1884, led by Professor W. D. Alexander, pictured here in a white hat. Hawaiian Historical Society.

Left: An early post-card proclaiming "Shark Fishing, Hawaii. Most fearless are the Hawaiian fishermen and many are the stories told of their prowess in hunting the man-eating sharks which are in the deep blue waters of the Pacific." This is a clear example of how nature is treated as an adversary. The conqueror stands beside his prey. Hawaiian Historical Society.

CHAPTER FOUR

Nature as Mediated Metaphor

. . . the entire earth is an immense patchwork of miniature terrae
incognitae . . .

Wright (1947:3)

K nowing a place involves more than knowing its
geography. It involves more than certainties
about cartography, more than an appreciation of
the beauties of landscape, more than a nostalgic attachment to a
configuration of natural features. It requires a careful, if unconscious,
ordering of fragmented knowledge, memory, and discontinuous
impressions. In other words the notion of place is a more elusive
matter than the usual sparse understandings about locations would
allow us to believe. It is through the kinds of accommodations that
the mainland migrants must make when they come to Hawaii that
these existential qualities emerge.

Our understanding of place is obscured by the scientific
view that what is of issue is subsumed by the rudiments of geography. That particular view is not cluttered by those qualities of
human experience that are deemed beyond the concern of science—sentiments, fears, the language of the senses, and so on.
Clearly it is the very existential poverty of the scientific image, as

in the case of a road map (Burke 1966:5), that renders it so valuable. Only in this way can attention be focused on a skeletal structure, devoid of imagery and emotions. Such poverty of symbol and detail suggests that in essence every place is like any place, and can be captured by a two-dimensional network of lines.

Each mainland *haole* talks eloquently of the experience of place. Each claims awarenesses which demand attention on arrival and continue to do so even after the Islands assume the status of home. They have come to a new place, unfettered by personal experience and unburdened by remnants of personal history. Yet it is not an unknown place. Rather it is familiar through a potent preconstructed imagery. It taps all the Western symbols about the South Seas. These images and sensations, the knowledge they prompt and the hopes they create, are mapped onto Hawaii. "Places are culturally defined." Susanne Langer (1953:95) reminds us, "location in the strict cartographic sense is merely an incidental quality of place."

Yet initial fantasies have the same existential blindness as road maps. They are constructed out of discontinuous symbols, selected for their visual power. As significant markers they keep the fantasy alive, but as blueprints to actual experience they lack pervasiveness and durability. They are meaningful only in the culture of expectations, but diminish in the face of actual acquaintance. Their significance fades with the newcomer's attempts to cope with ambience, ambiguity, and ambivalence. Far too often the fantasies become discrepancies, some of them irreconcilable. Fantasies depend, after all, on an absence of surprise and challenge.

So Hawaii is seldom a fulfillment of the promise produced in imagination, but rather a potential onto which the promise must be mapped. Perhaps it is this very task of mapping the promise onto the potential, of working at it, that separates the tourist from the serious immigrant. The tourist, in a cocoon of imagery, carefully managed and protected by a multinational corporate industry, is permitted to glide through a place in synthetic safety. It is this protected state that causes Sandford and Law to wonder, tongue in cheek, how "package-trip British tourists see nothing strange in the fact that hundreds and hundreds of miles of the Mediterranean seaboard have been built up in the image of their dreams" (1967:89; quoted in Relph 1976:59).

The mainland migrant, consequently, expends efforts to make of Hawaii a place that echoes the familiarities of the fantasy, something that resounds comfortably with the recognizable meanings of mainland culture. It could be argued that the transformation in the world view of the migrants is the turning of Hawaii into a familiar place, another version of home. The elements that constitute their mainland home are elements that have always resonated with their lives and have given them authenticity and security. In the process of mapping fantasies and familiarities onto Hawaii, the migrants come to recognize new stances. This chapter is an ethnography of these experiences.

Fantasy and Familiarity
as Livable Place

It is a philosophical commonplace to observe that Occidental consciousness characteristically sees the individual as distinct from nature. It views humans in the biblical sense—a separate inspiration of the Creator, His greatest creation. Humans are not a part of the heavens or of the earth. Indeed the sole destiny of the human is to tame and order the wildernesses found in the rest of creation. It follows that the environment is in a sense foreign; nature is potentially an enemy and one's own body is essentially a separate entity. New places, therefore, constitute the threats of the unknown. They are heavy with difference, shock, and inauthenticity. They veil, in the Western consciousness, potential danger. Thus separateness is the basic tenet of the Western world toward any environment, particularly a new one.

That this view is not universal is also well known. Most non-Western cultures tend to view the person as one with, or part of, the natural order. Indigenous Hawaiian culture is no exception. The Hawaiian relationship to nature was one of "subjective identification," one of "being-one-with-natural-phenomena." This becomes activated in the cultural sense of dependence and obligation,

"discrimination of the real, the good, the beautiful and the true . . .
feeling of organic and spiritual identification with the *'aina* (homeland) and *'ohana* (kin)" (Handy and Pukui 1958:28).

A hidden paradox faces the Western person in a new
place. On the one hand there is cherished fantasy potentially challenged by actual discovery. A struggle to maintain the illusions en-
sues. On the other hand there is alienation and the threat of unknown places which, like unknown nature, must be brought to hand
and put to order. Western consciousness demands that such foreign
matters be brought into the realms of established knowledge. This
is, in a sense, the task that faces whites in Hawaii.

How do the *haoles* from the mainland go about ac-
complishing familiarity and order? How do they do this in the face
of retaining some of the mystery and the fantasy that brought them
there in the first place?

Places are complicated puzzles which are "sensed in a
chiaroscuro of setting, ritual, routine, other people, personal experience, care and concern for home, and in the context of other
places" (Relph 1976:29). It is all these features that are the necessary
components of human rootedness. This rootedness is often given
that heavily romantic and emotive label "home." Such a notion is
probably universal. Even those who are considered placeless—migrant workers, sailors, hoboes, gypsies—have definite notions of a
home, a possessed place (Tuan 1977:158).

Knowledge of the Islands proceeds from an initial contact with a space that is meaningless except where it is colored by
the haze of fantasy. Images of "Blue Hawaii" and Diamond Head,
caressing winds and electric guitars prove insufficient to meet the
demands of actual Hawaii. It has been observed, for example, that
the emptiness of the prairies induces anxiety, "the anxiety of meaninglessness." But then, as the same quotation avers, "the human
mind asserts itself, its abiding courage returns and over this clear
Thoreauvian sky, men erect their frail lathings of belief and carpenter
their configurations of meaning and assurance" (James 1970:151).
In other words, an attempt is made to map personal experience
onto the empty space. The result is a frame characterized by isolated
meaningfulness in a sea of meaninglessness.

These patches of meaning, out of context and without wider cultural import, are constructed from the necessities of daily living and form the initial cognitive map. A newly arrived man, describing his loneliness and isolation in the early weeks, noted that his movements were essentially controlled by five locations. The five emergent familiarities he identified were: the house he and his family rented, the place of his work, the local supermarket, his childrens' school, and a local beach the family frequented for recreation. These had obvious visibility and provided for him a fragmented structure made sensible by experience. Another described overcoming his initial disorientation: "It took me just ages to learn how to get from one place to the other. All the one-way streets. Where best to park. The quickest routes and the most traffic-free times." Such familiarizing is common to each newcomer. The environment is given a personal stamp.

The quote from Wright highlighting this chapter suggests that the entire world is made up of miniature *terrae incognitae*. It captures the nature of the migrant's encounter. For the *haole* the Islands present themselves as full of meaningless spaces that enclose a few concentrated symbols familiar in fantasy. The Hawaii of the imagination, the Hawaii of the dreamer is quickly asserted and its cherished features recognized and protected. Indeed, it is reinforced continually, even long after the feeling of home has been established, in observations such as "I still look out from my apartment *lanai* sometimes, sense the wonder of it, and feel that I'm in a different world." Such consciousness recalls the South Sea idyll daily, and informs the *haole,* in partly conscious ways, of the reasoning that brought him or her to the Islands. The notion of having reached a distant and treasured place persists.

Concomitant with the recognition of a paradisiac ideal goes the unspoken imperative that landscapes are to be admired and that nature is to remain undefiled and innocent. This is in accord with other Western views which tend to see human involvement as somehow polluting. Despite modern tendencies to emphasize and even centralize the relationship of humans to nature (Heisenberg 1958), the very idea of paradise and utopia, indeed of landscape itself as something to be gazed upon, seems to require that the observer have a remote, uninvolved status. Ideals are, by definition, to be striven for rather than realized. They are a promise unsullied by human presence and human discontent.[1]

The mythic promise that brought Europeans to Hawaii is frequently recreated. By reminiscing the migrant restructures and reinforces a commitment to the dream.

> When I got off the plane, I felt almost as if I was entering water, the air was so heavy and so warm. Even though you could not smell flowers, it was as if the air were a flower. Such a heavy sort of feeling—the unbelievable warmth. It was like stepping off into the heart of a flower.

One informant recalled his arrival in the thirties:

> As we came around the corner, on the ship, you could smell the island in those days—out at sea—frangipani—the flowers. It was overpowering early in the morning. And, I felt at home, right then.

Others rail at the destruction of paradise, the destruction of their dream. They blame either the more recently arrived mainland *haole* or practitioners of life-styles which they view as doing violence to the landscape

> When I first came here two years ago, that wood was—was so beautiful. But, now, you can't stand it. There's old abandoned cars all over. There's tents pitched everywhere you look, and piles of trash. Nobody cares to even take the trash away. And, besides this, they don't even dig latrines, so you can smell—it's really an awful smell through there. And, I'm just glad that those people aren't allowed to come and live on our beach because it would really be a mess. And, the state hasn't done anything to make them leave.

The phrase "the rape of Hawaii," first voiced by the media in criticism of exploitation and crowding, has entered the vernacular. It implies the rape of the Hawaii of fantasy, the destruction of what I have elsewhere called "the ecology of hope."

> . . . really dirty people have gone to Maui. They've lived on the most beautiful beaches; they've lived off the people. Like—five years ago, people would say, "Sure. go and live off my fruit tree." Then, all the fruit trees were raided.

The lament for a lost paradise is as common a theme in the 1980s as it was in the 1960s and 1970s. The rape is not merely of the land, but also of people's sensitivities:

> These people were living in loin cloths. That's fine, really nice, if everyone could adjust to this; but, it offends people, especially on Maui. And they've lived there all their lives. And, it bothers people because they really want the land to be virgin—and it's not going to be for very much longer.

A major feature of *haole* creation of place, therefore, is the protection of the cherished paradise, the *raison d'être* for their presence. This protection of the natural, this concern with ensuring an untampered state, is a dominant theme in the history of Western cultures and is aptly reflected in the history of white migration to Hawaii. This protection has taken many forms, some of them contradictory. The early missionaries attempted to guard the Hawaiians themselves from licentiousness and sin by leading them through preordained paths of righteousness. The counterculture invasion of the 1960s and 1970s declared their esteem for the integrity of the natural and were vigorous in its espousal. Through it all the entrepreneurs and the tourist industry recognize that their most valued capital lies in conserving natural beauties. That both entrepreneurs and tourists destroy under the guise of preservation is an irony of ideologies.

Nature the Adversary: Humanizing and Challenging

Besides the guardian relationship to nature sketched above, there also occurs in Western consciousness a darker vision: nature as adversary.[2] Like its obverse, this vision seems to be characterized by the separation of the human from the natural order: Nature is, once again, bestowed with "otherness." In the previous case otherness aroused in the romantic and liberal conscience every protective sentiment ever directed toward those unable to care for themselves. In the latter case the otherness is threatening and the demand is for the mastery of an adversary.

The theme of nature as threat takes several forms in the mind and experience of the migrants. Some they bring with them, but many develop out of the very tourist poster features that constitute Hawaii as the South Seas paradise. The water environment, so important in the life of Hawaiians, for example, constitutes not only a beauty fitted to the South Seas vision, but also a potential hazard. It demands continual alertness on the part of a swimmer, surfer, sailing enthusiast, or snorkeler. It is an uncaring medium. One should not swim too far for fear of sharks. One should stay within reach of others for fear of dangerous undertows or sudden incapacitation. One should be wary of the ocean floor for fear of coral. One should be aware of moray eels and Portuguese men-of-war. The sensitivities thus required for human safety suggest a continual battle, jockeying for a control that is at best contingent.

Tropical vegetation, so picturesque in the detached remoteness of sunset photography, takes on unexpectedly uncomfortable dimensions. Newcomers learn to walk around certain trees "because they shed those sharp little pods that hurt your feet." Palm fronds—there can be no more tropical cliché—become night-time anxieties as one waits for a withered one to fall on the roof. Mangoes in season, hang heavily in the trees or splatter across the roads in "unbelievable abundance," and suddenly come to signal the onset of "mango itch." Finally the very coconut trees that fringe the idyllic tropical beaches take on a more practical dimension. One man with arch self-depreciating amusement described his ritualistic practices of avoidance and concentric circling in the neighborhood of coconut trees:

> I remember Abbott and Costello movies when I was a boy—all those coconuts that used to fall on their heads. It's not really a phobia with me. Others have said so too. I'm always telling the kids to make big circles around coconut trees, and they're always forgetting. I've never seen one actually fall, but . . .

The mainland migrant discovers in these ways that life on the mainland and idyllic postcards do not prepare the newcomer for the eventualities of the chosen domicile.

But nature also provides more disquieting adversaries in the forms of life that bore and scuttle and flutter and hop. The perimenters of the newcomers' resting place have to be modified and new strategies created in a silent negotiation for territory. The islands, the newcomer discovers to his or her discomfort, teem with minute life which, although embarrassingly unimportant in relation to "things that really matter," nevertheless demand ongoing attention.

> I've been raised around plenty of animals and plenty of bugs. *But,* my first experience with cockroaches was the worst in the whole world. My first night on Maui—I'd heard about cockroaches—these were the earthy kind—they came from outside; they're about two inches long, two to three inches long. Okay, I'm walking down the hall. I have my shoes on, luckily. Walking down the hall towards the shower. Here are *six* big two-inch cockroaches—*six of them*!! They weren't going to part their ways for me. They started chasing me! I didn't know what to do. So, I ran like hell for my room and waited for them to take the corner—you know. *Then*, the next day, I jumped in the shower and looked up and there's this huge king spider. This spider had to be, in diameter, at least four inches around. I looked up and thought, "You stay on your side, and I'll stay on mine." *Then*, the mosquitos! I used all kinds of insect repellent. Then, I finally decided if they liked me, they liked me. Another thing that really scared me were the centipedes. Now, I've seen two in the last two days *here*. Right here. My cat caught one and put it on the carpet. You hear all these stories. I had this friend—he loved stepping on them. Once, he had his slippers on. Stepped on one. It curled up and bit his toe, and he was sick for two weeks.

What is obvious is that the informant not only constructed a good story, but she has, as Kepes puts it, created "monsters." He noted that "when unprecedented aspects of nature confront us, our world model inherited from the past becomes strained; the new territory does not belong to it. Disoriented, we become confused and shocked. We may even create monsters, using old outworn images and symbols in an inverted negative way" (Kepes 1956:18).

Another informant carefully instructed me on the subtle sophistication of Hawaiian ecological equilibrium, which he, of course, considered appropriate knowledge for all to have. He was aware of the historical advent of certain flora and fauna to the islands and the rates of growth and decline in various facets of the environment. He vividly depicted the benign coexistence of various insects and other forms of animal life, in particular bufo toads, gecko lizards, termites, and mosquitoes. I was suitably impressed by this display of erudition and the latent claim to Hawaiianess that it implied. As if slightly abashed by his own immodesty in claiming both of these highly desirable statuses, he added that two years' residence and all of his acquired knowledge had not prepared him for a recent occurrence.

> I woke up in the middle of the night and went to the bathroom in the dark a couple of nights ago. I sat sleepily on the toilet. Something touched me—brushing against my anus and testicles. I leapt up and hit my elbow on the towel rack. When I turned on the light, I saw one of those huge black moths—you know, the kind that measures six inches across—in the toilet bowl, violently flapping his wings.

Such territorial competition on occasion involves pronounced conscious maneuvers to ascertain rights and yet retain some semblance of protecting the natural. The following story indicates how an informant driving a car bargains over road space with bufo toads:

> When I come home at night, in the dark, there *they* are in the middle of the road, blinded by the headlights, like so many large black stones. Sometimes, I put out my headlights—our street is so quiet and dark— wait a few moments—then, put them on again to see if they have hopped away. Then, for those still there, I try to weave past them. I hate to see them squashed all over the roads. Besides, they're good ecologically. I've met guys who collect them to take them to their own gardens in parts of the islands where they're less numerous.

Additional sensibilities develop. The housewife learns to look furtively into cupboards to avoid tactile surprise in the form of lizards and cockroaches. "My first week here, I opened the door to take out a cup, and this *thing* flashed past my vision. I shrieked and dropped the cup." The home owner continuously glances over the woodwork, ever alert to the revealing powder of termites. Some talk of visions of armies of termites contentedly chomping away at their very home and shelter. One woman, her mouth twisted in disgust, told me:

> When the termite season starts, they swarm around the lights; and, then, while the light is on, they drop their wings and get ready to mate. And, then, they're on the floor—like fat little ants. Ugh!! They're horrid—just horrid.

A notable way in which Western cultures have dealt with nature has been to frame it in human metaphors. This makes of the threatening force a human, and hence knowable, adversary. The thinking of the eighteenth and nineteenth centuries was of this kind (Barkan 1975; Rees 1975). Ruskin's careful comparison of the mountains of the earth to the muscles on the anatomy of a man is probably the most literate attempt to flood nature with human imagery (1888:267). If actual anatomy or physiology could not, however, be evoked, writers were content to draw comparisons with the products of the human mind and hand. In the organic and mechanical imagery so familiar to the nineteenth century, Nature became synonymous with great architectural and cultural achievements. Thus mountains became for Wordsworth "solemn temples" and pines, "mountain walls," and skies became for the historian Frederick Jackson Turner "giant cathedrals."

Another way that technological cultures humanize space is to make it readily recognizable by placing familiar cultural artifacts on it such as buildings, roads, and other markers. These are the way places are widely known in Europeanized settings. Places are also made into commodities. This is particularly apparent in Hawaii where landscapes and views quickly become appropriated and traded on the tourist market. These acts are direct expressions of power over nature. They imbue locations with the most directly understandable meanings. The relationship of the self to such places is immediately apparent.

Yet it is importantly a part of *haole* experience to be aware of the ancient Hawaiian way of knowing places. In indigenous Hawaiian culture places are identified not by transforming them to Western patterns, but by sacred connections or mythical experience. The presence of deities announces itself in ways completely beyond the reach of newcomers and is deposited in elusive details of land-scape.

The significance of place in non-Western cultures is aptly captured by Rapaport when he compares aborigine and European conceptions. As an example, he notes that "every individual feature of Ayers' Rock is linked to a significant myth and the mythological beings who created it. Every tree, every stain, hole and fissure has meaning. Thus what to a European is an empty land may be full of noticeable differences to the aborigine and hence rich and complex" (1972:3). For the Hawaiians, as for the Australians, the landscape is a document of cultural history. Western documentation, by com-parison, is deposited in technology and architecture. The making over of the history of the Islands is recorded in the increasingly visible developments. It is widely remarked on by those who have been in Hawaii for some time to recognize an escalation in this area. "Lahaina is beginning to look more like Sausalito than Sau-salito." The tower cranes, which frequently dot the skyscape of Waikiki or other parts of Honolulu, are called, pejoratively, the "national bird of Hawaii."

Many mainland *haole* are torn between the conscious-ness into which they were born, which advocates "domestication of the landscape," and the consciousness born of their commitment to honor the authentic and indigenous. It is part of their romantic self-image that they should acknowledge the poignant truths of na-tive Hawaiian beliefs. They are concerned that various places are endowed with mythic history and frequently acknowledge this in awkward and self-conscious ways:

> I've experienced mystic things there. I have great respect for the
> gods of Kauai. They're very vivid and very alive . . . I'd heard about
> this when I came over six years before on a tour. There are a number
> of well-known examples, like hotels built on sacred burial grounds
> and the hotel structures fall down . . . Something that actually hap-
> pened to me . . . it was a rainy day and we went back into the
> Hanakapiai Valley, which is about three miles in off the road, . . .
> the same Kalalau Valley which has an eleven mile trail . . . And now
> just within the last year or so the trail that's been cut into the sacred
> Hanakaiai Falls . . . Six of us walked up to the falls from our camp
> area . . . I had heard, but forgotten, that one should not pick anything

on the trail. It's not only a state law, it's also a sacred law . . . because bad luck can come to you if you do. We picked an example of six or eight different kinds of things—you know, giant ferns, giant leaves, and beautiful trailing flowing things—and all this rain. We got up to the Falls; we were laughing and enjoying ourselves. I think that the goddess of the Falls interpreted this as a sacrilegious act—to have picked all this, and to be spirited and jovial. When we got there, big boulders started falling down the cliff into the pool at the bottom. We'd heard of people being killed there; and there were offerings at the base of the pool—offerings of giant ginger—and ti-leaf offerings. And, the rocks came very close to us, and we moved away, and larger rocks came down. If vibrations or paranoia mean anything at times like this, we all, without saying a word, knew that the Falls wanted us to leave. It's very simple—We could not stay—we were not welcome. We knew that death or harm would come to us if we did not leave. I was very superstitious about it. But—I must say that no one, that day, was stoned. It's easy to have such thoughts when you're hallucinating. We were fresh, alive, vital.

All too frequently the white people of Hawaii stand uncomfortably with one foot in the reasonable, rational world of North America and the other in the mystic truths of an ancient and strange culture. All too often in seeking possible interpretations for untoward happenings, they turn with alacrity to timeless inevitabilities as the following story reveals:

I was driving along this country road on the Big Island in the late evening. I didn't know the area; I'd never been there and was somewhat lost. It was just pouring rain, torrential rain; the windshield wipers just wouldn't wipe it away. I saw this big, heavy Hawaiian woman standing beside the road—soaking wet—just standing there. She made a slight wave, and I stopped. She asked if I were going to some little village—I didn't catch its name—but, she said it was on the road—and, could she have a ride? So, I said, "Fine." The car heaved over on her side when she got in. She didn't talk much, and neither did I, for I was concentrating on driving. I did glance over, however, and she didn't seem to have any pupils—just the whites of her eyes! I thought that maybe she was blind. It was spooky, and I felt prickles on my neck. Anywway, she got out of the car at this little village. I told some local people about it later. They said there was no such road as the one I had been on. They all said that the woman had been Madame Pele.

The Pele in the story is the Hawaiian goddess of the volcano, much feared even in the Hawaii of the late twentieth century. Stories of meeting Pele, usually at the approach of evening when she is believed to be about and visible, are passed around the community. In all stories she is treated with a wary respect.

Nature as adversary is even more pervasive than the foregoing would suggest. It is institutionalized in a familiar undertaking which comes under the rubric of pleasure, an activity which has, in itself, no specific pragmatic end. The activity is usually called sport. It is culturally condoned and advocated pursuit which comes from an epistemology of conflict where the protagonist is pitted against a real or symbolic adversary. Sometimes this is a personal opponent, but as often as not it is nature herself who assumes the adversary position. It is nature which is to be subdued and conquered in swimming, skiing, gliding, hiking, fishing, hunting, mountaineering, canoeing, sailing, and, in the most Hawaiian of all sports, surfing. What are being defied are the laws of *nature*, whether they be the laws of physiology or anatomy, or the laws of physics or geography.

In surfing culture, in particular, the epitome of this relationship to nature is most visibly revealed. Innumerable tales of heroism and super-human skills lace the folklore of the surfing community. Person against gigantic or treacherous wave is the inevitable theme (Finney and Houston 1966). The rules of the surfing game demand that the surfer test human skills and strengths against the capricious variability and naked power of the sea. The language of surfing is full of the complexity and uncertainty of the adversary. There is talk of "seas," presumably in the plural to indicate their ability to transform themselves from the benign to the unpredictable and violent, and moreover, to be deceptively many-faced. Waves can be "easy combers," "fast or slow curlers," "spillers," "plungers," or "bone crushers." Much speculation goes into estimating "swells" and determining "wave size." Presumably the glories of victory are only appreciated in terms of the malevolence and power of the adversary. Months and years of effort are spent in perfecting the intricacies of angling, footwork, body stance, and weight distribution. Care, approaching the precision of scientific inquiry, is involved in collecting data on the mechanical and existential qualities of various surfboards, on the production systems of their makers, and on the properties of the materials of which they are made. An aesthetic appreciation is coupled with the excitement engendered by a particularly graceful or dangerous example of "shooting the Banzai Pipeline."[3] An avid interest in surfing publications reveals the fullness of the commitment: "and I started subscribing to the *Surfer* magazine. It was like the Bible to me. I read it from cover to cover."

Much of the adversary status of person to nature is mediated through the human body, a theme which I shall develop below. In the arena of sport the body is viewed as an instrument to be perfected to its limits in order to meet the various challenges. It assumes a technical status where its hidden possibilities and covert powers are to be enhanced by scientific plan. This is not, however, the only confrontation with the body provoked by the new domicile. While the body occupies a position of tacit obviousness, the new place introduces a discourse with body which is unexpected.

The Body Transformed

In keeping with the notion of separateness of self from nature, the human body becomes the repository of this separateness. The Western world view tends to endow the body with incorporative qualities which enclose the private within from the public without. It gives the body an enveloping character, secluding some enigmatic essence which exists in a tension with the natural world outside. Perhaps as the safe haven for the cogitating being, the body introduces a discontinuity with the rest of nature.

Imposed on this secluding function is the idea of the infinitely perfectible human body, a goal to be striven for and, presumably, eventually attained. There is an inordinate concern with bodily imperfections, which if unchangeable are to be concealed.

Thus ponderous, heavy, unathletic, lacking in agility are undesirable conditions of the body to be rejected and changed. It might be argued that the Hawaii of imagery holds out a perfected vision, although none of my informants alluded to any aspirations for this when they lived on the mainland. Once in the Islands, however, they report an emerging understanding about their bodies, a different imagery, a fulfillment of tacit hopes in this area. This involves a change in their view of self, a sense of well-being and health, a release from previous strictures, and a shifting of the private-public boundary. The body as visible becomes more common, suppressing old concerns about external opinions and evaluations.

> I used to hate getting into my suit. My waist was too fat, my legs too thin, my arms too flabby, breasts—ugh! But now, I don't care. I just get into my two-piecer, and . . .

To the migrants the promise is the same as that felt by their predecessors in the nineteenth century. It is a promise of freedom, presumably a release from the artifices of mainland expectations. The alternative offered is an exchange of what is presumably synthetic for what is seen as "natural."

> I've seen a formal wedding—women in muu-muus, men in aloha shirts. These are people who sort of wouldn't dress that way in Oshkosh. It gets rid of a helluva lot of superficial burdens so that the immediacy of one's self can be reflected with creative energies . . . They really want freedom. People are more able to think of themselves.

As this person indicates there are appropriate benefits for the individual psyche. It implies an emergence of one's self with the release of one's body from various strictures. This, after all, is a common belief engendered by contemporary psychology.

The transformation that seems to occur is one of increasing continuity with the environment. In contrast to initial conceptual breaks between one's body and nature, new bonds are forged and the newcomer begins to act more in consonance with the tropical surroundings. The spoken and unspoken separateness become more amorphous. Informants admit to either loosening their previous commitments to notion of body, or at least being able to identify their resistance. Some report a magical symbiosis with environment, where health and fitness are the rewards. The tendency is to treat this as an unexpected discovery.

> There's no doubt about it. We all feel better here. The kids don't get their colds, and I just feel healthier. Also, there's nothing like being able to get to the beach every day after work. I feel younger, more boyish—a Tarzan.

The body reborn is a common theme. The rebirth seems to gain its vitality from the natural environment and in all events involves the movement of the body closer to the existing milieu. One man, in subtle self-mockery and penetrating critique of ascribed cultural definitions of aging, debilitation, and ugliness, projected himself a half century into the future. He envisioned himself still living in the same place on the North Shore, still in full retention of bodily agility.

> I see myself a hard, lean, older man—a kind of mean old guy—no, not grouchy—but I won't take any guff from any kids. I can see myself walking down the beach, *real* hard and *real* lean, and *real* tanned, and strange dogs kind of cowering from me, and stuff like that. I can see myself walking in that direction out towards the point with a pair of old swim trunks on. There, I've got myself about ninety. I don't picture myself leaving this place at all—just a little meaner, a little grizzlier, a few more lines on my face. I can still see myself, at that age, being actually a better surfer—surfing Sunset even better than now.

Not only has he successfully met his natural adversary, age, but he has bodily become as indefatigable and unconquerable as *nature* ever was. In short, in a brilliant piece of transformation, he has become his adversary.

Few of my informants could be as lucid about their visions, but most made claims on belonging to the Hawaiian environment. Much of the belonging was transmitted through the acquired color of the skin. A color acquired without overexposure (like tourists) or underexposure (like "sickly" mainlanders) was the appropriate symbol. A color several hues darker than the one naturally ascribed was the aspired goal. The belief, widely held, of course, is that such color enhances one's attractiveness and suggests, in almost Veblenian fashion, that one possesses that most envied commodity, leisure. Indeed, for the sojourning transitory population, who come to Hawaii "to have a rest and to get a tan," the Islands offer perhaps little more than evidence of conspicuous consumption. Yet this is, undeniably, an overriding attraction for the contemporary traveler (MacCannell 1976). The subtleties of a new kind of color bar are indicated by the following:

> I kept looking at people in mainland cities and feeling very uncomfortable, until I analyzed it and found out that I was dismayed. They were all white. Certainly I wasn't used to seeing so much white skin displayed—because it was a fish-belly, sick, jail-white color—a sick person's color, you know. There's an awful tinge to city people on the mainland. They have this ungodly, unhuman, sickly white—like they all have T.B., or some disease. They stand out like the proverbial sore thumb.

It is only the relative newcomer, however, who will refer pointedly to the matter of tanning. "We like each other better with a tan," one recently arrived informant offered as a semi-serious reason for moving to the Islands. Once again, the appropriate color of skin reflects an emerging sense of unity with the environment; actual, in that it is acquired in the perusal of an outdoor life, and existential, in its more profound implications.

Indeed, the display of being part of Hawaii becomes increasingly important in the early months which are characterized by a keen sense of awkwardness and exclusion. Tanning seems to offer some superficial claims. A black woman from New York describes her experiences in this way:

> Well, I thought, "I'm not going to come this distance and miss out on anything." I thought, "Well, I'm black—I'm not going to worry about having sun stroke, or anything." Unfortunately, it's not true, for I was overexposed, and I was sick for a couple of weeks. It left a bad taste in my mouth.

The fusion with environment does not always occur. For some the discontinuity is not only naggingly apparent, but increases with the length of time spent there. One of my informants, who was to return to the mainland within months of the time I spoke with her, gave the alienation and separateness as an adequate reason for departure.

I never realized what environment can do to you. I always thought I could live *anywhere*—and give me six months and I could adjust to *anything*. And I *can* adjust—it's not that I can't, but I don't particularly want to. I don't like the non-change of seasons; I do like the colder weather. The environment does affect me an awful lot in that the warm weather does make me awfully tired—this is a physical thing. I do not like sweaty people. I really don't. I don't like body odor. This may be peculiar to me; perhaps everyone does not feel this way. This really offends me—the idea of constantly perspiring; that whole element really bothers me. And, therefore, it has affected our life sexually. It really has. And, this is one of our biggest problems here.

The natural world of Hawaii, therefore, is encapsulated for the newcomers as a bodily metaphor. They come alienated from nature, timorous in their relation to flora and fauna, rooted to mainland conceptions of themselves in an adversarial position. In the acculturation process they discover a comfortable niche, an emerging bodily fusion with the world outside.

Silent Demands of Time and Space

With a consistency I could not ignore, my informants reported experiencing time and space in ways that drew their attention. While much of the learning about new places is so congruent with everyday expectations as to pass unnoticed, every now and again some incident promotes enlivened awareness. In these particular incidents time or space "just seemed different."

The Western tradition is replete with everyday acknowledgments of these issues as something demanding attention. The mundane activities of the day are meaningful in spatial terms such as "open and closed space," "crowded spaces," "eating up space," "feeling space and conquering space," "being spaced out," and so forth. Even our own technological creations are described in spatial terms. For example, buildings "tower above one" or "fall in on one." Similarly, time is viewed as a commodity, frequently analogously with money. Thus one can "make it," "lose it," "gain it," "waste it," or even "borrow" it. It can be a luxury if in abundance or a deprivation if in short supply. As a commodity it can be vested with consciousness and power and can be "an enemy" or "on one's side."

One of my informants, in describing his past, is particularly vivid in noting altering perceptions of social time, restricted social and physical spaces, and in alluding to a restructuring of cognitive geography. He sketches his continuous movement westward across the North American continent to the Pacific. He begins his story in the '20s in New York.

> At the age of twenty-one, I was Fearless Fosdick—you know—out of New York. All New Yorkers were so superior to everyone else in the world. I had to take a couple of years of batting down, I was such a nuisance. My New York superiority! And a definite change in pace in life—this was the most marked thing I noticed. In New York, with my youth, everything was fast—a flash. Quick, quick, quick! I had to let down in Los Angeles; their pace was slower. I was elbowing people out of my way on the streets—"Get out of my way"—you know. Then, I came down to the Los Angeles pace of doing things. And, then, when I came over here, I had the same thing all over again. The pace here was quite different. People got in my way again [laughter]—brushing upon me. And this is true, not only physically, but in thought. They don't think as fast. The New York pace of thinking was faster than Los Angeles; the Los Angeles pace of thinking was—oh, immeasurably faster than Honolulu.

At this point in his narrative I asked him how he became aware of these matters, what cues had informed him and led to his observations.

> You say something to a person and they just look at you with this blank expression. You're talking so fast, or you're thinking so fast, that it takes them X seconds to arrive at understanding what you say and then thinking up an answer, and so on. So, the whole process is prolonged . . . I went to Fiji a few years ago, and I found there— at least to me—Fiji was exactly as it was in Honolulu when I first came in '37. And, much more enjoyable now than it would have been then because, now, I understand, I have gone through the Honolulu pace and come down to it. So, now, I'm able to move

into Tahiti, Fiji, and places like that, not to be irritated at the slower pace. I understand the reasons for it and can go along with it.

This particular informant, in keeping with a sentiment, widely shared by those who had migrated in earlier times, bemoans the destruction of the Hawaii he knew in fantasy and even in past reality. He explores the changes he experiences, continuing to use his chosen paradigm of time and space.

Well, the utter destruction of all the things that I enjoyed most—principally, the friendliness of the people. And the pace has gone up to where it is now, at the Los Angeles pace, or beyond it. The tension has risen from nothing to X thousandth percent. Your mobility has come down. The thing that I think irritates me the most, and drives me up the wall, is the noise. The lovely quiet we used to have—and the noises were what I call "natural noises" of pleasant, happy people, instead of strident electronic screams. These are the things that bother me. I feel I "escaped" from New York, at just the right time, before New York became the sodden sewer it is today. And, I escaped from Los Angeles before it, too, went the same way. The smog had only moved up to the middle of town, Westlake Park, when I left there. They had smog, but they didn't recognize it, or talk about it. But, it was visible up to the center of the city then; but now, of course, it's the entire Pacific Coast is covered with it. But I got out. The way I put it is that I've had two cities shot out from under me, and *now* Honolulu has been shot out from under me. If I was able, if I had the funds, I would go somewhere else . . . My trouble now is that I can't stand the cold. I have arthritis and I burn up with the pain. I'm miserable. I'd have to go south, somewhere in the Pacific. And, all of these countries, at least the ones I've been in, hate Americans. Depending on the country, the degree of hatred, they can make it very unpleasant for you. And, with limited funds, this is my chief trouble, I don't know where I can go. I made three big transplants—two big transplants. I'm a little too old for making another major transplant. I could do it at the age of twenty-one, thirty-seven, but can I do it at the age of seventy-two? I doubt it. And it offers no advantages, physically or financially, because the costs of living on the other islands are higher than here—and, here, they're higher than anywhere else in the world. So what are you gaining?

He continues to lament the destruction of his paradise, bringing forth a commonly accepted notion that social space and social distance are inversely connected. With decreased physical space he conceives of an increased social disengagement.

> Horrible! Well, I'd use the term "sewers." It's the only term that fits. They're just a flowing mass of pollution—water, people! The last time I was in New York—they're [the people] the most horrible, impolite . . . You speak to a person—you're trying to find directions, some help—and they glare. They don't look at you, they glare—this horrible muscoloid glare. You know this horrible muscle-type of person, who has muscles instead of a brain? And there you stand, with your mouth open, and no help. I avoid Los Angeles like the plague. When I'm forced to go there to change planes, that's all I do. And the same thing is happening with San Francisco. I don't want to go there anymore. And Chicago. And, I only go there because I have to change planes to see my son up in Michigan.

Time and space, as these ethnographic examples suggest, are experiences conceived in interactional, existential, and technical terms. They are shaped in the round of everyday life in consort with those around us. While they are inner experiences, understood and felt, they are also technically accurate measures. My informant has brought together all three notions into the account he has given of his coming to Hawaii.

Time is a construction which permits the recognition of events, the creation, or conversely the avoidance of linear order. It allows for the acknowledgment of the beginnings and ends of events, the awareness of durations, and, if necessary, frequencies. It permits such things as histories and futures. In short, it is a powerful, abstract ordering device.

Although it is undoubtedly culturally determined, time has some uncoded qualities which makes it possible to negotiate and mediate the experience. Thus differential demands can intrude on our accepted ways of thinking about time. This happens to the mainland *haole* who suddenly comes to a recognition that time is differently coded in the Islands and that previously accepted notions must be examined in the light of new demands. Time, like space, had always been invisibly, unconsciously, present. Now it becomes visible, a topic for consideration and for reflection. Such experiences are not new to the migrant to Hawaii but seem to reside in the experiences of most people who change cultures and domiciles. Nash alludes to the discrepancy of time codes in his portrayal of Americans in Spain (1970:130) and it appears to be commonly felt by most North Americans overseas (Cleveland et al. 1960:31).[4] A young man, recalling the first days of his arrival in the Islands, depicts the interactional negotiation of time through having the matter brought forcefully to his attention. His destination was a remote Hawaiian community which he reached after a day of traveling by various means and after spending many hours searching for the correct location. Dejected by his own slowness, weariness, and confusion, he is greeted by a local Hawaiian:

> I remember the first thing he said to me: "You all move so fast. People who come fresh from the mainland are really, really speeding." He says, "It's going to take you about two weeks to slow down." I thought, "Aw, what does he mean?" But, he meant that our method of speech, the way we moved around, the way we were all so organized, and the way we were so concerned about where we were going to sleep and when we were going here and there . . .

Within a short period the new culture of time has become well integrated into the pattern of a newcomer's life and it takes the arrival of another uninitiated person to force attention on the difference once more.

> I just want to sit down and slow down. What I like here is that it's slower. A friend came and saw me driving at 45 m.p.h., and he's used to me doing over 60. He said, "You've really slowed down." You sort of balance out because the island is smaller. No sense in hurrying. You're not going any place.

The informant has quite unconsciously tapped a cultural dictum: in Western cultures time and space can be made sense of in terms of each other. It is possible, therefore, to describe the distance of various locations by the amount of time that it takes to reach them, to give books intriguing titles like *What Time Is This Place* (Lynch 1972), or to produce a film ostensibly about tourism and label it *If This Is Tuesday, This Must Be Belgium*. The discovery that comes with the choice of Hawaii, however, is that restricted space, inflexible boundaries of ocean, and isolated geography come together to expand time. In short, by limiting geographical possibilities, time is slowed down.

> My husband traveled. We were never together . . . The Utah district covered a matter of six states. This is why he was never at home. The industry wasn't concentrated in Salt Lake. It was all over Idaho, Montana, eastern Nevada, northern Arizona, and into eastern Colorado. And he even went up into Oregon sometimes. And, if they were short of help on the West Coast and they'd call him to fly to the San Francisco office and help out . . . So, it was really awful. He was away all the time—every week. Sometimes he'd get home for weekends and, sometimes, it would be a month before he got home. And then he'd be home a couple of days. It got to the point where we were almost ready to be divorced. We had to get to where he couldn't travel—where it wasn't hurry, hurry, hurry. We're happy here. Of course, we're more free now. He was just here three weeks when he had to go to the Marshalls for three weeks. But that's unusual. And, then, he's been to Johnston Island and Guam, but only for a week at a time. And, that's all in eight years. That's pretty good.

The notion of shorter spaces and longer time organizes a sense of duration differently. Previous ideas about how long it takes to do things and what it is appropriate to accomplish are changed. The most common experience reported to me is the matter of taking trips by car. What would have been a short excursion on the mainland is now defined as a major undertaking.

> . . . like Kailua, for instance. It takes less than twenty minutes to get there on the freeway, but it seems too far away to bother going. I used to think nothing of driving for hours in the Bay area, or in Los Angeles.

Some informants very carefully see the slowness of time, the leisurely pace, as a clear outcome of indigenous Hawaiian culture. They interpret it as a notably different ordering of priorities. One man, still undergoing the stresses of acculturation, attempting to retain mainland notions of time and industry, harbors a critical note in his observation.

> Nobody cares about fixing anything. There's a kind of basic *mañana* for us. There's a slight lazy quality. If I let go, it could go that way. All the fast pace has been brought in. All those "go-go" people are

from California. If it were left to the people here, it would just be luau, luau, luau, and surf, surf, surf. Everyone goes to the beach. They say, "We don't need the money. We'll pack up the family and a picnic and go to the north shore!"

The relative slowness of Hawaiian time is captured in such mainland concepts as "island slows," "Maui slows," "pineapple time," "island time," "Mexican time," or even "mañana." The reference to Mexican time is probably to be expected as the actual experience of most migrants to Hawaii has usually not stretched beyond the boundaries of the continental United States. Here any difference in time code, particularly a slower pace, is labeled, somewhat pejoratively, in recognition of the southern neighbor.

This new system of Hawaiian time is immediately obvious to the incoming mainlanders. It alerts a time sense completely parallel to, and unknown by, the world of the precision clock. It resides in a cognitive order the machine cannot capture.

In learning to live in Hawaii, then, a new sense of time must be acquired. The same is true for that other existential awareness, space. Like time, space is an ordered metaphor, where spaces between individuals and objects are culturally regulated. It is an intricate competence and it is imperative for the smooth unproblematic management of daily commonplaces. It permits one to act and yet not to offend others. For the hopeful migrant, then, to understand space well is to behave in it like a Hawaiian.

Unordered space is humanly troublesome. Either its openness is an invitation to regularize or a potential threat. If its boundaries are not immediately apparent, then the imperative is to define them or, failing that, to negotiate them. Such symbolic understandings are most clearly demonstrated in the claims to territoriality on an open space like the beach. It is a continually shifting space, moving from relative emptiness to stages where less and less space is allocated to more and more people. All of this is accomplished by tacit agreement. At times an equidistant and rather simple positioning seems to be the determining factor. Yet other factors seem to affect allocation. The degrees of movement affected by the beachgoer, the age, sex, and ethnicity of individuals, the amount of paraphernalia accompanying the person, and other such matters seem to play an important part. Stranger distance is a mediated entity, which in actually measurable space may vary markedly within a very short period of time.

> This is known as my spot on the beach, I think. At least no one has ever taken it—people always sit at a respectful distance. I can tell if they want to strike up a conversation by where they sit and whether they give that meaningful ogle . . . I always try to go in the morning, before Hanauma Bay gets crowded. It's hard to find a place, and I end up going right to the end of the beach.

To violate the silent code of space usually causes doubt, suspicion of malicious intent, or other well-recognized reactions to this kind of meaninglessness.

> I was amused the other day. I was sitting on the beach, reading a book. This young, handsome, local kid, about twenty years younger than me—he came over this huge stretch of sand right for me, playing his guitar. Good God! I couldn't conjure up any reason. He stopped and knelt before me. All the reasons that fleeted across my mind, but the one it turned out to be. The real one—to try and save my soul for Christ.

Space, unlimited space, luxurious space, space that promised few boundaries is part of the Hawaiian fantasy. Now it is a threatened commodity in the eyes of many mainland migrants who came to seek it. Encroaching populations, mainly of their own kind, are viewed with distinct distaste. Old timers bemoan the lack of government controls on migration and immigration. Others sheepishly indicate that if they had their way they would try to keep all prospective settlers out. Young people who come for surf, sun, and tropical wilderness upbraid others like themselves for the same reason. They accuse them of abusing the environment, desecrating nature and local Hawaiian sensitivities alike.

> These people arrive from the mainland—and, even myself I have an instant bias against them. I have no right to. But I love the local people. I get pissed off when I see the tourists coming around. I get pissed off when I see all the building and developing. The local people have been kicked back into the hills into the slums of Kalihi. Americans want this or that valley or seashore, with all their money, and all the people have to split. And, the Orientals have the island sewed up—and, now the Japanese are buying up places and property right and left. It's just too crowded.

Other mainland migrants evaluate their own presence:

> Actually, to be truthful, it's getting to the point where I'm seriously considering moving somewhere else. Because it's not what it was when I first came. I went to the Holiday Mart last Sunday to cash a check. I couldn't walk, I couldn't move, the lines were so long. It suddenly clicked in my mind that this is what Hawaii is going to be like in maybe five or ten years.

The lure of the beaches, so central to the Hawaiian fantasy for many a newcomer, comes in for consideration. Many complain that the paradise of untrammeled sands of previous years are spoiled by "noisy teenagers," "slobs fooling around," "people parking themselves and their towels right on top of me," "inconsiderate bastards trampling sand in my eyes as they walk past," or "objectionable people who don't respect your privacy."

> The first year I came here I went surfing every day before I went to school—like at five o'clock in the morning. I came here in '66. It was still not so crowded. I'd be the only person there. Or, perhaps, one other person. Just an unbelievable feeling—being out there on a surfboard, looking at Diamond Head. And just no one else. It was a real haul, I savored it! . . . The last time I went it was so crowded I didn't enjoy it. No matter when I went to the beach, weekday, weekend, I used to be able to meditate, relax. Not any more.

Spatial constriction is believed to be a condition from which all mainlanders suffer regardless of the density of the population or the amount of development. This condition is encapsulated in local vernacular as "rock fever" or "island fever." Its symptoms are a claustrophobic anxiety brought about by the smallness of the island and the lack of geographic space on it. Its etiology is described as the person's inability to extricate himself or herself from mainland mental sets on time and space. One informant clearly suffered from all of the symptoms:

> We've seen everything there is to see. We like to go out for a drive every weekend. And, now there's nowhere else to go. We've driven around the island so many times already. It only takes a few hours. It'll be nice to get back to the mainland. I feel imprisoned out here.

In conclusion, then, if nature and place are human metaphors and cultural constructions, a move from one setting to another makes this very thing visible. The metaphors, compact and intricate packages of knowledge, become exposed for consideration. Old ideas retained in tacit consciousness are tapped by circumstances and held up to everyday demands. Here they are changed.

Thus places become domesticated. Nature in its many forms becomes accommodated. Yet, as Relph has written, "places are fusions of human and natural order and are the significant centres of our immediate experiences of the world" (1976:141). The significant implication here is that the human order, as well as the natural one, contributes to the sense of place. I have already noted the separateness of human and natural in Western epistemology. It now remains for me to acknowledge the experience of white settlers in a new human environment, to depict the paramount importance of other ethnic groups in their daily existence. The next chapter will deal with the impact of these relationships in the mainland *haole's* developing knowledge about Hawaii.

CHAPTER FIVE

Rituals of Inequality: Ethnicity and the *Haole*

Every society contains a repertoire of identities that is part of the "objective knowledge" of its members.

Berger (1966:107)

Caucasians arriving in the Hawaiian Islands encounter some everyday realities with considerable surprise. They come with ethnic attitudes comfortably intact and middle class values nourished and unquestioned through a lifetime of certainty. In order to live in Hawaii, however, they must accommodate some alien ideas. It surprises and even shocks some of them to realize that they are *haoles* and, moreover, *mainland haoles*. This surprise is the first stage of a subtle transformation wherein previously unquestioned beliefs meet an unexpected test. New constraints and relationships demand different social performances. Inevitably the recognition comes that as a *haole* one must fit into a variety of world views. Only in time will these views become clear and understood with any insight. For the present there is only the awareness of a new position in a new social setting. Not only is there a new way of classifying others, but there is a new way of ordering the positions of these classifications.

the newcomers find themselves in an unexpected place in this new order.

By now it is clear that *mainland haole* as an ethnic description is applicable only in Hawaii. It has neither context nor significance elsewhere. It is unlike any of the designations by which other immigrant groups have come to be known. Unlike Papua New Guinean or Laotian it does not necessarily refer to a national entity. Unlike Oriental or European it does not necessarily refer to a continent or a cultural region. Unlike *kotonk*, a Japanese person from the mainland, or *Buddha-head*, an Oriental person, it is not necessarily heavy with pejorative innuendo. Rather it reflects two turning points in Hawaiian history. It draws together two historical processes and thereby unites two of Hawaii's most pressing social problems. Just as the *haole*, or foreigner, is the quintessence of all that pressed in on the Hawaiian way of life in the nineteenth century, so the *mainland haole* is the quintessence of all that is pressing in on the Islands in the twentieth. Thus the present-day white migrant from mainland North America is the visible reminder of converging imposition.

For some time now, spurred on by the conferring of Hawaiian statehood, the migrants from the mainland have accounted for most of the burgeoning population.[1] In this they repeat the surge of American immigrants in the nineteenth century. The migrants of today, undoubtedly like their predecessors of earlier times, encounter already established positions, with the result that, for the first time in many of their lives, a sense of their unconscious and unavoidable involvement in history and politics, in economics and power, become apparent.

This chapter concerns itself with the coming together of diverse cultural notions about the meaning of human differences. It attempts to add a few more strokes to the portrait of the *haole* by portraying his or her inevitable meeting with the ethnic groups of Hawaii. More importantly it tries to demonstrate what happens to tacitly held ideas when they become culturally transplanted and to show what occurs when a previously taken-for-granted morality becomes questioned. It sets out the history of a set of ideas challenged by circumstances and experiences. The set of ideas is Western liberal consciousness.

Certain issues are raised in this part of the ethnography. How does experience mediate belief? How is social morality negotiated? How do experiences become coded into existential certainties? How does culture shape reasoning? The aim is to show people searching for the ideas that would permit them to exist in a livable world. The ideas which come up for examination are a complex, integrated set commonly referred to as the "Western consciousness." More specifically they are those ideas which are identified as having to do with how one should respond to human differences. The experiences which raise these questions for examination are the daily contacts between mainland *haole* and others in Hawaii and the former's growing awareness of their own place in the social milieu.

Surely, one might reason, the recognition that some people are the same and others are different is a cultural commonplace. Yet, obviously, the cultural categories of distinctiveness vary greatly. The orders and hierarchies into which these distinctions are placed vary as well. Similarly, the reasoning about *why* the differences are noted and *to what end* is also culturally defined. Perhaps all that can be said is that all human minds separate, associate, analogize, and refine. They are all attuned to consistency and variation. Perhaps this is where universality ends.

One of the crucial distinctions that Western cultures make is that of ethnicity. Other differences, such as sex and age, race and class, have long been recognized categories. As such they have long done the work of alienation and the ordering of social priorities. Ethnicity, however, is of recent vintage. At least ethnic revivalism is of recent vintage (Patterson 1977:147). The white migrant comes to the Hawaiian Islands well endowed with one particular sense of the moral order of ethnicity and of the position of the white person in this order.

Sensibilities about Differences: The Mainland Legacy

Caucasians arrive in Hawaii with a legacy of ideas and attend to the world accordingly. Spun from such beginnings their expectations about the people of Hawaii are predetermined. It may well be an unconscious creed, but it floods their experience in Hawaii with meaning, evaluates it, and often finds it lacking. Particularly poignant for them, inducing comment and even fervent discontent, is that they find themselves at a disadvantage. In their eyes they are the victims of what they can only view as violations of what they thought was an indisputable moral code. As they assume that the code is, or ought to be, universal, any infractions become matters to be remedied.

This code could be referred to as the liberal conscience, a perspective congealed out of a long history of ideas in Western culture. It includes assumptions about ethical behavior, about the nature of human beings, about the responsibilities of social life, and other such moral precepts. What I wish to raise in this argument is the part of this code that addresses the appropriate ways of dealing with the fact that some people are different.

Whether one refers to it as a liberal ideology, or, more invidiously, as "possessive individualism" (MacPherson 1962), or "cultural narcissism" (Lasch 1978), its message is clear enough. One practices it assiduously in politics, unconsciously in daily life, and evokes it in rhetoric. When absent, it becomes overbearingly obvious. So what constitutes this set of moral beliefs?

Paramount in it is a notion of equal worth, reflected in the strong belief in rights to individual expression, in freedom from tyranny, and a God-given right to expect that these virtues be protected. For the academically inclined the ghosts of Bentham, Hobbes, Locke, John Stuart Mill, and the great English and French libertarians appear, as does the more familiar Declaration of Independence. Locke's suggestion that humanness is freedom from others embodies the liberal ideology. This ideology promises a kind of universal security with maximum safeguards. These rights and freedoms, the expected protection that goes with them, constitute the fundamental liberal attitude toward ethnicity and race.

Everyday the ideology is produced in familiar epitaphs: All men are born equal. Human differences, like beauty, are only skin deep. Everyone has the right to liberty and the pursuit of happiness. Freedom is everyone's right as long as it does not harm others. Protecting the rights of others is a duty and an honor. These are the unquestioned promises. Within these parameters one has the right to pursue personal gain.

Basic to all of this is the underlying assertion that somehow people are the same in a more fundamental sense than they are different (MacPherson 1962:272). Thus differences are seen as being surface and consequently inappropriate for ascertaining inequality. It is quite immoral, therefore, to discriminate by skin color or other visible difference.

Any history of Western culture, however, indicates that most inequalities derive from perceived differences. The twentieth-century liberal conscience, so much the central actor in this chapter, seems to have evolved as the answer to these centuries of history. Whereas previously differences were to be punished, conquered, subdued, or eradicated, they are now to be honored. This is a philosophical commitment and an unvoiced expectation. It is this virtue, and the sensibilities that go with it, that guarantee happiness (Bredvold 1962:7) and ensure security.

Can one really claim this liberal consciousness for the mainland *haole*? It is common, both in and out of the social sciences, to maintain that world view is determined by occupation and social position. Further, it is equally common to attribute liberality to the well-educated middle class. The Hawaiian record leaves little doubt that those migrating from the mainland are overwhelmingly in the professional, business, and technical fields (Department of Planning and Economic Development 1982:table 10). As further evidence of this a study of the American national character done by scholars from the Institute of Statistical Mathematics in Tokyo makes some relevant assertions about Hawaiian residents. They envision four types of Americans: "the model citizen," or one who believes in the American system and emphasizes the individual; "the revolutionary," who distrusts the social order and is a high self-achiever; the "Archie Bunker" type, who believes in the system but is not successful because he does not perceive the society as a whole; and finally, "the rich liberal," who can be critical of the system while reaping its benefits. The Japanese scholars note that mainland migrants, and indeed the majority of Honolulu residents, come from "the model citizen" or "rich liberal" variety (Research Committee on the Study of Honolulu Residents 1980:67–68).

Celebration of Differences:
Ethnic Pluralism

As differences are asserted to be superficial, therefore, in essence they cannot be threatening. How are these obvious differences then to be viewed? They become defined as valuable in themselves. What is valuable is uniqueness and, in the American ethos, uniqueness is to be cherished. In this creed, therefore, ethnic groups become ends in themselves. To-be-themselves is thus a natural as well as a moral right. If they are indeed ends in themselves, how is this in turn to be handled? There is the unspoken assumption that somehow, logically and nonabrasively, these groups fit into a whole, into a system. To this whole, or system, they are seen as making their individual "contributions" (Peter 1981:56). This, in turn, is viewed as socially enriching.

The foregoing assumptions are fundamental to understandings held by those of liberal conscience. One such understanding with a long history is that of the "melting pot," which is dominated by an imagery of basic compatibility and congenial borrowing. Ruled out of this image are grating differences which usually embody potential conflict. The "melting pot" promises the eventual realization of universality, under the guise of evolving homogeneity. Ideas such as these dominated decades of social scientific thinking, as well as decades of social policy.

Another assumption of more recent vintage is the cultural or ethnic pluralism paradigm, wherein conflict is avoided by permitting both freedom and coexistence. Once again the understanding is that the whole is infinitely improved by the very differences of its parts. A commitment to this ideology is displayed in familiar ways, such as enthused advocacy of ethnic cuisine, vigorous claims that "one of my best friends is . . . ," or bemused tolerance for ethnic personalities or customs. These are rituals of equality. They legislate against the threatening imperfections that emerge out of wealth and status, privacy and leisure (Manning 1976:14). Thus pluralism is a social construction purposely intended to diffuse conflict.

The diverse structure of Hawaii makes it the paradigm case of pluralism. It has long been depicted in official and everyday versions as a "racial paradise." Every tourist brochure suggests it and every innocent tourist proclaims it. There is nothing new in this metaphor. Nor is there anything new in the backlash that its saccharine promise creates. While it is in the interests of some to prove that racial paradise is an appropriate epithet for the Hawaiian Islands, it is in the interest of others to debunk this assertion just as vigorously.

The notion of paradise does not rest only with the simplified fantasies of tourist tracts and airline trade magazines, but is woven into scholarly works as well. Taking the "melting pot" as his pervasive imagery, the executive assistant to the United States Secretary of the Interior in 1932 envisioned the "ultimate Hawaiian" as a composite of all the races of the Islands. He wrote reassuringly that research at the University of Hawaii had refuted the old theory that unions of unlike races produce inferior individuals (Du Puy 1932:115). He asserted that prejudices and conflicts did not exist and that race was not a social question unless raised by an outsider. Using the same notion of an ultimate universality, in 1937 Sidney Gulick projected the coming of the Neo-Hawaiian American race (Gulick 1937). Books such as these could not be written in the 1970s or 1980s. The contemporary analytic style ranges from critical and doubtful to downright condemning.

In the prophetic year 1941 Joseph Barber published *Hawaii: Restless Rampart*, bringing to light the economic stresses and social issues involved in the possibility of statehood. He pointed to Japanese economic interests in the Islands and the conflicts between Caucasians and Japanese. He reported that the Caucasians were threatened by what they saw as Japanese encroachment into various industries and by Japanese migration from rural plantations into the city. He noted that they even accused the Japanese of having plans for the political destiny of Hawaii (1941:136–37). What in 1941 was an accusation, the Caucasians of the latter part of the century experience as a foregone accomplishment.

Barely more than a decade after statehood the analysis and rhetoric had changed considerably. Wright *The Disenchanted Isles* (1972), Gray *Hawaii: The Sugar-Coated Fortress* (1973), Rapson *Fairly Lucky You Live Hawaii* (1980), McDermott et al. *People and Cultures of Hawaii* (1980), and Wooden *What Price Paradise?* (1981) exemplify the newest answers to the pervasive cultural paradise phenomenon. Wright concentrates on issues which he calls the "boiling melting pot," the "dividing line," and economic oppression by the *haole* establishment. Gray presses in relentlessly on white military and Big Five power, on Japanese political involvement, and Chinese economic interests. Both Gray and Wright give attention to the completely unjust plight of the Hawaiian. Rapson gives his book the subtitle *Cultural Pluralism in the Fiftieth State.* McDermott et al. use an open pluralist paradigm and Wooden assumes a tacit pluralism. In their acceptance of coexistence these works seem to echo an earlier sociological work, Andrew Lind's *Hawaii: The Last of the Magic Isles.* Lind notes that despite the fact that many residents of Hawaii seem satisfied with an apparent lack of racial tension, the Islands hold "no magical formula for exorcizing the evil spirits of racial discord and distrust in other parts of the world . . . Nor is there reason for believing that a benign climate can absorb the truculence, pettiness, and selfishness in men's dispositions any more in these Islands than elsewhere in the world" (1969:97).

The Comfortable Paradox

The ongoing celebration of difference is not without its critics nor without its inherent paradoxes. Ethnicity is, after all, a social construction. As a social construction it reflects familiar ideologies and principles which, in their turn, permit ready taxonomies of people. While these principles and ideologies have wide consensus they often appear purely arbitrary (Lieberman 1968). Thus one could assert that ethnicity and ethnic pluralism are purely arbitrary but perhaps necessary fictions. Herein lie the paradoxes which occasion the most acerbic of criticisms.

For example, it is openly recognized that the fiction of ethnicity does some of the work of "race," but is devoid of much of its sting. Ethnic pluralism applauds a wide assortment of identities. The free display of one's identity is, in Western culture, tantamount to some kind of spiritual human right. Thus, acknowledging identity through the ideology of pluralism releases people from foregone suspicion and distrust. It allows for familiar, workable stereotypes, making interaction easier. In short, the principle of ethnicity regulates our knowledge of others and supports it by ready answers.

Depending on their theoretical or political orientation, the cynical critics of ethnic pluralism are liable to condemn rather harshly. Not only do they see in the exercise of universalism and in the surface professions of equality a touch of *noblesse oblige,* they also see the purposeful restrictions and exclusions which make possible the practice of privilege. Some, like Patterson (1977:11), assert that pluralism is the intellectual antithesis of universalism, that it is a reactionary, conservative, and essentially hostile bourgeois principle, giving some groups (and presumably not others) the moral license to live with clear differences and privileges.

It can be argued that far from providing cohesion, pluralism is ultimately socially divisive. One of its basic rationales is the Western bourgeois notion of the right to identity. Further, even if one came to support the notion of identity as a moral expectation for all, one could neither thereby become one of the powerful, nor could one claim unity with them. "One is Scots, Welsh, or Irish to the extent that one differs from the English . . . the converse is not true" (Gorer 1975:156). Undoubtedly on the Hawaiian scene as well, one is something else because one is not Hawaiian, Japanese, Caucasian, or whatever group seems to be currently the holders of privilege. A sense of exclusion is a component of ethnic awareness. Some critics would suggest that ethnicity is a new version of alienation. The notion of "ethnic" in and of itself implies something other than the norm, the unquestioned and taken-for-granted. It suggests an outside status. In the guise of equality and freedom, then, ethnicity could be a justification for ghettoized exclusion.

For some, therefore, pluralism is a kind of ethnic aloofness, a segregation that is a new form of colonialism. It is a hypocritical chauvinism whose true character is hidden beneath placatory romantic rhetoric. Yet as a way of organizing the world its power is undisputed. Supported by Western liberalism, offering apparent freedoms, it allows such unsavory and unacknowledged parts of the Western consciousness as "capacities for consumption and acquisition, for emulation and competition, for status-ranking, for domination and subjection, for the inflicting and the acceptance of suffering, or indeed for malevolence, cunning, degradation, destructiveness, and brutality of all conceivable kinds" (Lukes 1979:147). The tautological character of ethnicity as an ordering principle ("insofar as an entire structure is infused by a single generating principle, this principle will be tautologically or repetitively implicit in all the parts"—Burke 1966:55) anchors it for much of contemporary history. Its apparent equality coupled with its inherent inequality make of pluralism a comfortable paradox. It is the product of a cultural hegemony powerful enough to revel in its own generosity and at the same time to create a containment policy that deals with divisiveness and conflict. Too often it is a policy vigorously espoused by those very people against whose interests it must ultimately legislate.

It is this paradox that the Caucasian migrants from the mainland experience. They come to know other groups in ways previously unknown to them. With the Western legacy unquestioningly in hand and an unequal world distantly present as a reminder, the *haole* come as viewers of their own liberality. They claim that they practice equality, fervently believe they should do so, and moreover are determined to do so. The problems of race associated with mainland North America are certainly part of their awareness, but are seen as malevolent cankers on the face of the life they left. Rank prejudice is the behavior of others, and they wish to be disassociated from it. Like all seekers after paradise, they are painfully innocent and just as painfully clumsy. They now find themselves in historically produced and culturally organized contexts for which they lack what Sahlins would call "historical structures of significance" (1981:8). They do not know the hard times through which this new knowledge has been tempered.

Certainly they have brought with them the notion of ethnicity as an organizing principle. Yet, as members of the class that was the moving force for that principle in the first place, their ignorance is that of the controlling faction. It is their perspective that has become the one recorded in official and academic documents. Yet their way of proceeding from the familiar, the case of the mainland, to the relatively unfamiliar, the case of Hawaii, is unexpectedly thwarted. Unforeseen insights await them. Both the ethic of racial accommodation and the art of racial management as developed on the mainland are inadequate to the new demands.

The Discovery of *Haoleness*

Possibly the most basic human reflection centers around developing a sense of who one is. This reflection is an ongoing process. Knowledge about oneself continually meets the subtleties of everyday interactions. The word we usually supply for this sense of self is "identity." Presumably one's identity is recognizable and the reactions to it predictable. Some aspects of identity seem to have the case of unwavering certainty, as in the case of being white, or female, or young. Yet this version of identity fails to account for the elusive qualities of self-awareness or the subtleties of experience. Even those qualities that seem to be unwavering, like age and color, respond to contextual demands. The gloss that identity seems to be, therefore, does not recognize that most aspects of it are as vulnerable as egg shells, as amorphous as whiffs of perfume. One's sense of self is never completely one's own property, but is always contingent on the tacit approval of others, their complicity in regacting appropriately. Certainly this is an interactionist and existential view of identity, where variability and legitimacy are essentially negotiated in each encounter. It is the view which led Strauss to use analogy of mirrors and masks (1959) and Goffman to talk of presentations of self (1959).

The process of learning about identity is inevitable for all newcomers to Hawaii. They learn in order to fit in, and conversely fit in in order to learn. The most salient awareness that confronts them is that they are *haoles*. As I have pointed out already, this discovery is made early, and its nuances continue to be encountered during their entire residence in Hawaii.

> Being a *haole*? Yes, I think the very first shock I had was being called a *haole* on my third day here. I thought I had been called "nigger." I couldn't believe it was said to me with the neutral kind of expression on the face that it was. It happened in a store. I thought I had been thoroughly insulted, with a coolness I couldn't believe either. See how innocent I was! I soon learned that it was relatively neutral. When I told *haole* acquaintances, they told me to wait until I heard "you *haole*," or "you damn *haole*," or "you fuckin' *haole*." I'm still learning its meanings even though I've been here six years . . . But I'm just much, much more cautious than I ever thought I'd be.

For the uninitiated the sting is informed by years of sensitivity to mainland racial problems. The mainland experience appears to be immediately self-evident:

> I was not able to handle the word *haole*. It used to bother me. On the job, I was called "*haole* boy," so I just quit . . . Since then, I've learned we aren't the only ones. I've heard *pake*, fenderhead, Buddha-head, even "you fuckin' slant eye" applied to others, so I don't care any more.

All the implications of *haole* status must be discovered. The intonations used with it, the very meanings of the word itself act as a barometer to the changing position of whites in the Islands. Its status seems to be deteriorating. This is revealed in sporadic efforts to replace the word *haole* with something more neutral like "Caucasian." The word, like its mainland counterparts "nigger" or even "Negro," is offensive to some. It is as if the word itself somehow stood apart and had nothing to do with the very identification process from which it derives. The word is questioned but the principle of ethnicity as a way of thinking remains unchallenged.

> *Haole* is inappropriate. I don't call myself *haole* anymore, I call myself Caucasian.

This assertion is honored not only by Caucasians. A Japanese professor at the university noted:

> I have used the word *haole* all the years I have taught here. Without even thinking about it. Everyone did. A couple of years ago one of

my students came up to me after class and said that he found the word *haole* offensive, and would I mind substituting the word "Caucasian." I have ever since.[2]

The Caucasians seem to be saying through their objections that they dislike having ethnicity become their most identifying feature. The notion of *haole* supersedes other identifying devices such as "bald man in green aloha shirt." For the first time in their lives many of them face their own ethnicity. Previously it had been quite irrelevant. Now, however, ethnic recognition determines interaction.

It is an old observation that white Anglo-Saxon North Americans are generally not viewed as ethnic but rather as the mainstream that makes ethnics of others. One sardonic account, however, suggests that there are considerable deprivations associated with this privileged position. "They are the only group," the anonymous writer suggests, "which did not encounter in the new world an established Western culture and thus were denied the character-forming experiences of discrimination and economic exploitation. Deprived of the wholesome loneliness of the newly arrived stranger, never having been called dirty, sub-human or different, this underprivileged group even had to wait until a war and the arrival of strangers made it possible to form its equivalent of the Sons of Italy, the D.A.R. One wonders whether we will ever succeed in assimilating it into the texture of American society" (Deutschmann 1978:416).

With eulogies to ethnic freedom on their lips, the mainland *haole* have seldom been challenged. They have not heard the radical assertions made by the likes of Patterson (1977:172) that ethnic relativism can quickly degenerate into unintended patronage. Nor have they been burdened with the possibility that what they see as equality and liberalism may be defined by others as the remnants of white colonial oppression. Nevertheless, Caucasians find themselves part of an emerging white ethnic group. They learn to be *haoles* in order to fit in. Not much of this learning, of course, is processed and publicly recognized. Rather it is usually a quiet, and even occasionally, a stormy transformation.

You see another new arrival come, and you find him being very obnoxious in his approach and attitude, and you realize that he's not doing anything you didn't do when you first got here. You see the eyes of people [local people] around him, and you feel they're feeling even stronger what you're beginning to feel. It takes a while, more than a year of sitting around, to be able to see the difference.

The transformation and discovery have characteristic features which the mainlander recognizes. The comfortable paradox is not quite so comfortable now. There are disjunctures between their expected status, their beliefs in equality and the realities they must accommodate. Caucasians discover they do not merely inherit their mainland position. Previous privileges are often denied them. They compare their position to blacks on the mainland.

I now know what it must be like to be black on the mainland. The poor black person must have it one hundred percent worse. I think that coming here was a rather good educational thing for us all, especially for my wife, and for my daughter—she's fourteen—and yes, even for me.

The Threat of Powerlessness

Among the early awarenesses for the newcomers is a taste of powerlessness. They may have some distant and academic understanding that power and privilege are unequally distributed, but usually that applies to others, somewhere else. The notion of inequality is central to the analysis of social critics and social scientists, but seldom is it a viable experience in the lexicon of the mainlander. The "oughts" of proper behavior cloud the issue and power and privilege become invisible forces. What might be seen as power by the cynical is quickly rationalized by the newcomer. It becomes translated into familiar cultural rationales such as "personality clashes," or merely unadulterated rudeness. If their own actions are construed by others as the exercise of privilege, they maintain that these very actions are essentially benign and motivated by moral correctness.

Generally speaking, Caucasians from the mainland are not strangers to cultural settings where power is wielded over them. That kind of power is, after all, part of everyday experience. This kind of exposure to power, which includes yielding to teachers, physicians, bank managers, and the like, is part of life. The morality of such power is accommodated under the warrant that knowledge and experience are unquestionably legitimate claims to having rights over others (Goodenough 1978).

The Hawaiian setting brings to the mainland migrant's attention the notion that power emerges in ways they would ordinarily consider illegitimate. When they are denied accommodations or jobs apparently on the basis of their whiteness and mainland origins, their liberal conscience is affronted. The usual explanations of rudeness or "bad character" begin to give way to the recognition that their ethnic affiliation is stigmatized. The notion that the stigma is supported by some kind of consensus is even harder to accept than the stigma itself.

> A few times I thought that they were just acting like delinquents, but then I noticed that they did not harrass Orientals. Also I just thought this or that Japanese person was cold, but then it dawned on me that they were just cold to us—yes, just because we were white.

The Caucasians soon begin to complain to each other. They note discrimination in politics, in economic pursuits, and in everyday interaction. These common experiences bind them to other whites and common efforts are made to find appropriate explanations for their diminishing status. While the majority complain about the state of affairs and note one incident of discrimination after another, a smaller number deny having seen or experienced prejudice. They routinely suggest that those who are discriminated against bring it on themselves by their own poor behavior and manners, and that Hawaii still is one place on earth where racial and ethnic harmony is to be found.

The arenas in which the perceived discrimination is played out are well known to all Caucasians who have moved to the Islands and have lived there long enough to have had experiences beyond the boundaries of the insulated tourist ghettos. The first disillusionment usually comes in mundane everyday interactions. The newcomers make purchases in stores, borrow books from the library, take their children to school, look for housing, and search for jobs. Sooner or later they confront their own whiteness, and come to understand that this very whiteness makes of them objects of suspicion, dislike, or ridicule. Consider the contrasts observed by a shopper in the treatment meted out to her and that accorded to Japanese customers:

> Like, we just went in one day to [Store.] [Store] is notorious for this. Like, I'd been waiting at a counter for a long time and two or three Japanese ladies'd come up. And when other people come after, invariably I will be pushed aside and others will be served . . . In fact, I'd been waiting a good twenty minutes. This sales lady kept pushing me aside and saying "Well? What do you want now?" and "How come you haven't found it?" You know, sort of things like this. *Really* rude, just *very* rude. Finally another girl, she was from a different counter, she came over and helped me. I mean, *she* saw it.

The same woman suggested that prejudice may have further ramifications than merely being ignored. She and her Chinese-Hawaiian husband attempted to exchange an item in a department store. They were accused of having purchased it elsewhere and of trying to dupe the store into exchanging something that had not been purchased there originally.

Most people I interviewed had in their memories some such incidents. Invariably the fact of their whiteness is used as the clue to the reported unpleasantness. They seem to believe that certain attitudes are inextricably connected to their visible ethnicity, and that certain occasions are legitimate arenas for the expression of these attitudes. They come to expect a particular kind of behavior from members of other ethnic groups and indeed rehearse and gear their own behavior to meet these vicissitudes. One woman describes how she either attempts to avoid exposing herself to such prejudicial treatment or uses her interactional skills to neutralize an expected altercation.

> When I see one of those really cold store clerks, or the Japanese librarian at our local library, I really quake inside. I try to be as meek, as humble, as I can. I ask their opinion and am terribly solicitous. Only then do I feel they cannot possibly be as horrid as they usually seem to be. This particular librarian is so bad that I often wait around until she leaves the desk, and then go up to another.

Ethnicity is also used to explain any unpleasant encounters around the important matter of finding appropriate housing. Many report that they are denied the right to rent certain places. If the landlord makes a decision to rent to someone else, ethnicity is a favored explanation for the rejection. The retelling is usually simplistic. The renter is seen as being rejected for being a Caucasian. There is no analysis concerning perceptions of the renter's personal integrity or the notion that this integrity is interpreted in cultural terms. There is little understanding that the island landlord's version of mainland renters could be the product of past experiences. There is little acknowledgment that such renters are seen as unreliable tenants who stay only for short periods. The rejected tenant does not consider the conventions of renting which examine matters such as the visible signs of local employment, numbers of children, and other extenuating circumstances. Ethnicity becomes the overriding explanation. The paradigmatic experience of mainland blacks, so loudly proclaimed in mainland presses, becomes the generating source for reasoning about their own rejections.

Other stereotypic knowledge about ethnicity does explanatory work in the white persons' attempts to cope with what befalls them. A common one is the supposed excessive cleanliness attributed to the Japanese, and the supposed view the Japanese are believed to have about Caucasian failures in this area. The Japanese view is usually depicted as completely irrational and it is maintained that their version of cleanliness is pushed to ridiculous limits in order to satisfy ethnic dislikes in a legitimate way. The following narration shows doubt as to whether ethnicity or cleanliness is at issue:

I don't know whether it's racial prejudice? I had a beautiful feeling towards Orientals until we moved to our house in Nuuanu Valley. I cleaned the apartment up for two days. Immaculate! Even so she charged $30 for cleaning. I had *wanted* to clean it up. When she came to inspect the apartment her daughter went around the place saying "this place is filthy." When John came back and told me, my bones were still aching from scrubbing that place. She deducted $30 for the lamp. We had paid our rent on time. It was terrible. I've gotten over it. I realize it was one incident, but it really hurt.

The Discrimination Story

It is in the daily arena of the work place that the mainland Caucasians' discovery of their inescapable whiteness is at its most dramatic. Finding employment, retaining it, and interacting with other groups in carrying it out prove to be unexpected occasions for ethnic recognition. Undoubtedly one possible analysis is to see the workplace as an area where ethnicity and power are inextricably combined. It could be argued that power is allocated or denied on the basis of ethnicity. Underlying such analysis would be a notion of limited resources and ethnically organized ways of distributing or claiming them (Despres 1975). While any situation could be made ripe for this kind of analytic treatment, Hawaii seems to be particularly à propos. The very history of Hawaii, at least as it is commonly written, would suggest that ethnic insularity and ethnic pluralism have been ways through which planters and other, usually white, elite could retain control and power. Ethnic insularity is given as an adequate explanation for the ineffectiveness of early unionism, which came to fruition much later in Hawaii than elsewhere. Indeed, unions like the International Longshoremen's and Warehousemen's Union (ILWU) are seen as strong forces for interracialism (Coffman 1973:77; Thompson 1978).

Caucasians tell a series of stories about their experiences. They become moral tales, with a worthy hero or heroine confronting odds powerfully constructed to defeat him or her. Each story depicts the battle between innocence and corruption. By implication the Western consciousness readily informs us of the ultimate moral victor. Meanwhile, however, the trials of Hercules, the anguished search of Ulysses, and all the accounts of good and evil known to the Western world are structurally incorporated into each story.

The first set of narrations has to do with the demise of innocence in the experience of searching for a job. It depicts the newcomer, resplendent with hope and skill, attempting to find a position. For reasons that are not clear (and because of the way the story must be structured, at that early point, cannot yet be made clear), the seeker is unable to procure one. Polite refusals are coupled with announcements that the position has been taken. In these weeks of endeavor the person inevitably approaches others, usually other white people, to relate the experience and to seek advice. Sooner or later certain cautionary tales are shared. One commonly heard, embellished with varying details to fit companies and persons, is the following:

> My friend saw this job advertised in the *Advertiser*. She phoned up and asked if the job were still available. She was told that sorry, it wasn't. Then the friend's girl friend, she's Chinese-Hawaiian, phoned up. She was told that the job was still available. A time for an interview was arranged.

The first instruction about ethnicity and about one's place in the order has now taken place. I heard this story many times, but do not ever remember hearing it as a first-person experience. This, perhaps more than anything else, shows its perseverance as common knowledge. The story is similar to a common mainland version where the black applicant is turned down over the telephone merely on the basis of his dialect, diction, or other speech characteristics which very clearly announce his or her race.

Other stories narrated by *haoles* have to do with being overlooked for employment despite obviously superior credentials. These tales usually involve considerable periods of painful discomfort in which the leading character, usually the narrator, attempts to understand the seeming rejection. The search for adequate reasons is often made a part of the narration, and the care in avoiding ethnic interpretations is made a commendable part of the moral fiber of the central figure. The next part of the story shows the slow coming to awareness of the probable explanation. The final events usually depict the wrong being righted.

> I know a girl who is an expert in the hotel management business. She knows how to handle all money, to keep accounts, and has considerable computer experience. She put in an application for a job in the new hotel. She didn't hear anything for a long time. When she phoned she was told "We haven't decided anything yet." This went on for some time, the same response. She was so obviously right for the job. She got a mutual friend who worked in the same hotel to find out about her application. He found it hidden, away

from the others, in a desk drawer. The Japanese employees had tucked it away. When the headman saw it he said, "My God, just what we need," and she was hired. There were five *haoles* working there, and now she is the only one.

Many of the ethnic success stories which come out of the work arena are structurally similar. They depict the overcoming of a series of Herculean obstacles after which the ethnically prejudiced villains get their come-uppance. One variety of story depicts the conquering of the negative stereotypes held about the *haole.* Usually the stereotype involves seeing the white newcomer as slow, lazy, bloated with self-importance, unable to work hard, impermanent, and generally unreliable. Through sheer perseverance, very obvious skills and abilities and intelligent foresight, the *haole* worker triumphs. The triumph usually concludes with the discriminators being taught a lesson and having to face the fact that the white person is extraordinarily able and gifted. The following is a story typical of this genre. The woman narrating is speaking of her first job working with "Japanese" nurses:

> Well, they'd load me down with an *impossible* task load for the day; and then, they'd be on my tail every minute. "Are you finished?" "Are you through?" It was just ridiculous. But, fortunately, I had been working in a hospital just as big and just as busy—even busier— because they have plenty of nurses here, all that they want. So I had been used to working very fast, and very hard. And that was a good thing. I think they thought I hadn't been a nurse for a while, but I had. If I had just been going back after ten or twenty years, like a lot of women do, I'd have been lost. Oh, my God!

The implication of the foregoing story is that the evil ones were forced to rethink their prejudiced thoughts and acknowledge the ultimate worthiness of the heroine.

Another set of stories involves an unjust banishment, a kind of testing of Job, where the hapless *haoles,* presumably working ably at their particular jobs, find themselves the objects of unexplainable forces which they come to see as ethnic prejudice. Despite their innocence and the depth of their sincerity they find the forces powerful enough to push them into the ultimate wilderness. There they struggle for a biblical period of strife and punishment only to eventually regain their rightful heritage. The stories usually feature the *haoles* as the objects of subtle and finally unmistakable prejudice, which culminates when they are unable to continue in their position. In the following, a man once in a state government office explains his decision to leave:

> I couldn't make out why they did not seem to like me. It was subtle stuff, like they didn't invite me for coffee or strike up casual conversations. Then when they promoted someone who was much less qualified than me, over me, I knew that it was nothing but prejudice because I wasn't one of their in-group. Things just seemed to get worse, until I finally left. I was the only *haole* in the department.

Thus, in these stories the evildoers triumph initially, but the inevitable ending is implied. While their punishment is not direct, the fact that the person left the setting, the fact that the person is now wary, suspicious, and presents a negative image of the co-workers, suggests an ultimate revenge. To cast the other as prejudiced permits the sufferer to be self-righteous. The implication is that, as we all know in these moral tales, the day of atonement will inevitably come. Right will triumph and the guilty will suffer for their evil ways. Since the late seventies, however, many stories indicate that some of the long-suffering heroes have hastened this mythical day of reckoning. They have declared discrimination and ethnicity clearly connected to their painful experience and have brought their suffering before the courts. These cases are reported in the papers and themselves become part of the lore.[3] They become common knowledge among Caucasians and suggest denouements for other stories of harrassment at work, or even, in some cases, actual dismissal.

> I got fired because he said I was a "dumb lazy *haole*." He said I didn't know what to do on the job. You know that some guys have taken their employers to court, one man took the State, or was it the Department of Education, to court.

The details of such common knowledge do not seem to be retained. "The public has a short memory" was the knowingly platitudinous comment by one of the main actors in such a drama.

When the story told seems to reach no comfortable conclusion, when virtue does not seem to triumph, another genre of tale is sometimes introduced. In this the thinkers of discriminatory thoughts become the targets of discrimination themselves, so that ultimately they learn the error of their ways:

> The one thing that is so almost hilarious to us is that the locals, the local Japanese . . . it's usually the Japanese that go to the mainland either for vacation or school . . . they come back crying the blues. "Oh my God, I was discriminated against. So and so wouldn't let me an apartment," and this and that and the other. "And people push me around." And gee, that's rough! Now you know what it's like! But a lot of them come back and they're just shocked. They find out that there's a world where Orientals are not in the majority. It comes as a surprise to them. Just a culture shock. No one understands them and kids laugh at them on the street and make fun of them. It's our moment of bitter triumph . . . There'll be big newspaper stories here on *this* prejudice. *Big* stories.

This is the ultimate punishment, the ultimate "bitter triumph."

If a story's conclusion is not depicted, our knowledge of narration structures, perhaps our very knowledge of the Western legacy about right and might, rushes in to provide one. The storyteller triumphs, either visibly or at least in moral rightness and moral strength. Each discrimination story is founded on the familiar "good triumphs over evil" structure of our own mythic domain. The goodness and skill of the hero determines this obvious conclusion. In each tale we are reminded of the exemplary moral character of the hero. In discrimination stories this takes the form of reminding the listener that the person tried to withstand the encroaching inevitabilities of a possible ethnic explanation. From time to time one may admit to having reasonable doubt about his or her own interpretation or the interpretations supplied by others. "There were some locals working there too, the people in charge were Orientals, but I'm not sure that this thing happened to me because I was white."

One denouement which serves to justify the anger and injustice in the stories is the steadfast correctness in the ultimate ethnic interpretation. This makes reverse discrimination or any retaliatory action, if only in the form of ethnic distrust, a moral thing. The evildoers will get their just deserts, either now or in the future by having to retract ugly thoughts, low opinions, and discriminatory actions in the face of strong contradictory evidence. In other words, the mainland legacy is implicit within the stories. Discrimination is discovered. Once discovered, there is a resurrection of the mainland notion of pluralism—peace through the glorification of differences.

The Paradox Turns

The mainland legacy has prepared the *haole* to live with what I have called the comfortable paradox. It permits cultural differences to endure. It makes these differences visible, and it honors and protects them. Yet by encouraging the principle of separate but equal, it engenders a system where the powerful perpetuate themselves and the powerless remain, perhaps in innocent bliss, cushioned by their own kind.

The *haole* are viewers of their own open-mindedness and liberty, the champions of equality and ethnic pluralism. They come as loud disclaimers of the horrors of racial discrimination on the mainland, indeed disassociate themselves from it. They tend to view Hawaii as a triumphant success in the area of racial equality. They attempt to avoid any resemblance to mainland inequalities in their new home.

Yet for them the paradox turns. Their mandate, that one ought to embrace separate but equal does not seem to work. By their own experience they conclude that this mandate is not shared. Violations of the liberal conscience appear one after another. Certain groups in Hawaii, it becomes apparent, embrace a notion of "separate but unequal." They seem to base this notion on the most unacceptable of variables, namely race, color, ethnicity. While some social and cultural discrimination might be countenanced, biological discrimination, or so it seems to the newly arrived *haole*, is wholly immoral. Those who practice "separate but unequal" on biological grounds are clearly guilty of moral turpitude. This kind of baseness makes it legitimate and, after all, natural, to discriminate against the perpetrators. The pain of this is that the *haoles* then violate their own principles.

Experience can only be identified and coded from a base of residual knowledge. Therefore, the interpretations the _haoles_ produce for the series of events and exchanges which they encounter come from repertoires forged in their past. By their own admission _haoles_ compare their experiences to those of black Americans. Perhaps few analysts working objectively from the outside, one eye on economic arrangements, the other on political ambience, would see much resemblance between the situations of the _haole_ and the black. These analysts would see nothing but differences in socioeconomic status, history, and privilege. All that is shared is the experience of discrimination. That _haoles_ choose to identify with blacks is a remarkable phenomenon which, more than anything else, shows the poverty of the white person's discrimination experience. Others had been ethnics, they themselves had been merely Americans. One Caucasian reflects about his own kind:

> A certain feeling, I don't know how widespread a feeling it is, but I know some segment of _haoles_ that come to Hawaii . . . feel that, somehow, _they_ are the Americans and that somehow the other people are foreigners. That somehow, you know, the _haoles_ are the ones that really belong here and really know what is going on and _we_ will really tolerate these other people, in a sense. We're liberal people and we're going to tolerate them. What if they were born here? We say "Yeh, but their parents weren't, their parents came here." But where did _your_ parents come from? Oh, they came from Poland or some place. But _that_ is totally different. You know.

Discrimination had previously been brought to their attention, and had been reflected upon with liberal concern. They knew it to be immoral by theory alone. Its actual experience remained forever somebody else's, made meaningful only through literary and journalistic depictions. A mere semblance of its actual agony was derived, in remote fashion, from a contemplation of staged protests and other displays in the media and elsewhere. It was a disembodied idea disseminated anonymously. Unlike pain or frustration it had no personal referent. It was not understood in its immediacy but rather, through an intellectualized romantic passion, in its second order abstractions.

This was all to change. The previous abstract heroism of Caucasians was to be transformed into the blood and guts of the actual experience. Many Caucasians are aware of and comment upon the reversal of the mainland doctrines of inequality. They frequently admit to what amounts to a biblical retribution. They "now know what it is like to be black."

In the new culture the mainland migrant comes to engage in a set of symbolic dramas. Every culture has such dramas within the repertoire of its expressive and interpretive discourse. They are familiar to all who are culturally competent. What is new to the *haole* is a cast of characters. I am referring to certain rituals to which the newcomer is introduced and in which his or her involvement is inevitable. These are those rituals of inequality unique to the Hawaiian islands.

Rituals of Inequality

I have made the assertion that ethnicity is not a physical fact but rather is the product of a consciousness shaped to see it. It exists as a tradition of cultural ideas mapped onto a population. These ideas assert certain kinds of agreed-upon social facts, which then serve as a warrant for other things. Their use becomes routinized, repetitive, and invariant. They make of inequality an ongoing phenomenon and reinforce the use of the concept of ethnicity as its appropriate interpretation. Thus to recognize, for example, one's *haoleness* is to succumb to ethnicity.

The response of the newcomer seems to fall into recognizable modes of reaction. One notable mode arises out of the assumption that equality is missing because they themselves have not behaved in a manner appropriate to the new setting. It is as if the pluralism and the equality, the happy coexistence they once envisioned is not working because they personally have not correctly portrayed their intentions and their eagerness to get along peacefully. By adjusting their behavior to a perceived tacit requirement, they believe that pluralistic equality will emerge. In this ritual the desire for equality becomes the topic of a kind of street theater, observable in public places. A degree of visible humility is affected, sometimes even an embarrassing obsequiousness. It might involve repeated, and often unnecessary, smiling, excessive politeness, deference to members of other ethnic groups, and overt restraints on loud talking and laughing. It is a ritual of self-denegration. Consider one man's depiction of his own behavior:

> I have learned from seventeen years how to get along. It requires a degree of humbleness . . . The Japanese don't readily accept you in, unless you have excellent manners from their point of view, which means no loud talking, no talking too much, very, very formal and polite. You don't demand anything. You request it. It's very low key.

I have observed Caucasians adopting deferential postures with store clerks, librarians, and others, attitudes they would consider unthinkable and unnecessary on the mainland where more direct and confrontational styles are favored. At gatherings and on buses a studied facial openness is frequently assumed, along with an uncritical stance and a quiet self-abnegating body posture. It is as if a display of public unworthiness was the essential requirement for the attainment of equality. Others behave in ways which suggest that they see interactional incompetence on the part of the local population. They seem to assume that their own behavioral style is natural and normal and hence rightfully to be expected of all. While admitting that their own presence may have some inhibiting effects, that it might cause withdrawal and coldness on the part of certain members of the Hawaiian population, they appear to believe that they are in the position to correct these behavioral inadequacies. This can be done, they assume, by heavy interactional demands in relevant situations:

> I believe in kneading them down . . . I become tremendously jovial and outgoing, and I force them to smile. There are ways of making them. When you put in half an hour you sometimes get the kind of reaction you need.

The belief appears to be that equality is deposited in the superficialities of interaction. Thus, being on the surface, it is, to all intents and purposes, entirely malleable. The ritual of righting behavior is characteristically in keeping with the mainland ideology that openness and a faithful display of one's feelings and intentions are desirable. The central premise appears to be that abrasive encounters are curable by activating the appropriate parts of one's own repertoire of behavior. The belief is that balance and predictability in interaction, being presumably within the participant's control, produce the required sense of community and equality.

Another reaction appears to be studied self-reflection. Problems with other ethnic groups become interpreted as somehow the product of one's own essential character or beliefs. As they come under reflection and criticism these beliefs begin to appear as faulty, as nothing more than falsely protected ignorance.

> Up until I came here, I was a real all-American, crew-cut—you know—American flag, apple pie, George Washington is a good guy. I didn't think we Americans could do any wrong. Tears used to come to my eyes with the Star Spangled Banner—really! That was where my head was when I first came. I'd never formed my own values.

Others, more closely in touch with the liberal consciousness, saw in the reactions of the other ethnic groups the inevitable backlash to "crass American power and insensitivity abroad."

A more self-righteous response is that the Caucasian, in being forced into the position of *haole,* is not only denied some kind of rightful individualism, but is also the object of injustice and even plain un-Americanism. Any display of violence and discrimination is an affront to the principles of equality and an erosion of standards. This is treated as curable, given a conversion to right-thinking and proper behavior. Nevertheless this apparent injustice is viewed as marking the demise of any euphemistic sentiment about ethnicity in Hawaii:

> The below-the-surface hatred—you know, all this malarky about this is the greatest melting pot, and all the races get together—this is strictly hokum dreamed up by emotional people, and easy bleeders, and all that bunch, and exploited by the Visitors' Bureau and big business. But the underground hatred here is the worst of any place in America, I think. On the mainland, it's expressed openly, here it's hidden. But the hatred here is much more intense. Well, on the street, they try to run me down into the curb, coming alongside and yelling "Get out of the way, you God damn *haole.*" Something ought to be done about it.

While there is no doubt that the response of some is that they do indeed live in an ethnic paradise, others just as fervently believe that ethnic confrontation is an inevitable part of life. They accept their position with ritualized resignation. Rather than seeing ethnicity as irrelevant and the rituals of attempted equality as its necessary corollary, they embrace inequality as the only healthy thing to do. They reason that they merely occupy another ethnic or racial niche, different only in its superficial qualities, with a new set of enemies and a new type of inhibition. Separatism is for them a way of life, inequality a predetermined human characteristic.

Unequal Ritual Partners: Adversaries

Experiences of powerlessness, repeated often enough, lead to understandings about how and, indeed, when they happen. Discrimination, to the Western mind, has to have perpetrators, and perpetrators are surely discoverable. Thus the knowledge that white migrants come to have is that two kinds of events threaten their comfort, and even their freedom. One is acts of violence, the other is acts of exclusion. The former are seen as directed toward white people, who serve as scapegoats for impotent rage translated into naked aggression.

> To keep the heat off whomever, everyone in Hawaii is letting the *haoles* take the brunt of social ills in my opinion. When they get built up into uneducated, unhappy people . . . those continuous negative dealings about a group called the *haoles* sounds like it's O.K. to hurt them. Especially true of the tourist, who is a nonentity. He is not someone you're going to see again. He's just another face in a crowded, crowded world and a crowded community.

The violence the *haoles* fear, the cases they read about in the newspapers, the beatings that are meted out to white enlisted men in the military, seem to come from a particular direction. The word they usually employ to describe the perpetrators is "locals." This is an intriguing category, which at some times seems to narrow to include a particular selection of ethnic origins, and at other times seems to expand to include anyone who resides in Hawaii. For some, however, the term encompasses all ethnic origins with the exception of *haoles*. This does not mean, however, that whites do not sometimes report being referred to as "local," an occurrence which they usually view with some satisfaction.

> I got up to the cashier and found I didn't have enough money to pay for the meal. "It's O.K.," she said, "you look like a local boy. I can trust you. Bring me the rest to-morrow." I felt really proud.

Thus the term "local" is both a reward and a deprivation. It acknowledges those native or belonging to the Islands and is widely used to deprive Caucasians of that cherished status (DiBianco 1980; Yamamoto 1979).

In recent years the Caucasians have grown increasingly more aware of frustrations and aggressions directed toward them by members of this ethnic category. They describe the category "local" as consisting of young people and if pressed they will supply vague ethnic derivations. Anyone with Hawaiian experience is uncomfortable with trying to supply definite ethnicity beyond "local." Some will offer the designation "Hawaiian," or will list some ethnic mixtures. In most descriptions the "locals" do not seem to include either Oriental or white islanders. Even when there is vague talk about an "ethnic mix," about Filipino, Hawaiian, Portuguese, and other origins, it is usually accompanied by an avowed reluctance to indulge in that kind of specification.

The seriousness of these fears of violence, their presumed origins and their apparent lack of premeditation is frequently a subject of comment. Some even see the fear as something white people create for themselves out of their relative ignorance:

> I've never found violence against us *haoles*. People tend to simplify. It's very easy to distinguish between a *haole* and an Oriental and if something happens between Orientals or "locals" . . . if you can't tell the difference between Japanese, Chinese, Korean, Samoan, Hawaiian—they're all Orientals or locals or something, you don't see it as an ethnic thing. But if a *haole* gets beaten up, then the *haole* is being picked on. I don't think there really is a widespread thing . . . I do think there is a long-standing thing between Hawaii-

ans and Samoans. If in a bar there's a group of Hawaiians and Samoans . . . oh, oh, look out, something's going to happen.

Others point with earnest conviction to rituals like "kill *haole* day" in the Hawaiian schools and ask whether this is not a very obvious example of prejudice or violence. Some indicate that on these days, when the hazing and badgering of white students is formalized, they keep their children home in order to avoid physical or psychological harm.

Acts of exclusion are more prevalent, however. The perpetrators are more readily identifiable. Most Caucasians report that confrontations with the Japanese range from benign and affable to cold and malicious. The usual accusations made by *haoles* are that the Japanese are exclusively committed to their own ethnic group, that they run the government of the Islands and noticeably exclude whites, that they dominate certain professions (such as dentistry), that they discriminate in hiring and renting and that they live completely separate social lives. The following effusive comments by a woman brought to my attention the fact that, despite her enthusiasm, there was another side to the Oriental encounter:

> Some of the local people are *so* nice, you could just kiss them. Some of the little Japanese and Chinese ladies, and some of the men, are just darling . . . *But* . . . some of them are cold.

Some of the encounters with the Japanese have been so significant, and are obviously so central to the work arena and everyday middle-class life, that most *haoles* have had many occasions to reflect upon the nature of those confrontations. Dealing with the Japanese was seen as being a problem for whites in general, and it was believed that only a small proportion of Caucasians enjoyed good relations with them.

> The only people who don't complain about the Japanese are middle-class housewives and those whose work doesn't have any contact with them.

Japanese-white relations are often labeled a "communication problem." This definition has the effect of diffusing the blame to a much less malignant source than sheer premeditated prejudice. In the work setting such problems typically manifest themselves in the following ways:

A response from a person just arrived is that the Japanese are not listening, or that they're not responding. They don't respond like we respond. They're very low key. They may not even acknowledge you. You find yourself saying "now, you understand what I mean?" Of course. They have all along. There are—just in the communication—there are still barriers. The Japanese still feel that we're barbarians.

Others indicate that it is difficult, especially in executive positions, to gauge the effects of transactions, or the intentions and thoughts of Japanese businessmen. They imply that the usual cues of whether approval is forthcoming, whether doubts exist, whether matters are proceeding satisfactorily—all the necessary interactionally produced knowledge—are missing. Hence the person doubts whether a move is a correct one, what a worthwhile suggestion would be, and the entire business procedure is rendered uncertain. Others comment on the elusive subtleties of having to save "face," when this is peripheral to the business at hand.

Others complain about the difficulties of having to suspend blame when poor decisions are made, and about the necessity to dilute decisions and mute group interaction. This apparent diffusing and sharing of decisions and responsibilities comes to be seen as deflating by those who have been socialized to more forthright mainland styles.[4]

If anything goes wrong, then no one is to blame. The decisions are so diluted. I found that very ego-deflating after a while. For God's sake! *I* made the decision, and if it gets screwed up *I* want to take the blame. I couldn't stand it any more, and then I left.

Beyond the "communication problem" whites complain about what they see as a Japanese hegemony. They readily point out that the "Japanese run the state government" and follow up this assertion with the name of the governor and the names of Japanese senators and congressmen. They believe that there are distinct difficulties not only for Caucasians aspiring to elected office, but even for those attempting to attain government, managerial, and clerical positions.[5] They define this as a matter of discrimination. Some even suggest that this is a Japanese attempt to take over the Islands completely. State officials themselves note that the imbalance results from past discrimination when the only jobs available to the

Japanese were positions within the government. The following man sees a powerful hegemony where the Caucasian in Hawaii is reduced to the status of the black man in the American south:

> The Orientals run the government, they run all the professions, they run the school system, they run this place. You want a hand out? Keep your mouth shut and be a good boy. That's the way it works. No one wants to call attention to this. It's like where I come from—the South. It's basically like this: "Nigger, you wanna live here? You keep your mouth shut." "Yessuh! You got any work for me today?"

As indicated most *haoles* also cite their own underrepresentation in the professions. They mention, in particular, education, and, in more recent years, dentistry.[6]

Many Caucasians note that there is an abrasive quality to much of the interaction that occurs between themselves and Hawaiians of Japanese ancestry. With their usual conviction about their own affability and approachability, they assume that the aloof Japanese response is occasioned by their own inescapable whiteness. Others are quick to add that they believe that the aloofness is probably also directed at other ethnic groups, although on the whole they are not completely convinced about this. Each Caucasian has some incident which, in his or her eyes, is paradigmatic of the relationship. Some mention coldness in the unavoidable contact in the round of daily life. They note that they are the last to be served, or that they are given a chilly reception, whereas other customers receive warmth and conviviality. In large work organizations Caucasian executives complain that Japanese typists have subtle ways of relegating their work to a staff member with lower status, or providing just the bare minimum in secretarial help. In friendship circles most whites admit that, while they may have multiethnic friends and are obviously proud of this accomplishment, the Japanese remain aloof, "clannish," and live in separate social worlds. Often those who claim to have Japanese friends, when the quality of the friendship is questioned, admit that the friendship exists only at the work place, that there is no visiting at each other's homes, or that it is, in some other way, a superficial friendship.

During the last half decade in Hawaii there has emerged toward Caucasians in particular the kind of tokenism that is so much a part of mainland life. The notion of "token white" formalizes the awareness of discrimination and signals some sense of responsibility on the part of the discriminators. It serves as a public declaration that discrimination actually exists. Caucasians often observe that in many places of work the *haole* is becoming like the "token black." Others noted that their continued employment seemed to rest more on their being the only white person in the establishment than on their particular skills. Obviously this denigration is considered a good cause for grievance. The words "reverse discrimination" are sometimes used to explain whites being underrepresented in places of work, where hiring policies seemed to favor other ethnic groups. "Reverse discrimination" is yet another product of the mainland liberal consciousness, and richly associated in their minds with mainland policies and employment practices.

Occasionally *haoles* note that the rituals of inequality to which they are exposed are particularly malignant. They tend to measure their own positions in ways classically produced by the Western world, namely comparing one's position to someone else's. "The *haole* has sunk to the level of the Filipino," opined one man with some bitterness. "He's fighting to be the last man on the totem pole." Others suggest that the ethnic discomfort sustained by mainland Caucasians is the prime reason for the increasing numbers returning to the mainland. A few use military imagery by observing that in order to survive many *haoles* are retreating to their strongholds at Kahala and Punahou.[7]

Thus discrimination stories develop adversaries. Even those who claim to have had no experience with discrimination and who continue to be fervent supporters of the American dream of separate but equal admit that there are a few "complainers and grumblers, and others unhappy with not being top dog." Knowledge about discrimination, if not direct experience of it, is widespread in the white community. The *haole*'s cherished ideology of separate but equal can only be sustained if the supposed equality is not challenged. When it is challenged, the Caucasians tend to analyze the threat in the form of ethnicity. Although economic pressures, competitive menaces, ominous deprivations, and the like are viable candidates for blame, the quickest response seems to be to isolate ethnicity, to group people accordingly, and to hold them responsible. This is not some kind of nasty quirk in Caucasian characters, but a culturally constituted way of accounting for various ills. Ethnicity, once again, seems to be the available resource. It allows for the emergence of a clear group of adversaries. The presence of human antagonists makes it possible to understand the cause more systematically, more intimately, and to plan one's response more knowingly. This kind of analysis comes as knowledge already at hand and already widely in use.

Organization of Stigma: Taxonomies and Stereotypes

The Caucasian quickly identifies major adversaries. Having done so, he or she discovers a principle, namely ethnicity, for isolating and classifying all. One can no longer be impartial, even euphemistically, but must be committed to recognizing ethnic differences. These differences are continually refurbished through daily interactions. It merely takes a few occasions, a few unexplainable events, and the slightest suggestions to reinforce cultural notions of ethnicity.

Stereotypes are a mixture of morality and social history. They reveal how people in a culture theorize about others and how, over time, such knowledge becomes infused with notions of morality. It is an empty exercise to attempt to determine whether stereotypes are true or false. This is immaterial. The importance of stereotypes is that in societies with heterogeneity and gaping social distances, in plural worlds like Hawaii, they facilitate interaction. At the same time that they provide an agenda for interaction, they award stigma or praise according to the dictates of the current moral order. They have a simplicity which serves as a superficial sense-making device. They assure consistency and consensus in interactions where possibilities and identities are numerous. They have an exaggerated and simple-minded quality which, in a culture that admires individualism, is viewed as particularly degrading.

Taxonomizing according to ethnic origin is obvious enough, but what is much less quickly discernible is the plethora of images distributed among the ethnic groups. These images come in the form of tacit knowledge built into each inter-ethnic encounter. More visible taxonomies are embedded in ethnic slurs and in a wide variety of ethnic jokes.[8] The culture is particularly rich in such stereotypic knowledge and lore. It has been persuasively argued that one of the functions of stereotyping and joking is social control (Douglas 1968; Warren 1974; Goudy et al. 1977). While this is no doubt an apt analysis, I suggest that the activity in itself posits a morally acceptable world by dwelling on the inappropriate. Stereotypes and jokes carry a panorama of the culture's "oughts."

The moral imperatives and the moral critiques are most visible in the Hawaiian version of an old riddle. One version of the riddle goes this way: One day three men went fishing—a Portuguese, a Hawaiian, and a Chinese. The boak sank and all three drowned. Why did they drown? The Portuguese drowned because he would not close his mouth, the Chinese drowned because he would not let go of his gold, and the Hawaiian drowned because he was too lazy to swim. Other versions add other ethnic groups, each of whom also drowns. The Japanese man drowns because there is no one he can copy; the Filipino drowns because no one tells him what to do, and so on.

The Caucasians sense the weight of the stereotypes which operate against them. They are loud, arrogant, and dripping with money. There are notions that they are rather stupid in the work place and unable to do a good day's work. Several jokes portray the Caucasians' insensitivity to non-whites, their ignorance, and their uncritical view of their own behavior. One particular joke, with the punchline delivered by the member of another ethnic group, makes this clear. Twice I heard the joke told with the punchline being delivered by a Japanese person: Two Japanese women were waiting at the airport for two Caucasian friends to arrive from the mainland. When they saw them coming one of the Japanese went forward to shake hands. "Hello, Joan! Glad to see you." "I'm Cynthia," the white woman replied. The Japanese apologized, "I'm so sorry. You know, all Americans look alike." The other joke centers on the same theme, the Caucasian's insensitivity: A Japanese man and a *haole* were at the graveside of their loved ones. After putting a vase of beautiful flowers on his wife's grave the *haole* saw the Japanese man putting a bowl of rice on the grave he was visiting. The following exchange took place: *Haole:* "When do you think he's going to come up and eat the rice?" Japanese: "As soon as your wife comes up to smell her flowers!"

Another stereotype directed against the *haole* takes issue with arrogance as well as ignorance, noting that the *haole* is too proud to speak pidgin. Caucasians are uneasy using pidgin, and often indicate feeling excluded because they are unable or unwilling to speak it.

> Nothing turns me off faster than *haoles* speaking pidgin. Because it's faked. Because it's not an ethnic thing. They're faking an ethnic thing to be accepted. Also, the way they do it. To talk a language at a level lower than they're capable of, it's just an awful thing . . . I hate the way people was *pau*. I'm *pau*! . . . trying to make out as if they're one of them. I never, never use their language like that. I'd feel silly doing it. It just doesn't belong to me.

Others report that their efforts to talk pidgin often make local people angry, as they seem to think that their inability to speak perfect English is being mocked. All too frequently Caucasians tend to see pidgin as inaccurate, as demonstrating only partial competence in the English language. Few of them have the perspectives recently developed with regard to black language, namely that its nuances and multiple meanings make it as sophisticated as straight American English.

Haoleness has as much to do with place as with race, with culture as with biology. Consequently there is a peculiar *haoleness* about non-white ethnics from the mainland. Before the annexation of Hawaii, American blacks were referred to as *haole eleele* (Lind 1969:110), literally translatable as black foreigners. Unfortunately, it is the experience of many blacks, particularly the middle-class ones, who may have migrated from the mainland to what they believed to be a racial paradise, that prejudices seem to migrate with them. Some observe that not only are they subjected to a number of the negative stereotypes that North American culture gives blacks (Abe 1945), but they also seem to inherit some of the unfavorable responses reserved for *haoles*. Similarly, Japanese from the mainland are distinguished from those of Hawaiian birth by being endowed with some of the disliked *haoleness*. They are categorized as *kotonk*, declaring their exclusion from the Japanese culture of Hawaii (Ogawa 1973:16-17). The term begrudgingly attributes to them a biological Japanese identity, but withdraws full Japanese recognition and status on the basis of the inevitable taint of the mainland. The adjective *haolified* is applied pejoratively to any person, regardless of ethnic origin. This denies all *bona fide* biological claims to ethnicity, and, on the basis of acculturation, renders individuals socially unacceptable.

While naturally enough they are only remotely aware of the details of the images about their own kind, Caucasians have a fuller grasp of the stereotypes awarded to other ethnic groups. They quickly indicate that the Japanese are opaque, clannish, secretive, nonresponsive, and power-hungry. In addition, they are as responsive to the Japanese stereotypes listed by Ogawa (1971) as are other Americans. They view them as upwardly mobile, educated, intelligent, good citizens, quiet, shy, clean, puritan, arrogant, thrifty, humorless, sly, and persevering. In fact, the only riddle in wide currency about the Japanese seems to capture the stereotype recognized by whites: Why is a Japanese like a banana? Answer: He's yellow on the outside, white on the inside.

The stereotypes for native Hawaiians, in one way or another, highlight the lowly socioeconomic position to which they have fallen. Yet, despite the denigrated status, they are much revered as the "original Hawaiians," as people with dignity and tradition. An aphorism commonly heard about the Hawaiian Islands is: "The Chinese own it. The Japanese manage it. The *haoles* visit it. The Hawaiians remember it." Another Hawaiian stereotype, which seems to have persisted from colonial days, depicts them as unspoiled and good-humored, if lazy (Finney 1961-62).

Laziness and a lack of intelligence seem to be the central core of much joking. The numbskull joke so familiar in Western cultures has its own version in the Islands. In general in its wider usage the joke operates using categories of place, such as towns or villages, categories of occupation, racial origins, and so forth. It has been used as scarcely veiled insults between quarreling families, disputatious neighbors, rivalrous work places, and other alienated groups. In Hawaii, however, it is employed almost solely as an ethnic insult. The brunt of the numbskull joke most frequently falls on those in more lowly socioeconomic circumstances. Thus Portuguese, Filipinos, and Hawaiians are those most commonly featured. Sometimes this dubious distinction is awarded to Samoans, and on occasion, less believably, to the other ethnic groups. The whites receive their share, depending of course, on the ethnicity of the teller.

Jokes, poised as they are between insult and camaraderie, between hostility and laughter, often reveal grossly exaggerated forms of the stereotypes. In jokes, perhaps more than elsewhere, stereotypes are made public. The Chinese, as recipients of the mainland Jewish joke, become the ones whose most noticeable characteristic is their wiliness with money. This portrayal is often supported by the whites, who note that much Hawaiian money is in Chinese hands, that the Chinese are wealthy, or that the Chinese own "all of downtown Honolulu." Other than this prominent stereotyped characteristic, in the eyes of Caucasians, the Chinese are seen as benign and friendly, as sociable and desirable as marriage partners. Sometimes they are by implication lumped in with the category "Oriental," as presumably are Koreans and others such as Taiwanese and Okinawans, but they are not usually isolated as adversaries.

Less prominent in the Caucasian's cosmology of ethnic images are the Portuguese and Samoans. Most whites seem to think that the Portuguese are great talkers, for so all of the jokes and much of the other imagery seems to suggest, but on the whole they have an unclear picture of what a person of Portuguese ancestry looks like or how he or she can be expected to behave. There is some notion on the part of whites that people called "locals" or "part-Hawaiian" sometimes have Portuguese blood in their background. They are, however, very conscious of the fact that the Portuguese eschew Caucasian ethnicity. The Samoans, on the other hand, have a very forceful stereotype. In the simplest of descriptions, Samoans are seen as big and quarrelsome. In some white communities there are tales which caution one against tangling with a Samoan. For example:

I stopped at the intersection and waited for the light to change. Someone honked behind me. It made me mad, he had no business honking. Then, he actually got out of his car and came up to me. As soon as I saw how big he was and that he was a Samoan, I changed my tune. When he growled something about "what are you waiting for?" I smiled and apologized.

Usually these anecdotes are told as humorous tales, with the joke on the teller in the classical position of a weakling confronted by a vision of superior size and strength.

A culture rich in ethnic variability, Hawaii is also a culture rich in ethnic pejoratives. The language of ethnic slur[9] does much of the work of declaring either excessive social distance or a special social intimacy. As is always the case, when ethnic slurs are used by those whose position is at a great distance from one's own, they are interpreted in their full nastiness. When used by those who have claims to intimacy or friendship, trust and permitted indulgence, they can be seen as privileged teasing and not to be interpreted literally. Working in inter-ethnic settings, most *haoles* assiduously avoid trading on presumed friendships by using slurs as declarations of intimacy. This is a closeness they do not dare to claim.

I hear them saying to each other: "Hey, you gotta Portagee mouth," or calling the Filipino technician a "Manang"—I'm not sure what that means except I think it is a tribe in the Philippines, a tribe that is not too bright. *I'd* never, never use them. If I did it would be very insulting.

Academic Stereotyping

There is a further type of stereotyping that needs mentioning. It might be referred to as an academically condoned ethnicity. Not only have various scholars from most of the known disciplines turned their attention to plural societies such as Hawaii, but they have played a major role in constituting what is known, and what is "respectable knowledge." By evoking the notion of impartial science, or perhaps at best impartial observation, they have set forth a series of elucidations and analyses. The analyses come under the rubric of expertise and a neutral stance. In an epistemological sense the works are a study of the status quo. They have not addressed themselves to new ways of thinking about, or new ways of committing themselves to, the very issues they address. They have merely done their part to keep the discourse on ethnicity activated. Perhaps my own efforts are bound by the same culture of neutrality and noninvolvement. The truths represented by them and by me are the truths of common sense transformed from lay into professional imagery. Perhaps, after all, they merely formalize some aspect of the knowledge previously part of the public domain.

Through the culture that characterizes the social and psychological sciences a certain kind of knowledge is produced. Scholars have done comparative work. The issue of ethnicity has been illuminated by showing how ethnicity has been used to explain other phenomena. When ethnicity itself is not at issue, members of one's own ethnic group are described without reference to ethnicity. On the other hand, in discussing the same issues, as, for example, education or sporting skills, members of an ethnic group not one's own are described in ethnic terms. (Bochner and Ohsako 1977). Other scholars have given ethnic identity questionnaires comparing three Japanese age groups in Japan, Honolulu, and Seattle (Masuda et al. 1973), or have compared social distance preferences along racial lines among white college students in South Africa and Hawaii (Kinloch 1974), or have compared judgments of facial expressions by three ethnic groups (Vinacke 1949b).

Another topic in the area of ethnicity that has interested academic culture is intermarriage (Nagoshi 1954; Schmitt 1971; Leon 1975; Meredith and Ching 1977). This presumably speaks to the social distance between various groups. With regard to social distance in particular, specific attention has been directed to the relationship of the two major ethnic groups, the Caucasians and the Japanese. The nature of their interaction has been studied (Bean 1954; Johnson and Johnson 1975). Interpersonal needs have been the subject of the focus (Meredith 1976) as has been the Caucasians' changing conception of the Japanese (Glick 1950). Samuels (1969, 1970), in particular, has devoted considerable attention to the issue.

Yet other academics have addressed the matter of stereotypes *qua* stereotypes—elucidating, quantifying, and documenting (Vinacke 1949a; Kurokawa 1971; Kinloch and Borders 1972). Both the observable characteristics and the content of the stereotypes are explored and analyzed. An example of this is the work on Japanese enterprise and achievement (Yamamoto and Mamoru 1974; Connor 1976), Japanese verbal behavior (Johnson et al. 1974), the high rate of Japanese suicides (Ibrahim et al. 1977), racial block voting (Lind 1957), and landlord preferences (Ball and Yamamura 1960).

The culture of academe turns the ethnic experience of Hawaii into a specific set of images. These images, like all images, reproduce the culture of the producer. In some sense they seem to decide *what is there*. As they come out of this particular culture the images of the last few decades are familiar, for they have entered the public discourse or, perhaps one could argue, have been derived from that discourse. They also liberally suffuse themselves throughout my own efforts. The ethnic imagery of academe is discernible in the following language: ethnocentrism, social distance preference and scales, race relations, friendship patterns, ethnic discrimination, racial codes, interactional, interpersonal and interracial attitudes, ethnic identity, and so on. These words come to speak a particular kind of truth, the truth of the academician and social scientist. Indeed, one could look at these academically built versions of ethnic difference and at the part they play in the organization of stigma. They might be seen as an inevitable Americanization, if not an intellectualization, of the issue. Perhaps, to put it more generously, they are an attempt at a universal culture, a culture in the name of a unifying science.

Theorizing, Cultural Reasoning and Negotiation of Guilt

Discrimination, stigma, stereotyping, and social distance go against the liberal grain. Stereotyping offends the sanctity of the individual, discrimination and stigma insult the doctrine of human rights, and excessive social distance is downright uncomfortable. Surely nobody deserves this seemingly irrational treatment. Its immediate implication is that either the offender, or those offended, are acting immorally, or if not that, then irrationally. Of course, race, color, or ethnic origin have long been declared immoral reasons for prejudice. Reluctant to believe that "mere" ethnicity, or worse, that peevishness or evil is the "real" reason for prejudice, the *haoles* try to find more adequate answers. They seem to believe that one is the cause of one's own suffering. Yet they feel innocent enough, as they expend considerable energy in putting rationality where for them only irrationality seems to exist. Out of their well-endowed liberal consciousness, they produce justifications. To find ritualistic enemies on the Hawaiian scene is easy enough. However, with typical liberal self-reflection, they try to understand and explain how they themselves could be the enemy.

Hence their theorizing is peculiarly mainland American. It is forged by puritanism and social responsibility, by the scientific imperative to find causes and origins, and by the compulsion to uncover evils and set them right. The theories reverberate with widely held academic analyses, a shared cultural reasoning, which appears in current scholarly tomes, as well as on the lips of the man or woman on the street. What makes the reasoning cultural is that it portrays what is considered an adequate analysis, a proper account, a persuasive argument, and indeed, what items of available knowledge are appropriate (Whittaker 1981b).[10]

These accounts are probably the closest we can come to what might be agreed upon as truths about discrimination. That there are many of these truths, just as there are many explanations, poses difficulties. But it was always so. Not only are there many possible cultural truths, but what makes it even more uncomfortable is that there is no authoritative indication of which might be the "correct" one, or even which might garner the most consensus.

What is the moral script that is brought to play? What are these theories that award rationality to the apparently irrational? They come in great variety, some contrary to each other, some obviously part of the same notions. The work they appear to do is to provide a sensible frame, a reasoning principle, which will continue to be useful in all cases and will always assure consistency of explanation. Further, they do the work so important to our moral consciousness, they award blame. Our thinking seems to be that if the blame can be given, the culprits isolated, then right will out. Western societies depend upon this notion. Finally, reasoning gives the comfort that only sense (as opposed to no sense, or nonsense), can give.

A common form of theorizing is that the reason for present-day prejudice is *historical.* The ghosts of Captain Cook, the early missionaries (if not their descendants), the early and late entrepreneurs, the perpetrators of annexation, and the strategists of World War II are paraded forth as having acted immorally and thus "naturally" having brought about the present situation. These were white people and their deeds were white deeds. Different historical events and persons are called forth to account for different kinds of discrimination. Discrimination against whites by the Japanese is explained in terms of World War II and the misery inflicted upon Japanese Americans both during and after the war. This is a well-recognized guilt on the mainland, as well as in Hawaii. Prejudice toward whites on the part of Hawaiians is accounted for by the beginnings of colonial domination and the continuing and deepening cultural and economic annexation. The taking of Hawaiian lands and the reducing of the native Hawaiian to the bottom of the ladder in his or her own land are seen as inevitably resulting in a deep resentment toward non-Hawaiians. With the other ethnic groups the historical roots of prejudice are said to center around the introduction of contract labor and the consequent decades-long subjugation of the peoples either on plantations or in rural locales.

The interesting aspect of the historical argument is that although it recognizes whites as deserving culprits, it adds an interesting twist. It posits the implication that blaming present-day individuals for acts committed by others in the past is neither just nor sensible. It suggests that shared skin color or geographical origin are not adequate reasons for delegating blame. In putting forth the historical reasoning some whites will even add that they have "no connection with those people a hundred years ago." In the following a man produces the classical argument and reflects, somewhat cynically, on his right not to be judged on the basis of the past.

When you go back in history . . . there's this deep-seated feeling that *haoles* have been at the root of every supposed evil that's ever happened to Hawaii. First of all Captain Cook founded the place. He should have left it alone. We'd have been a lot better off. Then the missionaries came. They screwed things all over. The U.S. government overthrew a sovereign monarchy and took over the state. It was all a bunch of conspiracy. It was the *haoles* that did it. The land was taken away by the *haoles*. The *haoles* have all the money, the *haoles* have all the jobs. The *haoles* live in Kahala. The "locals" live in Kalihi. I guess it all depends on how thick your skin is, in a sense, as to whether you feel *you* should bear some guilt for, maybe, what somebody did 200 years ago. More *haoles* are hated, because they are *haoles*. Stereotyping is what we have here.

In a sense this argument is ultimately diplomatic. It acknowledges the rightness of the prejudice while at the same time absolving the guilt of those who receive it. By neutralizing historical responsibility and by nullifying the ethnic connection, the *real* reason is placed on matters that are known to be inappropriate to present-day Hawaii. These inappropriate matters are, of course, events that happened so long ago that to force them to figure in present analysis can only be seen as willfully vindictive.

   Another equally common way of accounting for prejudice is manifested in the *scapegoating* theory. This theory states that all the social ills that plague a population build up into an unbearable tension which must be released. The most "natural" place to release this tension is against some person or group. This perspective is widely supported and fully documented in authorative, socio-psychological literature. The whites in Hawaii sometimes reason that because they are visible due to their whiteness and are seen as being in positions of power, they are the inevitable targets of the anger and frustration of the disadvantaged. Most of the acts of violence become transformed into "scapegoating" incidents. The theory has a strong "it's human nature" component to it. It inevitably makes of the whites hapless, innocent victims, once again in an unhappy position because of their color and simply because they are energetic and enterprising. The perpetrators of scapegoating become unthinking, uneducated, cloddish, and brutal. They are saved from being thoroughly evil only by another common reasoning gambit from Western cultures which suggests that they are brutal because "they really cannot help it" or that "society has done this to them." Scapegoating invariably explains the actions of those lower on the socioeconomic scale rather than the actions of economic competitors or those obviously in positions of power. Thus, generally, prejudice on the part of the Japanese is not seen as scapegoating. On the other hand, acts instigated by "tough locals" are seen as acts of frustration and scapegoating. A man who declares a loss of freedom in Hawaii because of prejudice, states a routine version of the scapegoating theory:

> . . . a bit of history that everyone buys about Caucasians responsible for all the social ills. Everyone gets on the bandwagon. Except the bandwagon they're on is that Caucasians are no good. Being one, I know. It's dangerous and people are dying as a result of it. You go back through the newspapers and show me one Japanese boy who's been killed in the last two years in a violent death. I'll give you fifty dollars. Caucasians can be singled out easily because of their skin. And because of this general community-wide put down of Caucasians which is fueled into vicious hate by people who haven't got a chance. They come from lousy home lives. They have no chance for economic survival. They're full of hatred and so this constant "damn *haoles*, damn *haoles*" . . . they sort of think—gee, even my peers think it's OK to take out frustrations on them.

Close to the scapegoating theory is the *basic human nature* theory. This argues that there is some kind of universal human nature and some kind of universals in the human condition. Some will have advantages and others will not. "The have and the have nots" is often put forth as an explanation for violence and prejudice. The dominant assumption is that this conflict is so basic to humankind that it is found in all cultures. Like its scapegoating version there is an almost mechanical imagery of the need to release built-up tension. It is as if humans were inelastic containers ready to explode. Indeed, the words "let off steam" are frequently applied. Much of the theorizing of the academic community (Freud is a case in point) is built on this kind of imagery.

By decreeing its basic properties, by implying that as humans we are all heir to them, the matter of blame is again diffused. Obviously one cannot push guilt onto the underprivileged and angry, for their anger and violence seems "natural" enough given the circumstances. If blame is to be given, theoretically at least, it should be given to those who presumably could do something about the state of affairs. Some Caucasians extend the blame to the "real" culprits, such as governments, peace-keeping institutions, and schools, which should be doing their job of isolating delinquents. Not surprisingly, the penal system, welfare workers, absent parental authority, and any number of well-known culprits are also implicated.

A theory commonly produced by those who take a more charitable view of the situation is a form of the familiar "personality clash" explanation. It is translated into what we in anthropology would call _culture and personality_. The notion is that personality is culturally determined. The reasoning is that a communication problem exists where various ethnic groups talk past each other, cannot understand each other, and hence naturally feel some alienation and prejudice. Therefore the blame cannot be placed on the individual. The individual is an innocent receptor who is invested with certain characteristics that lie beyond his or her choice. Hence social forces, culture, environment, and so on determine the differences in personality that account for interpersonal friction. The individual is again absolved of responsibility.

What may be called the _backlash_ theory argues that there are social inevitabilities to hegemony. Thus, as the existing white hegemony wanes a negative backlash against all Caucasians is inevitable. The assumption is that in the natural order of things, hegemonies cannot continue and must eventually experience strong reaction. In other words there are deep historical processes which determine the inevitability of events and this has essentially very little to do with individuals, societies, policies, or any consciously constructed events. It is a fated turning of events, the only possible end to more than a century of privilege and power. The reasoning usually appears in the following form:

> Well, it is bound to happen. We have controlled things long enough. We really have it coming. The whites have been _it_, and now they no longer are. Of course they [Hawaiians] dislike us . . . and now other groups, like the Japanese, have come to take our place.

Finally, the most prevalent of all theories is one that appears in a variety of forms. It could be called _deserved prejudice_.

It is the theory that argues that prejudice is rational after all. If one examined the behavior of whites and their arrogance, greed, and stupidity, one would have to conclude that the prejudice levied against them is deserved. The liberal consciousness of the mid-twentieth century is revealed in all its propensity for self-criticism and guilt. The theory is reflected by the claim of many Caucasians that they are often ashamed of their own kind:

> I've become, in a sense, anti-*haole*. I'm very much against my own culture for what it is . . . I've stopped trying to help newcomers. "Oh, you've just arrived? When are you going to leave?"

Others reveal their intense embarrassment with the brash or arrogant behavior of others from the mainland. Particularly irksome are the unwritten assumptions of other *haoles* that good things exist on the mainland and that the people of Hawaii are essentially backward. Embarrassment with mainland ignorance is revealed by a young mother:

> My father still thinks we're living in grass shacks. He's never come out. When Douglas was born, he wanted him flown to the West Coast immediately. He doesn't believe there are doctors here. In fact, when I told him who the baby's cardiologist was, that his name was Gerald Muramoto, he was just floored. He had him checked out because he was worried that the child would not have the proper care . . . Found out that he was highly respected all the way across the country. He graduated from Harvard Med School, did his internship at Columbia, he did his residency at Boston Childrens', and did his cardiology at Yale. Respected all over the mainland and he is written here for his opinions. When Daddy found this out, his image improved considerably, but he said "I can't understand why a doctor like that is living in Honolulu." I said "Daddy, he's Japanese. His family for several generations has been living here by *choice,* not because he couldn't get a job elsewhere."

Others cite cases of Caucasians who have lived in the Islands for a considerable numbers of years, even decades, and cannot pronounce Hawaiian names, have no friends other than *haoles,* have no interest in, or knowledge about, Hawaiian tradition. They still do not know what *mauka, ewa, makai* or *koko* mean. Obviously the appropriate commitment and involvement are not there.

Many note what they consider to be uncouth behavior by other *haoles* as another source of painful embarrassment. Loud talking, disrespect for island customs and people, and sheer greed are often cited:

> Recently we were setting up an art exhibit down at the shopping center here. We were putting on this fantastic spread of food. And along came a couple of guys . . . packs on their backs, just arrived, and looking at this. "Hey, wow, man, look at this." And already people were looking at them and thinking "Oh, no!" Then they say in loud, brash tones "What's all the food for?" Then someone replied that it was for an art show. And, then, because it's the way to be, added, "Take some if you like." "*Really? Wow*!!!" And they walk over and start taking food, they really start digging in . . . Because there are so many cultures here, you have to learn that just because you're told to take something, you don't always do it, or you do it in as much moderation as possible. They were just slobbering away.

In the counterculture era of the early seventies and late sixties such behavior was particularly observable. Members of the counterculture complained about those of their own kind who came and, in uncouth ways, "exploited," "took advantage of," and generally made themselves objectionable to the local people. "You offer them a banana, and they take five bunches."

This reasoning asserts that not only is the prejudice against Caucasians plausible, but it is even moral and properly deserved. The fact that prejudice exists should not be cause for surprise. White people, after all, are objectionable. Like all of the various forms of reasoning, this particular one does the same work of negotiating guilt. By admitting and even embracing guilt, another ethic is relied upon, namely that admission of guilt is itself a kind of absolution. One should not continue to punish those who have already admitted their guilt and are punishing themselves.

The reasoning produced by Caucasians could be seen as part of a struggle to deal with the threats to what is seen as a proper, and even an adequate, existence. While willing to take ethnicity seriously, they condemn as unjust the fact that it makes unequal demands and distributes unequal benefits. Ethnicity may indeed be the metaphor that makes the Hawaiian puzzle knowable, but it is not acceptable if it results in immoral behavior.

Ethnicity as *Lingua Franca*

Cultural accounts are informed by a mass of common knowledge passed from person to person and recommended for being the valid, usable, and somehow "real" reason for the plight of the *haole*. Whiteness, and in particular whiteness that still bears a mainland taint, is enough to account for what come to be seen as *haole* troubles. There is a large body of accumulated knowledge built around the concept of ethnicity which accounts for what in some other culture may be merely bad fortune or the will of the gods. Snippy store clerks, secretaries who give one's work low priority, management passing one over for promotion, inability to be heard, not being hired or, conversely, being fired, and all the possible woes that plague the work front become experiences that are suffused with meaning when ethnicity is suggested as the inevitable *raison d'être*. So strongly is the culture suffused with this organizing principle that it is difficult to even describe the problem without identifying the protagonists in ethnic terms. Second, it is not possible to produce an analysis of the troubles without resorting to ethnicity as an analytic resource.

Perhaps just once again the mainland legacy which so carefully produced the ultimate of the liberal doctrine—ethnic pluralism—determines the ethnic Hawaii. Perhaps the only way to write of culture is to assert that one can only experience what one can think. One can only think what one can think. Had the Western cultural hegemony been less determining for all the various cultures that have come together there, it would have been possible to glimpse alternatives. In my view ethnicity is the *lingua franca* of a place like Hawaii, an inescapable inevitable. Other possibilities are mere fantasies, hypothetical promises.

That other possibilities exist lies within the Caucasian purview. Indeed, many newcomers refuse to accept the readily available ethnic paradigm. Operating on some residual scientific imperative they attempt to test it out, to withhold judgment until it is inevitable, to vigorously disbelieve because it runs afoul of their liberal hopes. One man explains how he tested out what he had called the "Waimanalo wilderness:"

I remember hearing years ago about Waimanalo. They're all locals and they hate *haoles* out there. And, oh God, *never* go to a bar out there. We went for a drive around the island one day and decided to go into a bar there. What the hell, we thought. We had a couple of beers. We had a pleasant time, nobody said anything. Nobody stared. Nothing like that.

If ethnicity is then a kind of *lingua franca,* other questions crowd in. One sees very clearly the cultural hegemony of the West, the historical experience of the Western world with "other cultures" and "strange people." One cannot overlook the human imperative to translate these into sense, to make the world of strangeness come into focus as the world that, despite everything, is a familiar one after all. Ethnicity and all of its precursors, and anthropology itself, seem to provide some of the language of sense. The task of anthropology is inordinately demanding—to take that orderly madness somewhere out there beyond the walls of home and make it comfortably real and reliably orderly.

The matter of what is now called ethnicity has been addressed with such energy on all fronts. Many a historical account or overview attests to this. Such overviews affirm the searching and sweating and finally acknowledge the denouement reached in contemporary affairs. This is true of public policy as much as it is of anthropology (Cohen 1978). Anthropologists, in some sense the seekers after the ultimate *lingua franca,* the transformers extraordinaire, have as true agents of the Western world accepted ethnicity and bent their efforts to constructing it into reality, an unavoidable presence, and an integral part of our understandings. We have documented, accepted, and given ethnicity the ring of truth, contrary as it might be to our cherished ethos of equality and relativism. Despite some serious questions that have been raised about the notion and the attempts to direct our questing into the practices it produces (Moerman 1965; Barth 1969), we have continued in our support of this knowledge.

It might be futile to argue that anthropology merely confirms common sense, for surely that cannot be denied. But it goes further. It provides the material and the inevitable evidence for why it is so. This is much more than a question of whether ethnicity is a reality or a myth (Lieberman 1968). "Reality" smacks of scientism and myth smacks of "mere" belief, the implication being that it is somehow not real. We have accepted ethnicity as an entity, we have produced knowledge in its name, provided biological facts, and somehow accorded it approval in commonsense thinking. Whether we think of ethnicity as real in some God-given sense or merely as a sense-making tool, whether we think of pluralism as a paradox or an enrichment, we have given our efforts to documenting it. We have produced more and more of the kind of material, which in a culture such as ours constructs not only documents, but, more importantly, constructs those very entities that signal truth. We have fallen heir to our own scientism, the inescapable and perhaps even vigorous perspective of our own culture. We have accepted biology as true and inevitable and have churned out biological fact after biological fact. Had we heeded the lessons of linguistics and seen ethnicity as a language, or as a grammar, we might have contributed to it more of our unmistakable humanism and less of our deep preoccupation with fact. Had we seen ethnicity as an example of Western discourse, as a hermeneutic, we might have fared better as ultimate interpreters and might have saved ourselves from building and contributing knowledge that we will one day find as unsavory as we now do knowledge about race.

Many questions can be raised about a consciousness that produces ethnicity. Not only does it produce the notion itself, it also diffuses it throughout many parts of the world. Why is it convenient and inevitable that the Western mind has something called ethnicity as an ordering device? What power does it permit its creators to wield? What elusive or even nonexistent matters does it make possible, probable, and undeniable. It makes ethnics of people, on the one hand, giving freedom, and on the other, taking it away.

Perhaps an appraisal of ethnicity as an organizing code, as a sense-making device, as a *lingua franca* would suggest an analysis of it as a metaphor. Packed into the language of ethnicity and into the rituals it evokes are many structural devices and knowledge parameters. Within the Hawaiian context any reference to ethnic origin has a set of residual understandings which are immediately activated. This is the case whether the reference has an official cast, such as Japanese or Samoan, or whether it talks the language of ethnic slur. Naturally and most immediately it is a descriptor in more than a physical sense. As an inevitable contrast-pair it activates one's own ethnic affiliation and decrees recognized rituals and beliefs. Status and prestige, deference and unassailed rights are clearly implied. Just as quickly the interactional modes that must be adopted, that are usual or traditional, become evident. Layers of stereotypes rush in to facilitate the interaction. Accumulated knowledge from one's own ethnic group, amply supported by previous experience, act as everpresent guides to behavior. The social barometers, which filter and organize beliefs, sort out and make available relevant items of information.

Ethnicity then is a language, a sense-making agenda, and a way of viewing the world. It is an encounter that takes existing ideas, ideas with history and durability. It challenges and questions them, uses them in the troublesome matters of translating the imponderables, and leaves them changed.

The phenomenon of ethnicity is a mirror reflecting first the Western world, second the anthropologist or other documenter, and third, more by implication than anything else, the differences among the peoples of Hawaii. That it is a mirror built to prescription and colored by history seems to matter very little. It is an idea which seeks, successfully I might add, its own evidence. It is an idea supported by the photographed visages in books of authority and pamphlets of touristic temptation. It is visible and effective. Many a decision and many a policy are produced in its name. This very book, by its title and by the very people I have agreed, or more likely chosen to group together, is merely an example of the pervasiveness of the metaphor. It verifies once more the Western consciousness.

All told I can only return to my initial notion that a portrait of Hawaii is a portrait of Western consciousness. Hawaii is a place and a fantasy that European imperatives fashioned, its way of life a reflection of an imagination and a history conceived and fostered thousands of miles away. In this analysis, then, the turbulence of these islands becomes one between competing dogmas—cultures, we in anthropology have called them—each as doggedly convinced of its own moral rightness. From its first English or Spanish "discovery" to its thousands of more humble daily discoveries, Hawaii has become a testing place, or perhaps a resting place, for the Western idiom. The knowledge this produces, for which the *haole* is the perpetrator and I its scribe, suggests itself as one of many possible packages of knowledge. It is embodied in each *haole* person, an innocent enough traveler. When it is seen, as it frequently is, as a consciously motivated and Machiavellian presence, pulled by the strings of distant economic giants, its malignancies and scars are made obvious. Imbued with intent and personalized for ultimate effect, it is operated with malice and foresight by powerful absent landlords. The choice of dialectic, the inclination for one theory or another are matters of individual conscience, economic intention, or moral impulse. I take the stand that all these are within the possible, all in a sense embody their own morality. When one abandons the inner certainty and integrity of fact, one can only construct knowledge in answer to imperatives, public or private, moral or aesthetic.

Thus no doubt, in good time, other Hawaiis will emerge to join those already created, to add to this particular one fashioned jointly by the Caucasian presence and my documentation. It may speak of the minds and actions of other ethnic travelers, or the interests and claims of other translators. As I obviously do not believe that somewhere there, in the blue of the distant Pacific, there is the *real* Hawaii, yet to be discovered in a *true* sense, written about without the infinite number of prejudices possible, these writings can only make the proverbial contribution. They will attest to the existence of other minds and other Hawaiis, as distant in time and space from this one as human imagination and tradition will allow.

Notes

1. Dialectics of Enterprise, Hope, and History

1. The Cook expedition offered a careful phonetic record for the native words of some eleven islands apparently considered by the Hawaiians as part of their geographic domain: 1) Owyhee (the derivation of the word Hawaii); 2) Mowee (Maui); 3) Ranai, or Orania (Lanai); 4) Morotinnee or Morokinne (Molokini); 5) Kahowrowee or Rahoorowa (Kahoolawe); 6) Morotoi or Morokoi (Molokai); 7) Woahoo or Oahoo (Oahu); 8) Atooi, Atowi, or Towi, and sometimes, Kowi (Kauai); 9) Neehhehow or Oneeheow (Niihau); 10) Oreehoua or Reehoua (Lehua); and 11) Tahoora (Kaula). Of these only Molokini and Kaula were uninhabited. Moving westward on the Hawaiian archipelago, Nihoa, like Necker, was once occupied, as remnants of stone ceremonial platforms have been found there. The Hawaiians at the time of Cook probably visited them for the collection of feathers used in the making of cloaks for their chiefs. At present only Hawaii, Lanai, Molokai, Oahu, Maui, Kauai, and Niihau are inhabited.

The original record was made by Captain King, who, after the death of Cook on the third voyage, had assumed command. Cook's death, parenthetically, was an unfortunate happening resulting from a lack of understanding and adequate communication. He was slain on the island of Hawaii in a skirmish with the Hawaiians. It should be noted that the events leading up to this included the British insistence on defining certain native customs as "thieving," and in killing a few natives as indications of their determination to discourage it. In a manner horrifying to the British, the body was dismembered according to Hawaiian custom and, only upon the persistence of Captain King, were parts of it returned. The Hawaiians were apparently horrified that they were seen as cannibals, and wanted to know whether such an abhorrent custom was common among the British. Many years later, one of the missionary wives recalled meeting a man on the island of Hawaii, who, it was said, had eaten the heart of Cook thinking it belonged to a pig. It should also be noted, however, that, despite this reverse, the expedition departed some months later with the Hawaiian people restored to their initial image of friendliness, grace, and generosity in the eyes of the British.

The possibilities of cannibalism provide for an intriguing debate. There is certainly ample evidence provided by scholars (Dening 1978) for its existence, yet one cannot avoid considering the epistemological preferences of Western anthropologists and historians to construct certain kinds of knowledge and decide on certain interpretations. In a provocative piece of scholarship Arens (1978) finds no satisfactory first-hand account of the approval of this act in any part of the world. This raises again the ever-present question about whether anthropology studies "them" or "us."

2. Anthropology has developed an extensive literature on millenarian movements. A competent review of anthropological theorizing and empirical work is offered by Weston La Barre (1971). His article outlines the extensive terminology which the area has developed: adjustment movement, awakening, chiliasm, collective autism, cult movements, cultural renewal, eschatological movement, holy war, messianic movement, nativism, prophetism, rebellion, reformative movement, religious innovation, revitalization, revivalism, revolt, syncretism, visionary heresy, and others (1971:9). The term he prefers himself is "crisis cult." There are obvious connections, as yet to be explored by anthropology, among millenarianism, utopias, and paradise. Any such explication would multiply the literature many fold. What is even less consciously attended to by anthropologists is the relationship between cultural discontent and migration. It is this relationship that is addressed in this volume.

3. It is perhaps amusing and more indicative of the epistemological and cultural context which weaned anthropology to note that some of its adherents in the South Seas and other exotic climes have permitted themselves the indulgence of doing anthropology while at the same time speaking to Western curiosity: Malinowski's, *The Sexual Life of Savages* (1929); Mead's *Sex and Temperament* (1935); Danielsson's *Love in the South Seas* (1956); and Suggs' *Marquesan Sexual Behavior* (1966).

4. Information on names of deserters, the ships from which they came, and the amount of bail set is recorded in voluminous pages in the Archives of the State of Hawaii. Also available are the Honolulu Harbor Authority volumes listing all discharged sailors and the names of their ships. Similarly, records are available on embarking and disembarking passengers from all ships entering the harbor. With sufficient time and resources, one could construct a thoroughly documented portrait of *malihinis* coming to Honolulu, the length of their stay, and the dates and means of their departure, if departures did in fact occur. Only through such means as these could some respectable clues be provided on the shifting population brought to the islands, and the names of those who were destined to remain.

5. Italics are Fayerweather's. His correspondence provides documents of some value, especially as it appears to be preserved in relative completeness, covers several decades enabling longitudinal access to the world of an expatriate of the nineteenth century. In addition to the letters of missionaries, whose perspectives have made up much of what has become the early history of the Islands, the letters of Abraham Fayerweather are among the few archival documents written by men not in the public eye. The letters of the missionaries are available at the Hawaiian Mission Children's Society. The Hawaiian Historical Society provides further sources. Together they have provided data for the writing of many histories. The letters of Fayerweather, however, are a relatively recent acquisition by the Archives, and I am grateful to Agnes Conrad for bringing them to my attention soon after their arrival. They are presumably eventually destined for publication in a comprehensive volume chronicling the geographic mobility of a nineteenth-century American family.

6. Whether this amount is, or was, verifiable, or merely the sum arrived at by fertile gossip, is not disclosed in the letters. The archives, however, record Fayerweather's marriage to the part-Hawaiian daughter of an American sea captain. The eldest daughter of this union, Julia, is recorded as becoming the wife of Ah Fong, a wealthy Chinese merchant, credited with being "a millionaire" in the early years of this century. So perhaps while Fayerweather's own life may not have been favored with a "large fortune," it did happen to his progeny.

7. A complete breakdown of the occupations of foreigners: 50 carpenters and ships' carpenters; 32 clerks and bookkeepers; 22 merchants; 19 storekeepers; 17 hotel keepers and victuallers; 14 mariners; 11 government officials; 11 stewards; 10 masons; 10 printers; 9 missionaires or missionary agents; 8 tailors; 8 blacksmiths; 7 farmers; 7 teachers; 7 shoemakers; 7 foreign consuls or commissioners; 6 painters; 6 retail liquor dealers; 6 cabinet-makers; 6 warehousemen; 5 physicians; 5 graziers; 5 coopers; 4 bakers; 4 tinsmiths; 3 teamsters; 3 sailmakers; 3 barkeepers; 3 judges (1 Justice of the Peace); 3 cooks, 2 each of laborers, lawyers, watchmakers, barbers, saddlers, shipmasters, caulkers; and one brick-maker; boatbuilder, bookbinder, roadmaker, sexton, king's coachman, surveyor, pilot, butcher, auctioneer, and agent of the Hudson's Bay Company. The paper noted that, because of the transitory population, some one hundred names were missing (Greer 1970).

8. *Haole* originally meant merely "stranger." Yet, as it quickly became obvious that the majority of strangers were white, it came to refer to whites. As in the early days the term itself is neutral in intent and derogatory only in context or with a string of appropriate adjectives.

9. It is interesting to note that the Portuguese in the Islands are allocated to a different ethnic category than Caucasians. This socially perceived difference is revealed in interaction and even in officially produced demographic figures. The census figures of 1940 were the first to place the Portuguese with other Caucasians. Undoubtedly their classification as Portuguese rather than Caucasian is a function of their non-European home at the time of migration, the islands of Madeira and the Azores, their occupational association with non-Europeans, and perhaps their one-time status as contracted labor.

2. Discovering the *Haole:* The Grammar of the Fieldwork Encounter

1. It is in the work of symbolic interactionists on socialization that the processes which could be called "fieldwork" are most explicitly revealed. The work of Erving Goffman is perhaps most outstanding in this regard, in particular his classic ethnography of presentation of self to others (1959). Also of relevance in this genre of work is Strauss (1959), Berreman (1962), Becker et al. (1961), Olesen and Whittaker (1968).

2. There are some insightful writings of the fieldworker as stranger: Nash (1963); Daniels (1967); Meintel (1973). Further relevant works on strangers: Wood (1934); Simmel (1950); Schutz (1964).

3. There is a familiar old question in ethnography: How do we know the informant is telling the truth? This question plagued many fieldworkers for decades (Dean and Whyte 1958) and still continues to puzzle some. It is obviously a question arising out of a positivistic paradigm, now rendered meangingless by interpretive anthropology and symbolic interaction. The notion of realities constructed in interaction and knowledge produced in a particular context renders the notion of bias and untruth completely impotent.

4. I have since recognized that nonpositivism is liberating in its faithfulness to the people studied, in depicting correctly their world view. Yet, actually practiced it is often conservative and oriented to the status quo (McNall and Johnson 1975). No doubt it can be diverted to a more action-oriented social science. "I would hope to see the consensual ethos of anthropology move from a liberal humanism, defending the powerless, to a socialist humanism, confronting the powerful and seeking to transform the structure of power" (Hymes 1972:52; Richardson 1975:528).

5. These categories have a commonsensical nature. One can appreciate their significance in everyday sensemaking by looking at official application forms where person-

hood is understandable only in terms of answers to these categories."Hippie" was a relevant category when I began my work but has an antiquated charm now.

6. An analysis of various anthropological texts would most clearly reveal professional ideology by directing sensemaking either to taxonomic techniques used or holistic understandings considered necessary. It can be seen in an analysis of the dozens of volumes in the Case Studies of Cultural Anthropology published under the editorship of the Spindlers, sometimes known as "The Holt Rinehart Series." Another traditional perspective on ideology can be found in the Human Relations Area Files and in the normative catalogue now in its sixth edition, *Notes and Queries in Anthropology* (1967). They seem to reveal generalization, comparability, relativism, and holism as being the sacred doctrines of anthropology.

7. The obvious parallels to this fieldwork "method" are the many studies of urban social networks. Whitten and Wolfe indicate that this is "a trend away from concepts implying relatively static cultural patterns or fixed social institutions and toward concepts implying adaptation and adaptability" (1973:717). Also relevant are Mitchell (1969); Bott (1957); Aronson (1970), among many others.

8. This particular example obviously derives from my fieldwork in the early 1970s during the conscription for the Vietnamese war. At this time many draft resisters found their way to Hawaii and many, like this young man, found temporary homes in isolated rural communes, remote villages, or even on beaches and in the hills.

3. The Migration Story: Organizing the Past

1. The reverse side of the coin in official statistics is equally interesting. The 1970 census showed 179,735 persons of Hawaiian birth (ethnic stock unknown) and surprisingly an almost equal number of persons born on the mainland and now living in Hawaii, 178,531 persons (Schmitt 1977:90). The census also reveals that 112,443 now living in Hawaii were living on the mainland five years earlier (Schmitt 1977:96). These figures suggest the coming and going rate of white mainlanders and not the back and forth movement of other ethnic groups.

2. The explanation for the drop in the numbers of people migrating in to Hawaii since 1977 is given by the Department of Planning and Economic Development (DPED) as reflecting "differential nonresponse resulting from questionnaire revision . . . A redesigned survey form was introduced in July 1978, and there is evidence that it resulted in a seriously reduced rate of response for intended residents. The survey form was further modified during the summer of 1979, but the response rate has apparently never returned to its earlier levels" (DPED 1982:1). The figures for those intending to reside in Hawaii read: for 1977, 18,485 civilians (plus 25,132 military); for 1978, 15,399 civilians (plus 24,077 military); for 1979, 12,577 civilians (plus 9,982 military); for 1980, 3,266 civilians (plus 10,656 military); for 1981, 3,459 civilians (plus 14,675 military) (DPED 1982: table 1).

3. Another version of this tension between mainland control and Hawaiian context, a kind of metropolis-hinterland relationship for the military, occurred during the period (1941–1946) when Hawaiian civil affairs were under military control (Anthony 1955).

4. Perhaps one of the more interesting reflections of such cultural assumptions is one which poses one cultural biographical codification against another. In putting the autobiographical account of a Cebuano Filipino man into text, Hart (1956) distinguishes the narrative supplied by his informant from the additions and elaborations that resulted from his own questions, which of course were destined to ensure the construction of an autobiography on a Western model. Schwalm (1980) and Gilmore (1978) make clear the features of cultural monuments inherent in biography and eulogy respectively.

5. It is important to indicate that these comments from a professional man were collected in 1971. Clearly, while the same imagery would reoccur in 1983, its descriptive details would pay more attention to the demands developed by both the women's movement and the Hawaiian national movement. It is very unlikely that at the present time he would talk about "girls" or even "chicks," at least given his age, namely the early thirties, and moreover in conversation with a female academic! He would also be very careful with his notions of "white man power." Even in 1971 his talk of white supremacy indicated his unacculturated status. He had actually been in Hawaii a mere two months. He obviously was unaware of the nationalistic tenor of Island life and intended the remark on white man power to provoke quiet amusement at his own expense.

6. Perhaps the most striking story of a life crisis was recorded by Thomson MacCallum (1934), and retold by Gavan Daws (1978:299). Its central figure was encountered by MacCallum in Samoa as a fellow employee in a trading firm. The tale had epic proportions, apocryphal dimensions, and the flavor of classic Greek tragedy. The man involved was known as "His Lordship," a title matched by his aristocratic bearing and monocled appearance. He claimed to be of high birth, rendered unfortunate by the coming together of a titled father and a barmaid mother. This union had been engineered by a wicked paternal grandfather, and on gaining manhood "His Lordship" was bent on revenge. He presented himself as a gentleman and seduced the old man's ward, a duchess. He revenged himself by impregnating the young woman. His own punishment came in the form of then falling in love with her. She, as bad luck would have it, had been promised to a prince. The seducer naturally felt himself under a curse and left to wander the world, feeling worthless. Because of his sense of honor, he felt he was forever unable to marry and have children. He reached Samoa. By fortuitous circumstance he was offered an adopted daughter by a dying trader. He refused. After explaining his refusal, he discovered to his amazement that the adopted daughter was his own child by the duchess. Presumably the duchess had confessed to her husband who had sent the child to distant relatives, who, as one would guess, turned out to be the dying trader in Samoa. Father and daughter were united, returned to England to find the prince dead and the duchess still willing to marry the early claimant of her virtue. Naturally the Victorian tale ended with the promise that they lived happily ever after. Daws uses the story to draw out an ever-present phenomenon among migrants when in a new country. They relinquish all old and presumably oppressive connections and emerge, not as one of the ordinary folk, but rather as expatriates of elevated status.

4. Nature as Mediated Metaphor

1. The literature on Western tendencies to idealize and romanticize nature is extensive. It stretches across many academic disciplines and the arts as well. Often it is seen as the inevitable outgrowth from biblical beginnings, through Rousseauian naturalism to contemporary American attitudes. It stretches from the Garden of Eden to "keep off the grass" signs and landscaped cemeteries. Many scholars address the contradictory nature of Western views. A modest indication of the proliferation of the writings follows: W. H. Auden, *The Enchafèd Flood* (1950); Alfred Biese, *The Development and the Feeling for Nature in the Middle Ages and Modern Times* (1905); Wilson O. Clough, *The Necessary Earth: Nature's Solitude in American Literature* (1964); Havelock Ellis, "The Love of Wild Nature," *Contemporary Review* (1909); W. G. Hoskins, *The Making of the English Landscape* (1970); William B. Hunter, "The Seventeenth Century Doctrine of Plastic Nature," *Harvard Theological Review* (1950); Hans Huth, *Nature and the American: Three Centuries of Changing Attitudes* (1957); Leo Marx, "Pastoral Ideals and City Troubles," *The Fitness of Man's*

Environment (1968); Nikolaus Pevsner, "The Genesis of the Picturesque," *The Architectural Review* (1966); Peter J. Schmitt, *Back to Nature: The Arcadian Myth in Urban America* (1969); Paul Shepard, *Man in the Landscape: A Historic View of the Esthetics of Nature* (1967); Henry Nash Smith, *Virgin Land: The American West as Symbol and Myth* (1950); George H. Williams, *Wilderness and Paradise in Christian Thought* (1962); Mary E. Woolley, "The Development of the Love of Romantic Scenery in America," *American Historical Review* (1897).

2. Again the literature on these matters attests to the awarenesses Western scholars have developed about this overriding and very important relationship. The notion of conquering and subduing the wilderness of the American frontier is a common way of dealing with the issue (Billington 1954; Moore 1957; Turner 1893), as are the ideas embedded in the notion of progress and technological development (Marx 1964; Gitlin 1979). That these views are the results of theorizing and hence subject to the changing winds of the history of ideas is also obvious (Glacken 1970; Huth 1957).

3. The Banzai Pipeline, made familiar to most North Americans in the annals of television beer advertisements in the early 1970s, is the surfer's proverbial ultimate challenge situated on the island of Oahu on the North Shore. The whole area is renowned for surfing beaches. The Pipeline is located in the Sunset Beach area, and constitutes for some the surfing mecca of the world. The name captures both the curl of the fast-breaking waves and the war cry of Japanese foot soldiers in World War II. The notion of the pipeline refers to the sense of being encased in a tube, with waves so high and so curled that the rider is in semi-darkness during the short fast ride. The Japanese cry is essentially a cheer uttered prior to going into battle, meaning "long-live" or "viva." Thus, to the surfer it suggests potential danger and violence. Other famous surfing spots include Makaha Beach Park on the leeward side of the island, where north and west swells of a characteristic variety make it a world renowned location used for professional surfing competitions, such as the Makaha International Invitational and the Duke Kahanamoku Hawaiian Surfing Classic.

4. Anthropologists have produced rather strong evidence of the relative codification of time. Not only have they observed different uses of time by the people they studied, but they have also experienced varying time structures themselves. Although a great deal of the work on time produced by anthropology has to do with cultural conceptions of ecological and subsistence cycles or with calendars, some cognitively sensitive work has also been produced: Bourdieu (1963), Doob (1971), Fabian (1983), Hallowell (1937), Hall (1959), Leach (1961), Geertz (1966), Maltz (1968). Provocative work has also been done by geographers (Carlstein et al. 1978); sociologists (Roth 1963; Schwartz 1975); philosophers (Poulet 1956; Husserl 1964) among others. Particularly relevant to understanding the Western consciousness and the notion of time is an exploration of photography—*Time in a Frame* (Thomas 1977).

5. Rituals of Inequality: Ethnicity and the *Haole*

1. The most recent official confirmation of this is from the year 1979 (Department of Planning and Economic Development 1982: tables 1, 18). It indicates that 39,476 arrived from the mainland United States (24,077 were military personnel and dependents; 15,399 were civilians). Among the migrants from other countries are: 5,016 from the Philippines, 1,192 from Korea, 586 from China and Taiwan, 365 from Japan, 286 from Vietnam, 135 from Canada, and 1,364 from various other countries.

2. This decision and the position it assumes is not universal as the following excerpts from letters to the editor of the university newspaper indicate: "As for the terms 'white' or 'Caucasian' I find Caucasian an awkward word and white reminds me of George

5. Ethnicity and the *Haole* 201

Wallace. Maybe I should like to be referred to as 'honky,' instead." (Martin Resnick, "Student Likes 'Haole,' " Letters to the Editor, *Ka leo o hawaii,* September 17, 1973.)

" 'Haole' simply means 'foreigner' in Hawaiian . . . Had the adventurers been Asians, the term would have been applied to them and the course of history would have been radically altered, but such was not the case. They instead have earned other names such as 'pake,' 'buddha head,' 'yobo' etc. . . . Anyone who is at all sensitive to language is immediately struck by the gentle and humorous nature of all these terms, certainly a tribute to the nature of the people who have witnessed the invasion and division of their native lands by succeeding waves of outsiders." (Mike McClory, " 'Haole' Stirs More Reactions," Letters to the Editor, *Ka leo o hawaii,* September 17, 1973.)

3. "Two Dentists Charge Racial Bias in $200,000 Suit against State Licensing Board," *Honolulu Star-Bulletin,* December 17, 1976, p. B4; Leslie Wilcox, "$1.5 Million Suit Cites Gov. Ariyoshi," *Honolulu Star-Bulletin,* July 30, 1977, p. B4; "Mainland Haole Charges Reverse Bias in Job Hunting Here," *Honolulu Advertiser,* February 17, 1978, p. A3; "TV Newsmen Lose Bias Suit," *Honolulu Star-Bulletin,* April 27, 1979, p. A12;" Lawsuit Charges Racial Discrimination in Isle Dental Exam," *Honolulu Advertiser,* March 20, 1979, p. G2; Gregg K. Kakesako, "State Government Hiring Questioned," *Honolulu Star-Bulletin,* May 4, 1979, p. A1; Stu Glauberman, " 'Token White' Tells Why He Forced Issue," *Honolulu Star-Bulletin,* May 5, 1979, p. A2; Ken Kobayashi, "State Pays $40,000 in Discrimination Suit," *Honolulu Advertiser,* November 14, 1979, p. A1; Ken Kobayashi, "Judge Rules Agency Was Biased: Says Caucasian Woman Was Qualified," *Honolulu Advertiser,* January 28, 1982, p. A3.

4. The Japanese business ethos, the social organization of Japanese business institutions, and the morality of Japanese interaction has been extensively covered in the literature (see Imai and Norbury 1975; Karsh et al. 1974; Inumaru 1977; Musashi 1982; Rohlen 1974; Selhi 1975; Tsurumi 1976; Vogel 1975; Yoshino 1968). The cultural patterns of personal behavior and the politics of cross-cultural interaction have also been richly documented (Doi 1973; Bennett and Ishino 1963; Ogawa 1971; Lebra 1976; Barnlund 1975).

5. Quite often the Caucasians are aware of figures which support the complaint. Though not always sure of percentages, they indicate that these are available and essentially support the argument. Figures compiled in 1978 for the Federal Equal Employment Opportunity Commission were reproduced in a front-page newspaper article on hiring discrimination in 1979: "Of the state's 11,047 permanent workers, 47.2 percent are Japanese American; 15.7 percent Hawaiian or part-Hawaiian; 15.4 percent Caucasian; 8.4 percent Chinese or Korean; 8.2 percent Filipino; and 5.1 percent 'other.' " (Gregg K. Kakesako, "State Government Hiring Questioned," *Honolulu Star-Bulletin,* May 4, 1979, p. A1). In answer to criticisms about the large percentage of Japanese in government, state officials often note that the Americans of Japanese ancestry (AJA) joined government service at a time when other jobs were not open to them.

6. A report presented to the Attorney General addresses the issue of bias in the admission of dentists to practice. While it notes that 85 percent of the dental board are of Asian ancestry, it adds that 81 percent of general practitioners are also Asian and hence the composition of the board is not surprising. It notes that 30 of 35 Asians passed the board exams in a two-year period, while only 28 of 74 non-Asians were successful. Among alternate suggestions for this success rate are: 1) Personality and intellectual ability may be higher for Asians, with perhaps a greater fear of failure; 2) Asian residents of the state may be more motivated because of family and peer expectations and motivation to practice in the home state is perhaps greater; 3) recency of training may lead to greater motivation to pass, against those already in practice elsewhere; and 4) dentists with specialization may not be as successful on general exams (Dunn-Rankin 1976).

7. There is an interesting tacit acceptance of a colonial past in this comment often given to me in a wry and knowing way by my informants. Kahala is a part of Honolulu with some of the most expensive real estate, mainly owned by the Bishop Estate, and long an almost completely Caucasian part of the city. The composition of this suburb is changing, however. Punahou is a private school established for the children of missionaries in 1841 and is seen as an elite institution. It provides both elementary and high school training.

8. The ensuing data on jokes are taken from a collection of between three and four hundred jokes and riddles collected during my years of fieldwork. I thank David Whittaker for sharing with me his own extensive collection.

9. The ethnic slurs common to the mainland such as Jap, Chink, Whitey, Nigger, and others are heard infrequently. Among those common to the Hawaiian scene are:

> **Portagee mouth**—loud talkers, loud mouth.
> **fufus**—fuzzy headed. Sometimes used for Samoans.
> **popolo**—black.
> **yobo**—Korean.
> **moke**—local type, Hawaiian, very derogatory.
> **slopes, slants**—Orientals.
> **kotonk**—Japanese born on the mainland.
> **flip**—Filipino.
> **Buddha head**—Oriental, Japanese or Chinese.
> **malasada**—Portuguese.
> **AJA**—Americans of Japanese ancestry (usually not a slur).
> **black dog**—Filipino. As they are known to have eaten dogs.

10. I do not doubt that were it possible to collect the many accounts provided for seemingly irrational events, there would be numerous structural similarities among them. Any culture has thematic possibilities for reasoning which may be converted to specific situations.

Glossary of Hawaiian Words Used in Everyday English Speech

In about the year 1820, the missionaries gave the Hawaiian language its first written form consisting of a simple alphabet of twelve letters: five vowels and seven consonants. The seven consonants are H, K, L, M, N, P, and W. They are generally pronounced the same as in English, with some exceptions. K is a bit softer than in English. L is as a soft L in English, but sometimes as a soft R. W is as a soft V or W in English. The vowels are:

A pronounced as the vowel in WASH
E pronounced as the vowel in DAY
I pronounced as the vowel in BE
O pronounced as the vowel in SLOW
U pronounced as the vowel in DUDE

alii   chief, king, the nobility, or aristocracy.
aloha   hello, goodbye, love, good feelings, a greeting; used as an adjective, verb, noun; used in a large variety of contexts: "*Aloha* Friday"; "She *alohaed* me";

"There's a lack of *aloha*"; and in signing notes, even official letters.

ewa	a direction in Honolulu; i.e., west, toward Ewa Plantation, now Ewa Beach.
hale	house.
haole	white person; foreign to Hawaii. "Ask that *haole* over there."
haole eleele	black person from the mainland.
hapa haole	literally "half *haole*"; part foreign; hence, part white; sometimes used to refer to other facets of Hawaiian culture, once traditional and now diverted to partly white ways, e.g., "*hapa haole* music"; "*hapa haole luaus.*"
heiau	temple; place of worship; used to refer to historic sites which were native ceremonial spots.
holoku	a loosely fitted long dress, with a yoke, sometimes a train, fashioned on the Mother Hubbard dresses worn by the missionaries.
hui	a club, society, or association. "I belong to the weaving *hui.*"
hula, hulahula	dance; song.
ka leo o hawaii	literally "the voice of Hawaii"; name of the student newspaper at the University of Hawaii.
kai	sea, as in Hawaii Kai, a suburb of Honolulu.
kamaaina	son of the earth; native born; old timer; a status with considerable prestige, leading to satirical comments by those not born in the Islands: *kamaaina* status depends on how much money one has.
kanaka	man; human being; native; now has a derogatory connotation and its use is avoided; in American and Canadian northwest the ethnic designation for descendents of Hawaiian and other Pacific island immigrants.
kapu	forbidden; taboo.
keiki	a child; signs may read "Playground for *keikis.*"
koa	a Hawaiian wood, used in making furniture, much valued; fine red wood once used for canoes and surfboards—*Acacia koa.*
koko	Koko Head; a promontory between Honolulu and other landmarks like Hanauma Bay and Makapuu Head.

kona	south or southwest; *kona* weather is hot, windless weather.
lanai	porch; terrace; "We ate on the *lanai*."
lei	necklace, usually of flowers or dried seeds.
luau	a feast.
mahalo	thank you; used over loudspeakers in public places and on signs in stores thanking one for patronage.
mahele	land division; usually used to refer to the Great *Mahele* of 1848. A redistribution of land between the king, chiefs and the government.
mai tai	a Hawaiian cocktail, well known in the tourist world.
makai	seaward; common in giving directions in Honolulu; e.g., "Drive *ewa* for two blocks; then, turn *makai* for one; then, *koko* (name of a well-known Honolulu promontory) to the store on the corner; then *mauka*, and there you are."
malihini	stranger; a newcomer.
malo	a loin cloth.
mauka	inland; uphill; toward the mountains; common in giving directions in the city of Honolulu.
menehune	dwarf; elf; by legend, the first pygmy peoples to have inhabited the Islands, whose culture is said to remain in some of the historic sites on the island of Kauai, and who are said to have many magical qualities, such as always accomplishing their work at night and turning to stone humans who perceive their efforts.
muu-muu	gown worn in Hawaii; a Mother Hubbard inherited from the efforts of the missionaries; a loose dress with a yoke, usually short sleeved or sleeveless.
nui	big; great.
pake	Chinese.
pali	a cliff; precipice; the Nuuanu Pali is a precipitous cliff in the Koolau Range, in the center of the island of Oahu, where Kamehameha I fought a deciding battle for control of the Islands.
pau	finished; commonly used by all ethnic groups. "Are you *pau*; if so, put your work on the front desk."
poi	pounded taro root, permitted to ferment, and a part of every Hawaiian meal; "the staff of life."
punee	a sofa; a bed; stores advertise "*pu-nees* for sale."

tapa   barkcloth made from a mulberry tree; designs of traditional *tapa* are used in decorating the haunts of tourists.

ti   any of several species of Asiatic and Polynesian shrubs, *Cordyline terminalis*; *ti* leaves are used in "grass" skirts.

wahine   a woman. "His *wahine* was there, too, so I couldn't say anything."

yakuza   not a Hawaiian, but a Japanese word. Used to refer to the Japanese or Oriental "Mafia" or underground.

References

Abe, Shirley. 1945. "Violations of the Racial Code in Hawaii." *Social Process in Hawaii* 9–10:33–38.

Aberle, David F. 1970. "A Note on Relative Deprivation Theory As Applied to Millenarian and Other Cult Movements." In Sylvia L. Thrupp, ed., *Millennial Dreams in Action,* pp. 209–14. New York: Schocken.

Agar, Michael. 1980. "Stories, Background Knowledge, and Themes: Problems in the Analysis of Life History Narrative." *American Ethnologist* 7(2):223–38.

Alexander, William D. 1892. "The Relations Between the Hawaiian Islands and Spanish America in Early Times." *Hawaiian Historical Society Report* 1:1–10.

Ames, Michael M. 1957. "Reaction to Stress: A Comparative Study of Nativism." *Davidson Journal of Anthropology* 3(1).

Anderson, Bern. 1960. *The Life and Voyages of Captain George Vancouver, Surveyor of the Sea.* Seattle: University of Washington Press.

Anthony, J. Garner. 1955. *Hawaii Under Army Rule.* Stanford: Stanford University Press.

Arens, W. 1978. *The Man-Eating Myth: Anthropology and Anthropophagy.* London: Oxford University Press.

Aronson, Dan R., ed. 1970. "Social Networks." *Canadian Review of Sociology and Anthropology,* Special Issue, 7:4.

Ball, Harry V. and Douglas S. Yamamura. 1960. "Ethnic Discrimination and the Marketplace: A Study of Landlords' Preference in a Polyethnic Community." *American Sociological Review* 25:687–94.

Banks, Sir Joseph. 1768–71 (1962). *Voyage in the Endeavour with Captain Cook.* MS journal. Sydney: Mitchell Library.

References

Barber, Joseph, Jr. 1941. *Hawaii: Restless Rampart.* New York: Bobbs-Merrill.

Barkan, Leonard. 1975. *Nature's Work of Art: The Human Body as Image of the World.* New Haven: Yale University Press.

Barkun, M. 1974. *Disaster and the Millenium.* New Haven: Yale University Press.

Barnlund, Dean C. 1975. *Public and Private Self in Japan and the United States.* Tokyo: Simul Press.

Barrot, Théodore-Adolphe. 1839 (1978). *Unless Haste Is Made: A French Skeptic's Account of the Sandwich Islands in 1836.* Kailua: Press Pacifica.

Barth, F. 1969. *Ethnic Groups and Boundaries: The Social Organization of Culture Difference.* London: Allen and Unwin.

Barth, Frederik. 1975. *Ritual and Knowledge Among the Baktaman of New Guinea.* New Haven: Yale University Press.

Baudet, Henri. 1965. *Paradise on Earth: Some Thoughts on European Images of Non-European Man.* New Haven: Yale University Press.

Beaglehole, J. C. 1966 (1934). *The Exploration of the Pacific.* 3d edition. Stanford: Stanford University Press.

Bean, Robert. 1954. "My Race Relation Experience at Work." *Social Process in Hawaii* 18:26–29.

Becker, Carl. 1932. "Everyman His Own Historian." *American Historical Review* 37(2)221–36.

Becker, Howard S. et al. 1961. *Boys in White: Student Culture in Medical School.* Chicago: University of Chicago Press.

Bennett, J. A. 1976. "Immigration, 'Blackbirding,' Labour Recruiting? The Hawaiian Experience 1877–1887." *Journal of Pacific History* 11:3–27.

Bennett, J. W. and I. Ishino. 1963. *Paternalism in the Japanese Economy: Anthropological Studies of Oyabun-kobun Patterns.* Minneapolis: University of Minnesota Press.

Berger, Peter L. 1966. "Identity as a Problem in the Sociology of Knowledge." *European Journal of Sociology* 7:105–15.

Berreman, Gerald D. 1962. *Behind Many Masks.* Ithaca, N.Y.: Society for Applied Anthropology, Monograph No. 4.

Billington, Ray Allen. 1954. *The American Frontiersman: A Case-Study in Reversion to the Primitive.* Oxford: Clarendon.

——1981. *Land of Savagery, Land of Promise: The European Image of the American Frontier.* New York: Norton.

Bingham, Hiram. 1849 (1969). *A Residence of Twenty-One Years in the Sandwich Islands.* New York: Praeger.

Bochner, Stephen and Toshio Ohsako. 1977. "Ethnic Role Salience in Racially Homogeneous and Heterogeneous Societies." *Journal of Cross-Cultural Psychology* 8(4):477–92.

Bogue, Donald. 1959. "Internal Migration." In Phillip Hauser and Otis Duncan, eds., *The Study of Population: An Inventory and Appraisal.* pp. 486–510. Chicago: University of Chicago Press.

Bott, Elizabeth. 1957. *Family and Social Network.* London: Tavistock.

Bourdieu, P. 1963. "The Attitude of the Algerian Peasant Toward Time." In Julian Pitt-Rivers. ed., *Mediterranean Countrymen,* pp. 55–72. Paris: Mouton.

Bradley, Harold W. 1942. *The American Frontier in Hawaii: The Pioneers 1789–1843*. Stanford: Stanford University Press.

Bredvold, Louis I. 1962. *The Natural History of Sensibility*. Detroit: Wayne State University Press.

Buck, Peter H. 1959 (1938). *Vikings of the Pacific*. Chicago: University of Chicago Press.

Burke, Kenneth. 1966. *Language as Symbolic Action*. Berkeley: University of California Press.

Carlstein, Tommy et al., eds. 1978. *Making Sense of Time*. London: Edward Arnold.

Cartwright, Bruce, Jr. 1916. "Some Early Foreign Residents of the Hawaiian Islands." *Hawaiian Historical Society,* 25th Report, January 17, 1917, pp. 57–64.

Castaneda, Carlos. 1968. *The Teachings of Don Juan: A Yaqui Way of Knowledge*. New York: Ballantine.

——1971. *A Separate Reality: Further Conversations with Don Juan*. New York: Simon and Schuster.

Chinen, Jon J. 1958. *The Great Mahele: Hawaii's Land Division of 1848*. Honolulu: University Press of Hawaii.

Clark, Jeffrey T. and John Terrell. 1978. "Archaeology in Oceania." In Bernard J. Siegel et al., eds., *Annual Review of Anthropology* 7:293–319. Palo Alto, Calif.: Annual Reviews.

Clemens, Samuel L. 1866 (1967). *Mark Twain's Letters from Hawaii*. A. Grove Day, ed. London: Chatto.

Cleveland, Harlan et al. 1960. *The Overseas Americans*. New York: McGraw-Hill.

Cobb, Edith. 1977. *The Ecology of Imagination in Childhood*. New York: Columbia University Press.

Coffman, Tom. 1973. *Catch a Wave: A Case Study of Hawaii's New Politics*. Honolulu: University Press of Hawaii.

Cohen, Ronald. 1978. "Ethnicity: Problem and Focus in Anthropology." In Bernard J. Siegel et al., eds., *Annual Review of Anthropology* 7:379–403. Palo Alto, Calif.: Annual Reviews.

Colby, Benjamin and Michael Cole. 1970. "Culture, Memory and Narrative." In Robin Horton and Keith Finnegan, eds., *Modes of Thought: Essays on Thinking in Western and Non-Western Society*, pp. 63–91. London: Faber and Faber.

Colby, B. N. and J. L. Peacock. 1973. "Narrative." In J. J. Honigmann, ed., *Handbook of Social and Cultural Anthropology*, pp. 613–35. Chicago: Rand McNally.

Connor, J. W. 1976. "*Joge kankei*: A Key Concept for an Understanding of Japanese-American Achievement." *Psychiatry* 39:266–79.

Cook, James. 1778 (1967). *The Journals of Captain James Cook on his Voyages of Discovery*. Vol. 3. *The Voyage of the Resolution and Discovery 1776–1780*. Part 1. J. C. Beaglehole, ed., Hakluyt Society, Cambridge: Cambridge University Press.

Cottle, Thomas J. and Stephen L. Klineberg. 1974. *The Present of Things Future: Explorations of Time in Human Experience*. New York: Free Press.

Creighton, Thomas. 1978. *The Lands of Hawaii: Their Use and Misuse*. Honolulu: University Press of Hawaii.

Dahlgren, Erik Wilhelm. 1917. *Were the Hawaiian Islands Visited by the Spaniards Before Their Discovery by Captain Cook in 1778?* Stockholm: Almquist and Wiksells.

Daniels, Arlene Kaplan. 1967. "The Low-Caste Stranger in Social Research." In Gideon Sjoberg, ed., *Ethics, Politics, and Social Research*, pp. 267–96. Cambridge, Mass.: Schenkman.

Danielsson, Bengt. 1956. *Love in the South Seas.* New York: Reynal.

Daws, Gavan. 1968. *Shoal of Time: A History of the Hawaiian Islands.* New York: Macmillan.

——1978. " 'All the Horrors of the Half Known Life': Some Notes on the Writing of Biography in the Pacific." In Niel Gunson, ed., *The Changing Pacific: Essays in Honour of H. E. Maude*, pp. 297–307. Oxford: Oxford University Press.

Day, A. Grove. 1960. *Hawaii and Its People.* New York: Duell, Sloan and Pearce.

Dean, John P. and William Foote Whyte. 1958. "How Do You Know If the Informant Is Telling the Truth?" *Human Organization* 7:34–38.

Dening, Gregory. 1978. "Institutions of Violence in the Marquesas." In Niel Gunson, ed., *The Changing Pacific: Essays in Honour of H. E. Maude*, pp. 134–41. Oxford: Oxford University Press.

Department of Planning and Economic Development, State of Hawaii. 1977a. *Hawaii State Plan: The Economy.* Vol. 1. Honolulu: State of Hawaii.

——1977b. *Hawaii State Plan: Socio-Cultural Advancement.* Vol. 5. Honolulu: State of Hawaii.

——1981a. *Hawaii's In-Migrants, 1980.* Statistical Report 146, May 7, 1981. Honolulu: State of Hawaii.

——1981b. *State of Hawaii Data Book: A Statistical Abstract.* Honolulu: State of Hawaii.

——1982. *Hawaii's In-Migrants, 1981.* Statistical Report 154, May 14, 1982. Honolulu: State of Hawaii.

Despres, Leo A. 1975. "Toward a Theory of Ethnic Phenomena." In Leo A. Despres, ed., *Ethnicity and Resource Competition in Plural Societies*, pp. 187–207. The Hague: Mouton.

Deutschmann, Linda Bell. 1978. "Decline of the Wasp? Dominant Group Identity in the Ethnic Plural Society." In Martin L. Kovacs, ed., *Ethnic Canadians: Culture and Education*, pp. 411–18. Regina, Sask.: University of Regina Press.

DiBianco, Paul E. 1980. " 'Localism' in Hawaii." *Honolulu Advertiser*, March 13, p. A19.

Doob, Leonard W. 1971. *Patterning of Time.* New Haven: Yale University Press.

Doi, Takeo. 1973. *The Anatomy of Dependence.* San Francisco: Kodansha International.

Douglas, Mary. 1968. "The Social Control of Cognition: Some Factors in Joke Perception." *Man* 3:361–76.

Dowling, John J. 1975. "Values and Objectivity." *The Human Context* 7:399–421.

Dumont, Jean-Paul. 1978. *The Headman and I: Ambiguity and Ambivalence in the Fieldworking Experience.* Austin: University of Texas Press.

Dundes, Alan. 1969. "Thinking Ahead: A Folkloristic Reflection of the Future Orientation in American Worldview." *Anthropological Quarterly* 42:53–72.

———1972. "Seeing Is Believing." *Natural History Magazine* 81(5):8–12, 86–87.

Dunn-Rankin, Peter. 1976. *Is There Racial Bias in the Admission of Dentists to Practice in the State of Hawaii?* A Report to the Attorney General of the State of Hawaii.

Du Puy, William Atherton. 1932. *Hawaii and Its Race Problem.* Washington, D.C.: GPO.

Ellis, William. 1827 (1963). *Journal of William Ellis.* Rpt. Honolulu: Advertiser Publishing.

———1831 (1969). *Polynesian Researches.* Volume 4. New Ed. Rutland, Vt.: Charles E. Tuttle.

Ellul, Jacques. 1968. *A Critique of the New Commonplaces.* New York: Knopf.

Ennew, Judith. 1976. "Examining the Facts in Fieldwork: Considerations." *Critique of Anthropology* 7:43–66.

Evans-Pritchard, E. E. 1963. "Introduction to Some Zande Texts." In I. Schapera, ed., *Studies in Kinship and Marriage.* RAI Occasional Paper No. 16. London.

Fabian, Johannes. 1983. *Time and the Other: How Anthropology Makes Its Object.* New York: Columbia University Press.

Fairchild, Hoxie Neale. 1955 (1928). *The Noble Savage: A Study in Romantic Naturalism.* New York: Oxford University Press.

Farrell, Bryan H. 1974. "The Tourist Ghettos of Hawaii." In M. C. R. Edgell and B. H. Farrell, eds., *Themes on Pacific Lands,* pp. 181–221, Western Geographical Series, Vol. 10. Victoria, B.C.: University of Victoria.

Fayerweather, Abraham W. 1831–1876. *Letters 1831–1876.* Archives of Hawaii, Microfilm job 125, Records of Hope T. Eldridge.

Ferdon, Edwin N. 1968. "Polynesian Origins." In Andrew P. Vayda, ed., *Peoples and Cultures of the Pacific.* New York: Natural History Press.

Finney, Ben R. and James D. Houston. 1966. *Surfing: The Sport of Hawaiian Kings.* Rutland, Vt.: Charles E. Tuttle.

Finney, Joseph. 1961–62. "Attitudes of Others Toward Hawaiians." *Social Process in Hawaii* 25:78–83.

Firth, Raymond. 1936 (1963). *We, The Tikopia: A Sociological Study of Kinship in Primitive Polynesia.* Boston: Beacon.

Ford, Julienne. 1975. *Paradigms and Fairy Tales.* 2 vols. London: Routledge and Kegan Paul.

Frank, Gelya. 1979. "Finding the Common Denominator: A Phenomenological Critique of Life History Method." *Ethos* 7:68–94.

Fuller, Gary and Murray Chapman. 1974. "On the Role of Mental Maps in Migration Research." *International Migration Review* 8:487–506.

Gamio, Manuel, ed. 1971 (1931). *The Life History of the Mexican Immigrant: Autobiographical Documents.* New York: Dover.

Geertz, Clifford. 1966. *Person, Time and Conduct in Bali: An Essay in Cultural Analysis.* Cultural Report Series No. 14, S.E. Asia Studies, New Haven: Yale University.

212   References

——1973. "Thick Description: Toward an Interpretive Theory of Culture." In *The Interpretation of Cultures*, pp. 3–30. New York: Basic Books.

——1976. "'From the Native's Point of View': On the Nature of Anthropological Understanding." In Keith H. Basso and Henry A. Selby, eds., *Meaning in Anthropology*, pp. 221–37. Albuquerque: University of New Mexico Press.

Gilman, Gorham D. 1970. "1848—Honolulu as It Is—Notes for Amplification." In Jean S. Sharpless and Richard A. Greer, eds., *The Hawaiian Journal of History* 4:105–56.

Gilmore, Michael T. 1978. "Eulogy as Symbolic Biography: The Iconography of Revolutionary Leadership, 1776–1826." In Daniel Aaron, ed., *Studies in Biography*, pp. 131–57. Cambridge: Harvard University Press.

Gitlin, Todd. 1979. "Domesticating Nature." *Theory and Society* 8:291–97.

Glacken, Clarence J. 1967. *Traces on the Rhodian Shore*. Berkeley: University of California Press.

——1970. "Man Against Nature: An Outmoded Concept." In Harold W. Helfrich, ed., *The Environmental Crisis*. pp. 127–42. New Haven: Yale University Press.

Glick, Clarence Elmer. 1950. "A Haole's Changing Conceptions of Japanese in Hawaii: A Hypothetical Approach Using a Social Typology." *Social Process in Hawaii* 14:1–10.

Goffman, Erving. 1959. *Presentation of Self in Everyday Life*. Garden City, New York: Doubleday Anchor.

Goodenough, Ward H. 1978. "Multiculturalism as the Normal Human Experience." In Elizabeth M. Eddy and William L. Partridge, eds., *Applied Anthropology in America*, pp. 79–86. New York: Columbia University Press.

Goodman, Robert B. et al. 1971. *The Hawaiians*. Sydney: Island Heritage.

Gorer, Geoffrey. 1975. "English Identity Over Time and Empire." In George de Vos and Lola Romanucci-Ross, eds., *Ethnic Identity: Cultural Continuity and Change*, pp. 156–72. Palo Alto: Mayfield.

Gotschalk, D. W. 1969. *The Structure of Awareness, Introduction to a Situational Theory of Truth and Knowledge*. Urbana: University of Illinois Press.

Goudy, W. J. et al. 1977. "Stereotyping as a Form of Attempted Social Control." *Sociology and Social Research* 61:350–62.

Gough, Kathleen. 1968. "Anthropology: Child of Imperialism." *Monthly Review* 19(11):12–27.

Gouldner, Alvin. 1976. "The Dark Side of the Dialectic: Toward a New Objectivity." *Sociological Inquiry* 46:3–16.

Graves, Nancy B. and Theodore D. Graves. 1974. "Adaptive Strategies in Urban Migration." In Bernard L. Siegel, et al., eds. *Annual Review of Anthropology* 3:117–51. Palo Alto, Calif.: Annual Reviews.

Gray, Francine du Plessix. 1973. *Hawaii: The Sugar-Coated Fortress*. New York: Random House.

Greer, Richard A. 1970. "Honolulu in 1847." *Hawaiian Journal of History* 4:59–95.

Gulick, Sidney L. 1937. *Mixing the Races in Hawaii: A Study of the Coming Neo-Hawaiian Race*. Honolulu: Hawaiian Board Book Rooms.

Habermas, Jurgen. 1968. *Knowledge and Human Interests*. Boston: Beacon.

Haddon, A. C. 1911. *The Wanderings of People.* Cambridge: Cambridge University Press.

Hall, Edward. 1959. *The Silent Language.* Garden City, New York: Doubleday.

Hall, James Norman. 1931. "The Art of Loafing." *Atlantic Monthly* 148:57–63.

Hallowell, A. Irving. 1937. "Temporal Orientation in Western Civilization and in a Preliterate Society." *American Anthropologist* 39:647–70.

Hammons, T. 1976. "Americans and Paradise: The Pacific Basin as a Literary Source." *Journal of the West* 15:102–16.

Handelman, Don and Elliott Leyton. 1978. *Bureaucracy and World View: Studies in the Logic of Official Interpretation.* St. John's, Newfoundland: Institute of Social and Economic Research, Memorial University of Newfoundland.

Handy, E. S. Craighill and Mary Kawena Pukui. 1958. *The Polynesian Family System in Ka-'U, Hawai'i.* Wellington, New Zealand: The Polynesia Society.

Haole, A. 1854. *Sandwich Island Notes.* New York: Harper. (Attributed to George Washington Bates.)

Harper, Ralph. 1966. *Nostalgia: An Existential Exploration of Longing and Fulfilment in the Modern Age.* Cleveland: Press of Case Western Reserve University.

Hart, Donn V. 1956. "Halfway to Uncertainty: A Short Autobiography of a Cebuano Filipino." *Journal of East Asiatic Studies* 5:255–77.

Heisenberg, Werner. 1958. "The Representation of Nature in Contemporary Physics." *Daedulus* 87:95–108.

Holzner, Burkart. 1972. *Reality Construction in Society.* Rev. ed. Cambridge, Mass.: Schenkman.

Honolulu Advertiser. 1978. "UH Dean Predicts a Pacific Oceanic Paradise." *Honolulu Advertiser,* March 2, 1988, p. B3.

Hormann, Bernhard L. 1982. "The Haoles." *Social Process in Hawaii* 29:32–44.

Husserl, Edmund. 1964. *The Phenomenology of Internal Time-Consciousness,* Martin Heidegger, ed. Bloomington: Indiana University Press.

Huth, Hans. 1957. *Nature and the American: Three Centuries of Changing Attitudes.* Berkeley: University of California Press.

Hymes, Dell. 1972. "The Uses of Anthropology: Critical, Political, Personal." In Dell Hymes, ed., *Reinventing Anthropology,* pp. 3–82. New York: Random House.

Ibrahim, I. B., C. Carter, D. McLaughlin, and M. N. Rashad. 1977. "Ethnicity and Suicide in Hawaii." *Social Biology.* 24(1):10–16.

Ige, Philip Keimin. 1968. "Paradise and Melting Pot in the Fiction and Non-Fiction of Hawaii; A Study of Cross-Cultural Record." Ph.D. dissertation, Columbia University.

Imai, Masaaki and Paul Norbury. 1975. *The Japanese Businessman.* Tokyo: Association Business Programs.

Inumaru, Kazuo Francesco. 1977. "The Japanese Business Community in Milan." Master's thesis, Cambridge University.

James, Stuart B. 1970. "Western American Space and the Human Imagination." *Western Humanities Review* 24(2):147–55.

Johnson, Colleen Leaky and Frank Arvid Johnson. 1975. "Interaction Rules and

Ethnicity: The Japanese and Caucasians in Honolulu." *Social Forces* 54:452–66.

Johnson, F. A. et al. 1974. "Social and Psychological Aspects of Verbal Behavior in Japanese-Americans." *American Journal of Psychology* 131:580–83.

Judd, Bernice. 1974. *Voyages to Hawaii before 1860*. Honolulu: University Press of Hawaii.

Judd, Gerrit P., IV. 1961. *Hawaii: An Informal History*. New York: Collier.

Kalčik, Susan. 1975. ". . . like Ann's gynecologist or the time I was almost raped." In Claire R. Farrer, ed., *Women and Folklore*. pp. 3–11. Austin and London: University of Texas Press.

Karsh, B. et al. 1974. *Workers and Employers in Japan*. Tokyo: University of Tokyo Press; Princeton: Princeton University Press.

Kemper, R. V. 1973. "Tzintzuntzenos in Mexico City: The Anthropologist Among Peasant Migrants." In G. M. Foster and R. V. Kemper, eds., *Anthropologists in Cities*, pp. 63–91. Boston: Little, Brown.

Kepes, Gyorgy. 1956. "Introduction." In Gyorgy Kepes, ed., *The New Landscape in Art and Science*. Chicago: Paul Theobald.

Kinloch, G. C. 1974. "Racial Prejudice in Highly and Less Racist Societies: Social Distance Preferences Among White College Students in South Africa and Hawaii." *Sociology and Social Research* 59:1–13.

Kinloch, Graham C. and J. A. Borders. 1972. "Racial Stereotypes and Social Distance Among Elementary School Children in Hawaii." *Sociology and Social Research* 56:368–77.

Kirch, P. V. 1974. "The Chronology of Early Hawaiian Settlement." *Archaeology and Physical Anthropology of Oceania* 9:110–19.

Kirshenblatt-Gimblett, B. 1975. "A Parable in Context: A Social Interactional Analysis of Storytelling Performance." In Dan Ben-Amos and Kenneth S. Goldstein, eds., *Folklore: Performance and Communication*, pp. 105–30. The Hague: Mouton.

Kittelson, David. 1971. "A Bibliographic Essay on the Territory of Hawaii, 1900–1959." *Journal of Pacific History* 6:195–218.

Kurokawa, M. 1971. "Mutual Perceptions of Racial Images: White, Black and Japanese Americans." *Journal of Social Issues* 27(4):213–35.

La Barre, Weston. 1971. "Materials for a History of Studies of Crisis Cults: A Bibliographic Essay." *Current Anthropology* 12:3–44.

Labov, William and Joshua Waletzky. 1967. "Narrative Analysis: Oral Versions of Personal Experience." In June Helm, ed., *Essays on the Verbal and Visual Arts*. Seattle: University of Washington Press.

Ladd, William. 1838. "Remarks Upon the Natural Resources of the Sandwich Islands." *Hawaiian Spectator* 1(2):68–79.

Langdon, Robert. 1975. *The Lost Caravel*. Sydney: Pacific Publications.

Langer, Susanne. 1953. *Feeling and Form*. New York: Scribner.

Lasch, Christopher. 1978. *The Culture of Narcissism: American Life in an Age of Diminishing Expectations*. New York: Norton.

Leach, Edmund. 1961. "Two Essays Concerning the Symbolic Representation of Time." In *Rethinking Anthropology*. London: Athlone.

Lebra, Takie Sugiyama. 1976. *Japanese Patterns of Behavior.* Honolulu: Univeristy Press of Hawaii.

Lee, Dorothy. 1959. *Freedom and Culture.* Englewood Cliffs, N. J.: Prentice-Hall.

Le Guin, Ursula K. 1969. *The Left Hand of Darkness.* New York: Ace Books.

Leon, J. J. 1975. "Sex-Ethnic Marriage in Hawaii: A Nonmetric Multidimensional Analysis." *Journal of Marriage and the Family* 37:775–81.

Leyton, Elliott. 1975. *Ravages of Industrial Disease.* Toronto: McClelland and Stewart.

Lieberman, Leonard. 1968. "The Debate over Race: A Study in the Sociology of Knowledge." *Phylon* 29(2):127–41.

Lind, Andrew W. 1957. "Racial Bloc Voting in Hawaii." *Social Process in Hawaii* 21:16–19.

——1969. *Hawaii: The Last of the Magic Isles.* New York: Oxford University Press.

——1980. *Hawaii's People.* 4th ed. Honolulu: University Press of Hawaii.

Lloyd, Geoffrey E. R. 1966. *Polarity and Analogy: Two Types of Argumentation in Early Greek Thought.* Cambridge: Cambridge University Press.

Loomis, Albertine. 1966 (1951). *Grapes of Canaan: Hawaii 1820.* Honolulu: Hawaiian Mission Children's Society.

Louch, A. R. 1966. *Explanation and Human Action.* Berkeley: University of California Press.

Lovejoy, Arthur O. and George Boas. 1935. *Primitivism and Related Ideas in Antiquity.* Baltimore: Johns Hopkins University Press.

Lowenthal, David. 1961. "Geography, Experience and Imagination: Towards a Geographical Epistemology." *Annals of Association of American Geographers* 51:241–60.

Luhmann, Niklas. 1976. "The Future Cannot Begin: Temporal Structures in Modern Society." *Social Research* 43:130–52.

Lukes, Steven. 1979. "The Real and Ideal Worlds of Democracy." In Aliks Kontos, ed., *Powers, Possessions and Freedom.* pp. 139–52. Toronto: University of Toronto Press.

Lynch, Kevin. 1972. *What Time Is This Place?* Cambridge: M.I.T. Press.

McArthur, Norma. 1966. "Essays in Multiplication: European Seafarers in Polynesia." *Journal of Pacific History* 1:91–105.

MacCallum, Thomson Murray. 1934. *Adrift in the South Seas: Including Adventures with Robert Louis Stevenson.* Los Angeles: University of California Press.

MacCannell, Dean. 1976. *The Tourist: A New Theory of the Leisure Class.* New York: Schocken.

McDermott John, Jr. Wen-Shing Tseng, and Thomas W. Maretzki, eds. 1980. *People and Cultures of Hawaii: A Psychocultural Profile.* Honolulu: University Press of Hawaii.

McHugh, Peter. 1968. *Defining the Situation.* Indianapolis: Bobbs-Merrill.

MacPherson, C. B. 1962. *The Political Theory of Possessive Individualism: Hobbes to Locke.* London: Oxford University Press.

McNall, Scott G. and James C. M. Johnson. 1975. "The New Conservatives:

Ethnomethodologists, Phenomenologists, and Symbolic Interactionists." *The Insurgent Sociologist* 5:49–65.

Malinowski, Bronislaw. 1929. *The Sexual Life of Savages.* New York: Harcourt, Brace, and World.

——1961 (1922). *Argonauts of the Western Pacific.* New York: Dutton.

Malo, David. 1838 (1903). *Hawaiian Antiquities (Moolelo Hawaii).* Translated by Dr. H. B. Emerson. Honolulu: Hawaiian Gazette.

Maltz, Daniel N. 1968. "Primitive Time-Reckoning as a Symbolic System." *Cornell Journal of Social Relations* 3:85–112.

Manley, Seon and Robert Manley. 1970. *Islands: Their Lives, Legends, and Lore.* Philadelphia: Hilton Book.

Manning, D. J. 1976. *Liberalism.* London: Dent.

Manuel, Frank E. 1965. "Toward a Psychological History of Utopias." *Daedalus* 94:293–322.

Marcus, George G. 1980. "Rhetoric and the Ethnographic Genre in Anthropological Research." *Current Anthropology* 21:507–10.

Maretzki, Thomas W. and John F. McDermott Jr. 1980. "The Caucasians." In John McDermott Jr., Wen-Shing Tseng, and Thomas W. Maretzki, eds., *People and Cultures of Hawaii: A Psychocultural Profile,* pp. 25–52. Honolulu: University Press of Hawaii.

Marshall, Donald. 1961. *Ra'ivavae: An Expedition to the Most Fascinating and Mysterious Island in Polynesia.* New York: Doubleday.

Marty, Martin E. 1978. "Migration: The Moral Framework." In William H. McNeill and Ruth S. Adams, eds., *Human Migration: Patterns and Policies,* pp. 387–403. Bloomington: Indiana University Press.

Marx, Leo. 1964. *The Machine in the Garden: Technology and the Pastoral Ideal in America.* New York: Oxford University Press.

Masuda, Minoru et al. 1973. "The Ethnic Identity Questionnaire: A Comparison of Three Japanese Age Groups in Tachikawa, Japan, Honolulu, Seattle." *Journal of Cross-Cultural Psychology* 4:229–45.

Maude, H. E. 1964. "Beachcombers and Castaways." *Journal of the Polynesian Society* 73:254–93.

Mead, George H. 1959. *The Philosophy of the Present.* Arthur E. Murphy, ed. La Salle, Ill.: Open Court Publishing.

Mead, Margaret. 1935. *Sex and Temperament in Three Primitive Societies.* New York: Morrow.

Meintel, Deirdre. 1973. "Strangers, Homecomers and Ordinary Men." *Anthropological Quarterly* 46:47–58.

Meredith, Gerald M. 1976. "Interpersonal Needs of Japanese-American and Caucasian-American College Students in Hawaii." *Journal of Social Psychology* 99:157–61.

Meredith, Gerald M. and Donna R. Ching. 1977. "Marriage-Role Attitudes Among Japanese-American and Caucasian-American College Students." *Psychological Reports* 40:1285–86.

Michener, James A. 1959. *Hawaii.* New York: Bantam.

Mills, C. Wright. 1940. "Stituated Actions and the Vocabulary of Motives." *American Sociological Review* 5:904–13.

Mitchell, J. Clyde, ed. 1969. *Social Networks in Urban Situations.* Manchester: Manchester University Press.

Moerman, Michael. 1965. "Ethnic Identification in a Complex Civilization: Who Are the Lue?" *American Anthropologist* 67:1215–30.

Moncrief, Lewis W. 1970. "The Cultural Basis of Our Environmental Crisis." *Science* 170:508–12.

Moore, Arthur K. 1957. *The Frontier Mind.* Lexington: University of Kentucky Press.

Morrell, W. P. 1963. *The Great Powers of the Pacific.* Historical Association Pamphlet G54. London: Routledge and Kegan Paul.

Mumford, Lewis. 1922 (1962). *The Story of Utopias.* New York: Viking.

Musashi, Miyamoto. 1982. *The Book of Five Rings (Gorin No Sho).* New York: Bantam.

Nagoshi, Kunio. 1954. "Some Observations Regarding Haole-Japanese Marriages in Hawaii." *Social Process in Hawaii* 18:57–65.

Nash, Dennison. 1963. "The Ethnologist as Stranger: An Essay in the Sociology of Knowledge." *Southwestern Journal of Anthropology* 19:149–67.

——1970. *Community in Limbo: An Anthropological Study of an American Community Abroad.* Bloomington: Indiana University Press.

Nash, Roderick. 1967. *Wilderness and the American Mind.* New Haven: Yale University Press.

Natanson, Maurice. 1969. "Introduction." In Maurice Natanson, ed., *Essays in Phenomenology,* pp. 1–22. The Hague: Martinus Nijhoff.

Nordhoff, Charles. 1874. "New England Folkways in Hawaii." *Northern California, Oregon and the Sandwich Islands.* Berkeley: Ten Speed Press.

Nordyke, Eleanor C. 1977. *The Peopling of Hawaii.* Honolulu: University Press of Hawaii.

Ogawa, Dennis M. 1971. *From Japs to Japanese: An Evolution of Japanese-American Stereotypes.* Berkeley: McCutchan Publishing.

——1973. *Jan ken po: The World of Hawaii's Japanese Americans.* Honolulu: University Press of Hawaii.

Olesen, Virginia L. and Elvi W. Whittaker. 1968. *The Silent Dialogue.* San Francisco: Jossey-Bass.

Patterson, Orlando. 1977. *Ethnic Chauvinism: The Reactionary Impulse.* New York: Stein & Day.

Peabody, Andrew P. 1865. *The Hawaiian Islands as Developed by Missionary Labors.* Boston: Proprietors of Boston Review.

Peirce, Henry A. 1880. "Early Discoveries of the Hawaiian Islands in the North Pacific Ocean: Evidences of Visits by Spanish Navigators during XVIth Century." *California Monthly Magazine,* September, pp. 3–8.

Peter, Karl. 1981. "The Myth of Multiculturalism and Other Political Fables." In Jorgen Dahlie and Tissa Fernando, eds., *Ethnicity, Power and Politics in Canada,* pp. 56–67. Toronto: Methuen.

Pitcher, E. G. and E. Prelinger. 1963. *Children Tell Stories: An Analysis of Fantasy.* New York: International University Press.

Polanyi, Livia. 1979. "So What's the Point?" *Semiotica* 25(3/4):207–41.

Poulet, Georges. 1956. *Studies in Human Time.* Baltimore: Johns Hopkins University Press.

Rabinow, Paul. 1977. *Reflections on Fieldwork in Morocco.* Berkeley: University of California Press.

Ralston, Caroline. 1973. "The Beach Communities." In J. W. Davidson and Deryck Scarr, eds., *Pacific Island Portraits.* Canberra: Australian National University Press.

——1978. *Grass Huts and Warehouses: Pacific Beach Communities of the Nineteenth Century.* Honolulu: University Press of Hawaii.

Rapaport, A. 1972. "Australian Aborigines and Definition of Place." In W. J. Mitchell, ed., *Environmental Design: Research and Practice*, vol 1. Proceedings of the 3d EDRA Conference, Los Angeles.

Rapson, Richard C. 1980. *Fairly Lucky You Live Hawaii: Cultural Pluralism in the Fiftieth State.* Washington D.C.: University Press of America.

Rees, Ronald. 1975. "The Scenery Cult: Changing Landscape Tastes Over Three Centuries." *Landscape* 19:39–47.

Relph, E. 1976. *Place and Placelessness.* London: Pion.

Research Committee on the Study of Honolulu Residents. 1980. *Honolulu Residents and Their Attitudes in Multi-Ethnic Perspective: Toward a Theory of the American National Character.* Tokyo: Institute of Statistical Mathematics, Monograph 1.

Reynolds, Stephen. 1823–42. *Stephen Reynolds' Journal.* November 27, 1823, to June 27, 1842. Honolulu: State Archives of Hawaii.

Richardson, Miles. 1975. "Anthropologist—The Myth Teller." *American Ethnologist* 2:517–33.

Ricoeur, Paul. 1971. "The Model of the Text: Meaningful Action Considered as a Text." *Social Research* 38:529–62.

Riemer, Jeffrey W. 1977. "Varieties of Opportunistic Research." *Urban Life* 5:467–77.

Ritchey, P. Neal. 1976. "Explanations of Migration." In A. Inkeles et al., eds., *Annual Review of Sociology* 2:363–404. Palo Alto, Calif.: Annual Reviews.

Rogers, Pat. 1975. "Gulliver and the Engineers." *Modern Language Review* 70:260–70.

Rohlen, Thomas P. 1974. *For Harmony and Strength: Japanese White-Collar Organization in Anthropological Perspective.* Berkeley: University of California Press.

Ross, Alexander. 1849. *Adventures of the First Settlers on the Oregon and Columbia River.* London: Smith, Elder.

Rossi, Peter H. 1956. *Why People Move.* New York: Free Press.

Roth, Julius A. 1963. *Timetables: Structuring the Passage of Time in Hospital Treatment and Other Careers.* Indianapolis: Bobbs-Merrill.

Royal Anthropological Institute. 1967. *Notes and Queries in Anthropology.* 6th ed. London: Routledge.

Ruskin, John. 1888. *Modern Painters: Of General Principles and of Truth.* Vol. 1. Sunnyside, Orpington, Surrey: George Allen.

Rust, Eric Charles. 1953. *Nature and Man in Biblical Thought.* London: Lutterworth Press.

Sacks, Harvey. 1972. "On the Analyzability of Stories by Children." In John J. Gumperz and Dell Hymes, eds., *Directions in Sociolinguistics*, pp. 325–45. New York: Holt, Rinehart & Winston.

Sahlins, Marshall. 1981. *Historical Metaphors and Mythical Realities: Structure in the Early History of the Sandwich Islands Kingdom.* Ann Arbor: University of Michigan Press.

Said, Edward W. 1978. *Orientalism.* New York: Random House.

Samuels, Frederick. 1969. "Colour Sensitivity Among Honolulu's Haoles and Japanese." *Race* 11:203–12.

———1970. *The Japanese and the Haoles of Honolulu.* New Haven, Conn.: College and University Press.

Sandford, Jeremy and Roger Law. 1967. *Synthetic Fun.* Harmondsworth: Penguin.

Sanford, Charles L. 1961. *The Quest for Paradise: Europe and the American Moral Imagination.* Urbana: University of Illinois Press.

Schenk, H. G. 1966. *The Mind of the European Romantics: An Essay in Cultural History.* New York: Frederick Ungar.

Schmitt, Robert C. 1968a. "South Seas Movies, 1913–1943." *Hawaiian Historical Review* 2:433–52.

———1968b. *Demographic Statistics of Hawaii 1778–1965.* Honolulu: University Press of Hawaii.

———1971. "Recent Trends in Hawaiian Interracial Marriage Rates by Occupation." *Journal of Marriage and the Family* 33:373–74.

———1977. *Historical Statistics of Hawaii.* Honolulu: University Press of Hawaii.

Schurz, William Lytle. 1939. *The Manila Galleon.* New York: Dutton.

Schutz, Alfred. 1964. "The Stranger." In Arvid Brodersen, ed., *Collected Papers II: Studies in Social Theory*, pp. 91–105. The Hague: Martinus Nijhoff.

Schwalm, David E. 1980. "Locating Belief in Biography." *Biography* 3:14–27.

Schwartz, Barry. 1975. *Queuing and Waiting: Studies in the Social Organization of Access and Delay.* Chicago: University of Chicago Press.

Schwartz, Norman B. 1977. "A Pragmatic Past: Folk History, Environmental Change, and Society in a Petén, Guatamala Town." *American Ethnologist* 4:339–58.

Searle, John R. 1970. *Speech Acts: An Essay in the Philosophy of Language.* Cambridge: Cambridge University Press.

Selhi, S. Prakash. 1975. *Japanese Business and Social Conflict: A Comparison of Japanese and American Patterns of Response.* Cambridge, Mass.: Ballinger.

Silverman, Sydel F. 1967. "Life Crisis as a Clue to Social Functions." *Anthropological Quarterly* 40:127–39.

Simmel, Georg. 1950. "The Stranger." In Kurt Wolff, ed., *The Sociology of Georg Simmel*, pp. 402–08. Glencoe, Ill.: Free Press.

Sinclair, Andrew. 1977. *The Savage: A History of Misunderstanding.* London: Weidenfeld and Nicolson.

Smith, Bradford. 1956. *Yankees in Paradise*. Philadelphia: Lippincott.

"Social Life in the Tropics." 1868. In Abner Kingman, ed., *Hawaiian Club Papers*. Boston: Hawaiian Club.

Speare, A., Jr. 1971. "A Cost-Benefit Model of Rural to Urban Migration in Taiwan." *Population Studies* 25:117–30.

Stevenson, Robert Louis. 1892 (1956). *The Beach of Falesá*. New York: Heritage Press.

Stokes, John F. G. 1939. "Hawaii's Discovery by the Spaniards: Theories Traced and Refuted." *Hawaiian Historical Society Papers*, no. 20, pp. 38–113.

Strauss, Anselm L. 1959. *Mirrors and Masks*. New York: Free Press.

Street, B. V. 1975. *The Savage in Literature: Representations of "Primitive" in English Fiction 1858–1920*. London: Routledge & Kegan Paul.

Suggs, Robert C. 1966. *Marquesan Sexual Behavior*. New York: Harcourt, Brace, and World.

Tagupa, William E. 1977. "Native Hawaiian Reparations: An Ethnic Appeal to Law, Conscience, and the Social Sciences." *Journal of Ethnic Studies* 5:45–50.

Terkel, Studs. 1974. *Working: People Talk About What They Do All Day and How They Feel About What They Do*. New York: Pantheon.

Thomas, Alan. 1977. *Time in a Frame: Photography and the Nineteenth-Century Mind*. New York: Schocken.

Thompson, David E. 1978. "The ILWU as a Force for Interracial Unity in Hawaii." In Dennis M. Ogawa, ed., *Kodome no tame ni: For the Sake of the Children*, pp. 496–512. Honolulu: University Press of Hawaii.

Thurston, Lucy G. 1882. *Life and Times of Mrs. Lucy G. Thurston, Wife of Rev. Asa Thurston, Pioneer Missionary to the Sandwich Islands, Gathered from Letters and Journals Extending over a Period of More Than Fifty Years*. Ann Arbor, Mich.: S. C. Andrews.

Townsend, Ebenezer, Jr. 1888 (1921). "Extract from the Diary of Ebenezer Townsend, Jr." *Hawaiian Historical Society Reprints*, no. 4.

Tsurumi, Yoshi. 1976. *The Japanese Are Coming: A Multinational Interaction of Firms and Politics*. Cambridge, Mass.: Ballinger.

Tuan, Yi-Fu. 1968. "Discrepancies Between Environmental Attitude and Behaviour: Examples from Europe and China." *The Canadian Geographer* 12:176–91.

——1977. *Space and Place: The Perspective of Experience*. Minneapolis: University of Minnesota Press.

Tuggle, H. David. 1979. "Hawaii." In J. D. Jennings, ed., *Polynesian Prehistory*, pp. 167–99. Cambridge: Harvard University Press.

Turner, Frederick Jackson. 1893 (1938). "The Significance of the Frontier in American History." In Fulmer Mood, ed., *The Early Writings of Frederick Jackson Turner*. Madison: University of Wisconsin Press.

Twain, Mark. 1889 (1923). "Welcome Home: To a Baseball Team Returning from a World Tour by Way of the Sandwich Islands." In *Mark Twain's Speeches*, pp. 145–49. New York: Harper.

——1967. *Mark Twain's Letters from Hawaii*. A. Grove Day, ed. London: Chatto & Windus.

References

Vinacke, W. Edgar. 1949a. "Stereotyping Among National Racial Groups in Hawaii: A Study in Ethnocentrism." *Journal of Social Psychology* 30:265–91.

——1949b. "The Judgment of Facial Expressions by Three National Racial Groups in Hawaii: 1. Caucasian Faces." *Journal of Personality* 17:407–29.

Vogel, Ezra F., ed. 1975. *Modern Japanese Organization and Decision-Making.* Berkeley: University of California Press.

von Kotzebue, Otto. 1830 (1967). *A New Voyage Round the World in the Years 1823, 24, 25 & 26.* 2 vols. Amsterdam: N. Israel.

Warren, C. A. B. 1974. "Use of Stigmatizing Social Labels in Conventionalizing Deviant Behavior." *Sociology and Social Research* 58:303–11.

Wenkam, Robert. 1974. *The Great Pacific Rip-Off: Corporate Rape in the Far East.* Chicago: Follett.

Wheeler, Stanton, ed. 1969 (1976). *On Record: Files and Dossiers in American Life.* New Brunswick, N.J.: Transaction.

Whitehead, A. N. 1932. *Aims of Education.* London: Benn.

Whittaker, Elvi. 1978. "The Ethnography of James Agee: The Moral and Existential Accountability of Knowledge." *Canadian Review of Sociology and Anthropology* 15:425–32.

——1981a. "Anthropological Ethics, Fieldwork and Epistemological Disjunctures." *Philosophy of the Social Sciences* 11:437–51.

——1981b. "The Mexican Presence in Canada: Cultural Reasoning and the Immigrant Experience." Paper Presented at the First Conference on Regional Impacts of U.S.-Mexican Economic Relations, Guanajuato, Mexico, July 1981.

Whittaker, Elvi and Virginia Olesen. 1964. "The Faces of Florence Nightingale." *Human Organization* 23:123–30.

Whitten, Norman E., Jr. and Alvin W. Wolfe. 1973. "Network Analysis." In John H. Honigmann, ed., *Handbook of Social and Cultural Anthropology*, pp. 717–46. Chicago: Rand McNally.

Wood, Mary Margaret. 1934. *The Stranger: A Study in Social Relationships.* New York: Columbia University Press.

Wooden, Wayne S. 1981. *What Price Paradise: Changing Social Patterns in Hawaii.* Washington, D.C.: University Press of America.

Wright, J. K. 1947. "*Terrae Incognitae*: The Place of Imagination in Geography." *Annals of the Association of American Geographers* 37:1–15.

Wright, Theon. 1972. *The Disenchanted Isles: The Story of the Second Revolution in Hawaii.* New York: Dial Press.

Yamamoto, Eric. 1979. "The Significance of Local." *Social Process in Hawaii* 27:101–15.

Yamamoto, Joe and Iga Mamoru. 1974. "Japanese Enterprise and American Middle Class Values." *American Journal of Psychology* 131:577–79.

Yarrow, Marian Radke et al. 1970. *Recollections of Childhood: A Study of the Retrospective Method.* Monograph of the Society for Research in Child Development, No. 138, vol. 35, no. 5.

Yoshino, Michael Y. 1968. *Japan's Managerial System.* Cambridge: M.I.T. Press.

Index

Abe, Shirley, 177
Aberle, David F., 18
Acculturation: analysis, xxx, 88; fieldworker's, xxiii, 197n1, 197n2; *see also Haole(s)*
Adams, Alexander, 28
Agar, Michael, 86
Ah Fong, 196n6
Alcohol, 27, 31, 38
Alexander, William D., 5
Alexander & Baldwin, 40
Allen, Anthony, 42
American Indian: early visitors, 42; contemporary population, 43
Ames, Michael M., 18
Amfac, 40
Analysis: advocacy and, xxvii; choice, xxiii-xxiv, xxvi; parts and wholes, xxv; possible paradigms, xxv; avoidance of, xxv; similarity and difference, xxv
Anderson, Bern, 19–20
Anderson, Rufus, 34
Anthony, J. Garner, 198n3
Anthropology: analysis in, xxv-xxxiv; bias, xxiii, 197n3; cannibalism, 195n1; choices, xxxiii; common sense, 190-91; creation of, xv-xxiv; as criticism, xxxii-xxxiii; ethnicity, 190–93; experience, xix; facts, xvii, 191; fieldwork traditions, 55–56, 61–62; folklore of, xvii, 61–62; generalization, 101; ideology, 20, 57–59, 62, 198n6; idioms, xxii; imperialism, xxviii-xxix; interpretive, xxvi, xxxii, 197n3; interpretive vs. positivistic, xxxii-xxxiii, 55, 57, 58, 63, 197n3, 197n4;

millenarian movements, 196n2; missionizing, xvii-xviii; morality, xxiv, xxv, xxxii; nature, 14; as order, xvi, 198n6; parables, xxi; reality, 190–91; researcher and, xvi; romanticism, xvii, 11; socialist humanism, 197n4; South Seas, 14, 196n3; task of, 190; theoretical commitments, xv, xvi; time, 200n4; tourism, xvii–xviii; traditions of, xviii–xix, xxiii; truth, xxxii, 191, 197n3; as Western knowledge, 14; *see also* Fieldwork
Archives of the State of Hawaii, 196n4, 196n5, 196n6
Arens, W., 195–96n1
Aronson, Dan R., 198n7
Australian aborigine, 124

Backlash theory, 186
Baldwin, James, xxx
Ball, Harry V., 181
Banks, Sir Joseph, 13
Banzai Pipeline, 127, 200n3
Barber, Joseph, Jr., 147
Barkan, Leonard, 123
Barkun, M., 18
Barnlund, Dean C., 201n4
Barrot, Théodore-Adolphe, 7
Barth, Frederik, 91, 190
Baudet, Henri, 13, 23
Beachcombers, 25–27, 28–29, 33–34, 36
Beach communities, 26
Beaglehole, J. C., 4
Bean, Robert, 180
Becker, Carl, 99

223